DAYTRIPS IN GERMANY

DAYTRIPS

IN

GERMANY

50 One Day Adventures
by Rail or Car

REVISED EDITION

by
Earl Steinbicker

HASTINGS HOUSE / PUBLISHERS
New York

The author would like to thank the following people, whose generous help and encouragement made this book possible:

Hedy Wuerz, of the German National Tourist Office.

Lucille Hoshabjian, of Lufthansa German Airlines.

Juergen Arnold, of the German Federal Railroad.

All photos are by the author except as noted.

First Published May 1984
Revised Second Edition January 1987

Library of Congress Cataloging in Publication Data

Steinbicker, Earl, 1934–
    Daytrips in Germany.

    Includes index.
    1. Germany (West)—Description and travel—Tours.
I. Title.
DD258.25.S74   1984   914.3'04878   84-4518
ISBN: 0-8038-9283-7

Printed in the United States of America

10 9 8 7 6 5 4 3 2

Contents

Introduction

Visitors to Germany can choose from an enormous range of experiences. There are magnificent cities and medieval towns to be explored, mountains to be climbed, history to be relived, and wines to be tasted. Few nations can match its scope of art, architecture, music, or natural splendor. The possibilities for adventures are endless, but the premise of this book is that nearly all of the very best attractions can easily be enjoyed on a daytrip basis. The pages which follow describe fifty of the country's most intriguing destinations and tell you, in step-by-step detail, exactly how to go about probing them on your own.

For convenience, the book divides Germany into three broad areas of tourist interest—Bavaria, The Rhineland, and The North. Each of these has one major city which, for reasons of transportation and accommodation, makes the most logical base for daytrips in its region. These are Munich, Frankfurt, and Hamburg. Other towns, of course, could be substituted as bases; and these possibilities are suggested in the text whenever practical.

Daytrips have several advantages over the usual point-to-point touring, especially for short-term visitors. You can cover a far greater range in the same time by seeing only those places which really interest you instead of "doing" the region town by town. They also lead to a more varied diet of sights, such as spending one day high in the Alps, the next in Munich, and the third in medieval Rothenburg.

The benefits of staying in one hotel for several days are obvious. Weekly rates are often more economical than overnight stays, especially in conjunction with airline package plans. Then, too, you won't waste time searching for a room every night. Your luggage remains in one place while you go out on a carefree daytrip. There is no need to pre-plan every moment of your vacation since you are always free to go wherever you please. Feel like seeing Würzburg today? Ah, but this is Monday, when its sights are closed, so maybe it would be better to head for the Black Forest instead, or take a stroll through Wiesbaden. Is rain predicted for the entire day? You certainly don't want to be on the Rhine in a shower, so why not try the wonderful museums in Cologne? The operative word here is flexibility; the freedom of not being tied to a schedule or route. You may run up more mileage this way, but that is easily offset by using one of the prepaid unlimited transportation plans described in the next section.

All of the daytrips in this book may be taken by train or car. Full information for doing this is given in the "Getting There" section of each trip. A suggested do-it-yourself walking tour is outlined in both the text and on the street map provided. Time and weather considerations are included, along with price-keyed restaurant recommendations and background information.

The trips have been arranged in a geographic sequence following convenient transportation routes. In many cases it is possible to combine two trips in the same day. These opportunities are noted whenever they are practical.

Destinations were chosen to appeal to a wide variety of interests. In addition to the usual cathedrals, castles, and museums, there are mountain peaks, wine villages, boat cruises, Roman ruins, country walks, salt mines, elegant spas, great seaports, places where history was made, places of literary association, medieval towns, and many others. You should really read through all of them before deciding which intrigue you the most.

Many of the attractions have a nominal entrance fee of some sort—those which are free will come as a pleasant surprise. Cathedrals and churches will appreciate a small donation in the collection box.

Finally, a gentle disclaimer. Places have a way of changing without warning, and errors do creep into print. If your heart is absolutely set on seeing a particular attraction, you may want to check first to make sure that the opening times are still valid. A source for this information is given for each daytrip.

One last thought—it isn't really necessary to see everything at any given destination. Be selective. Your one-day adventures in Germany should be fun, not an endurance test. If it starts becoming that, just stroll over to the nearest café, sit down, and enjoy ourself. There will always be another day.

Happy Daytripping!

Section I

Getting Around

All of the daytrips in this book can be made by rail or by car. Which of these you choose depends on purely personal factors, but you may want to consider some of the following information before deciding.

BY RAIL

The **German Federal Railroad** *(Deutsche Bundesbahn, or DB)* is among the finest in the world. It operates about 20,000 passenger trains a day, serving some 6,000 stations; as well as an extensive bus network connecting small villages and rural areas with the rail network. The system is presently being expanded to allow the running of extremely high-speed *InterCity Express (ICE)* trains, due to begin service in the near future.

There are very few places in Germany which cannot be reached by rail. Equipment now in use varies from the sleek *InterCity (IC)* expresses to some rather quaint railcars. If you enjoy riding trains you will savor each type for the special and diverse experiences it offers.

Seasoned travelers often consider riding trains to be one of the best ways of meeting the local people, and making new friends. It is not at all unusual to strike up an engaging conversation which makes your trip all the more memorable. You can also get a marvelous view of the passing countryside from the large widows, and have time to catch up on your reading.

All trains operated by the Federal Railroad belong to one of the following categories, as indicated on schedules and departure platforms:

TEE—*Trans Europ Express.* The only train in this category in present operation on the German railroad is the famous "Rheingold," a first-class-only luxury service following the Rhine River between Amsterdam and Basel with an added year-round section between Mainz and Munich—stopping at Darmstadt, Heidelberg, Stuttgart, Ulm, and Augsburg en route. This added section continues on to Salzburg during the summer months. The *Rheingold* runs once a day in each direction and carries a premium surcharge, although this does not apply to holders of first-class railpasses. Reservations are suggested.

IC—*InterCity Express.* These swift, modern trains run at hourly intervals between about 50 major cities and towns within Germany and to neighboring countries. Connections with other expresses are very convenient, and many IC trains now stop at the Frankfurt airport for the benefit of air passengers. All trains of this category carry both first- and second-class cars, with a choice of compartment or open seating. The first-class—as well as some of the second-class—cars are air conditioned. Many of the newer second-class cars are now designed to accommodate handicapped passengers. Food and beverage service is continuously available at your seat or in the dining car. Most IC trains are equipped with radio-operated coin telephones. Attendants on board can help you with such details as hotel or car rental reservations while you speed along. There is an additional charge to ride IC trains, called a *Zuschlag,* but this does not apply to most railpass users. Reservations are suggested during peak travel times.

D or **FD**—*Express trains.* sometimes made up of older equipment, these expresses serve more towns than the ICs, and run nearly as fast. The FD trains feature a *"Quick-Pick"* buffet car with inexpensive meals and drinks. There is an extra charge *(Zuschlag)* for distances of less than 50 kilometers *(about 31 miles),* although this does not apply to most railpass users. Seats can be reserved if desired. All trains in this category carry both first- and second-class cars.

E—*Eilzug.* These semi-express trains frequently use older equipment, rarely offer food or beverage service, and primarily serve smaller towns. Both first- and second-class cars are available.

N—Called *Nahverkehr* but usually not given any particular designation, these locals make many stops and can take you to very rural locations. Much of the equipment is old and sometimes rather quaint, although there are some modern N-trains. First class is not always offered.

S—Usually made up of high-speed ·modern equipment, these commuter locals serve the outlying areas near large cities, and operate as subways within the city. They usually carry both first- and second-class cars.

Buses operated by the Federal Railroad, marked "DB," connect rural areas with train stations in larger towns, and fill in for rail service during off-peak hours. Railpasses are accepted.

Schedules for train service can be consulted at the information offices *(Auskunft)* in stations. While there, be sure to check the return schedules as well to avoid any possibility of getting stranded in some quaint medieval village. Tables of departure *(Abfahrt, on yellow pa-*

A New ICE Train (Photo Courtesy of German Federal Railroad)

per) and arrivals *(Ankunft, on white paper)* are posted throughout the stations; and are arranged in time sequence using the 24-hour clock. Thus, a departure at 3:32 p.m. would be marked as 15.32. Be sure that you are looking at the correct table, not one for a nearby city. Some stations, notably Munich's *Hauptbahnhof*, have free printed schedules for popular destinations. A few, including Munich and Frankfurt, feature self-operated computer terminals in which you enter your destination and approximate time frame, and receive a free printout in German, French, and English of all the possible routings within that period. Watch out for the word *"Umsteigen,"* or the letter "U," which indicates a change of trains. The best way to check schedules, however, is to purchase a schedule book—called a *Kursbuch*—which is available in both national and regional editions at a modest price. The compact Thomas Cook Continental Timetable, sold in some travel book stores in North America, by mail from Forsyth Travel Library (P.O. Box 2975, Shawnee Mission, Kansas 66201; phone toll-free 1-800-FORSYTH for credit-card orders), or at Thomas Cook offices in Britain, is very useful although it does not list *every* local service.

You may want to make **reservations** for long trips during peak periods, especially on TEE or IC trains. Railpass holders must pay a small fee for this. The reservation will assign you a specific car and seat number. Those traveling without reservations should be careful not to sit in someone else's reserved seat, which is marked by a card at the compartment entrance or above the seat.

A RAIL TRAVELER'S GLOSSARY

Abfahrt	Departure
Ankunft	Arrival
Anschluss	Connection
Ausgang	Exit
Auskunft	Information
Ausland	Foreign
Ausser	Except
Bahnhof	Train station
Bahnhofwirtshaft	Station restaurant
Bahnsteig	Platform
Bergbahn	Mountain railway
Besetzt	Occupied
Besonderheiten	Special particulars
Bestellung	Reservation
Binnen	Inland (domestic)
Damen	Women
DB, Deutsche Bundesbahn	German Federal Railroad
Eilzug	Semi-express train
Einfache	One-way
Eingang	Entrance
Eisenbahn	Railway
Erste Klasse	First class
Fahrgast	Passenger
Fahrkarte/ Fahrschein	Ticket
Fahrplan	Timetable
Fahrpreise	Fare
Fahrrad am Bahnhof	Bicycle rental in station
Fahrt	Journey
Feiertage	Holidays
Fensterplatz	Window seat
Fernzug	Long distance train
Frauen	Women
Fremdenverkehrsverein	Tourist information office
Fundbüro	Lost-and-found
Garderobe	Checkroom
Gefähr	Danger
Gepäck	Luggage
Gepäckabfertigung	Baggage check room
Gepäckträger	Porter
Gleis	Track
Haüptbahnhof (Hbf)	Main train station
Herren	Men
Hin und zurück	There and back (round trip)
Kofferkuli	Luggage cart
Kursbuch	Official timetable book

Kurswagen	Through car to indicated destination
Liegewagen	Inexpensive sleeping car with bunks (Couchette)
Männer	Men
Münz-Zugtelefon	Pay phone on train
Nahverkehr	Local train
Nichtraucher	No smoking
Nur	Only
Ohne	Without
Platzreservierung	Seat reservation
Postamt	Post office
Raucher	Smoking
Reisebüro	Travel agency
Reiseproviant	Food & drinks to take along
Reserviert	Reserved
Richtung	Direction
Rückfahrkarte	Round trip
S-Bahn	Commuter rail line, may operate as subway inside large cities
Schaffner	Ticket collector
Schalter	Ticket window in station
Schlafwagen	Sleeping car
Schliessfach	Luggage locker
Schnellzug	Express train
Sitzplatz	Seat
Sonderrückfahrkarte	Reduced price excursion ticket
Speisewagen	Dining car
Täglich	Daily
Triebwagen	Rail car
Tunnelbahnhof	Underground train station
U-Bahn	Subway, Métro, Underground
Umsteigen	Change (of trains)
Verbindung	Connection
Verboten	Forbidden
Verkehrsbüro, Verkehrsverein, Verkehrsamt	Tourist information office
Wagen	Car (of train)
Wagenstandanzeiger	Train make-up diagram
Wartesaal	Waiting room
WC	Rest rooms
Wechselstube	Money exchange place
Werktage	Weekdays (Mon.–Sat.)
Zoll	Customs
Zu	To
Zug	Train
Zuschlag	Supplementary fare
Zutritt verboten	Do not enter
Zweite klasse	Second class

It is always best to arrive at the station *(Bahnhof)* a few minutes before departure time and go directly to the track platform *(Gleis)* shown for your train on the departure board. There you will usually find a sign marked *Wagenstandanzeiger* which shows the exact makeup of every express leaving from that platform, including the location of each car. This serves two major purposes. First, you won't have to make a last-minute dash when you discover that the first-class cars stop at the opposite end of a long platform. Secondly, and more important, it shows which—if any—cars are dropped off en route to your destination.

The **routing** and final destination of each car is shown just outside its door as well as in its vestibule. First-class cars are marked with the numeral "1" near the door, and with a yellow stripe above the windows.

Most express trains offer a **food and beverage service** of some sort, as indicated on the schedules. Riding in a regular dining car or self-service *"Quick-Pick"* car can be a delightful experience, but beware the pushcarts in other cars which sell well-shaken cans of warm beer. You are much better off stocking up on snacks and refreshments at the station and bringing them with you, as most Europeans do.

Railpasses can be an incredible bargain if you intend to do any real amount of train travel. Ask your travel agent about them before going to Germany, as they are difficult—but not impossible—to purchase once there. The German Federal Railroad *(DB)* accepts the following passes:

EURAILPASS—the grandaddy of them all, allows unlimited first-class travel throughout 16 West European countries, excluding Great Britain. It is available for periods of 15 or 21 days, or 1, 2, or 3 months. The Eurailpass includes a wide variety of fringe benefits, such as free Rhine river cruises, some free buses, discounts on some popular mountain railways, and several free international ferry steamers.

EURAIL SAVERPASS—an economical version of the Eurailpass which offers the same first-class travel benefits as outlined above, but for groups of 3 or more people traveling together. Between October 1st and March 31st the group size can be as small as 2 persons. This pass is available for a period of 15 days only, and the rail travel must always be done as a group.

EURAIL YOUTHPASS—this low-cost version of the Eurailpass is available to anyone under the age of 26 and allows unlimited second-class travel in the same 16 European countries for periods of 1 or 2 months. It does not cover express train surcharges, but the fringe benefits are pretty much the same.

The **GERMANRAIL TOURIST CARD** *(DB Tourist Karte)* is valid for unlimited travel in West Germany only, and offers a substantial saving over the Eurailpass. It is available in both first- and second (coach)-class versions, for periods of 4, 9, or 16 days. Fringe benefits include a discount on Rhine, Main, and Mosel river cruises, some free buses, a large reduction on a round-trip rail ticket to West Berlin (transit visas are free on all trains), and free bicycle rentals at hundreds of rail stations with the option of dropping off the bike in another town.

The **GERMANRAIL "JUNIOR" TOURIST CARD** is available to persons under the age of 26 and provides unlimited second-class rail travel in West Germany only for periods of 9 or 16 days. The fringe benefits are the same as those for the GermanRail Tourist Card described above.

All railpasses must be **validated** at a train station on the first day of actual use. The first and last days of validity will be entered on the pass at that time. Be certain that you agree with the dates *before* allowing the agent to write them in.

If you intend to take several of the daytrips in this book, and especially if at least one of them is to a distant location such as Berchtesgaden, Trier, or Goslar, a railpass will probably wind up saving you a considerable amount of money. Even if the savings are less than that a pass should still be considered for the convenience it offers in not having to line up for tickets, and the freedom of just hopping aboard almost any train at whim. It also makes practical the use of extra-fare expresses *(TEE, IC, D, or FD types)* for even short distances, and encourages you to become more adventurous—to seek out distant and offbeat destinations.

The 5 passes described above are sold by most travel agents, who also have current information and prices, and by mail from the Forsyth Travel Library mentioned on page 11. Alternatively, you could contact the nearest GermanRail office. In North America these are located in New York, Boston, Chicago, Denver, Houston, Los Angeles, San Francisco, and Toronto. The address of the New York office is:

GERMANRAIL
DB
747 Third Avenue
New York, NY 10017

Phone (212) 308–3100

Those who have decided against a railpass, or who reside in the countries covered and therefore cannot buy one, still have some money-saving options. Before purchasing a full-fare ticket you should always ask about special one-day excursion fares which may be applicable to your journey. 24-hour passes are usually available for use on the type "S" trains in and around major cities. Remember that a surcharge

(Zuschlag) is required for all rides on TEE or IC trains; or on D or FD trains for distances of less than 50 kilometers *(31 miles)*. This does not apply to most railpass users.

Germany also has a few privately owned small railroads, which do not accept railpasses but may grant discounts to their holders. The only ones which pertain to the daytrips in this book are the rack-railways on the Zugspitze and Wendelstein peaks, and the steam train at Chiemsee.

BY CAR:

Many tourists prefer to explore Germany by car, especially when several people are traveling together. The country's extensive network of superhighways *(Autobahnen)* is world-famous for its virtually unlimited speeds. And Germans do tend to drive *very* fast, frequently over 100 miles per hour. Autobahn routes are marked by the letter "A" preceding their number, while the letter "E" indicates international routes. Secondary roads, including those of the "B" category, have strictly enforced speed limits. The use of seat belts is mandatory at all times, and penalties for driving while intoxicated can be quite severe. Driving in German towns is often tricky, what with the one-way streets *(Einbahnstrassen)* and numerous pedestrian zones.

A brief glossary for drivers is provided on page 18. For more comprehensive automotive terms, you may want to use a pocket-sized phrase book, such as *German for Travellers* by Berlitz.

Cars may be rented from a large number of agencies at airports and in major towns, including some familiar American firms. The German Federal Railroad *(DB)* has an arrangement with InterRent for car rentals at major train stations, reservations for which can be made at the stations or even on board IC trains. The fly-and-drive plans offered in conjunction with transatlantic flights on Lufthansa and some other carriers can save you a great deal of money over what it would cost to purchase these services separately. Full details on current offerings are available from your local travel agent, who should be consulted as far ahead as possible since advance purchase is required.

BY AIR:

Lufthansa operates an extensive **domestic air service** which you may want to use in traveling between the base cities, particularly from Munich to Hamburg or vice versa. Pan American, British Airways, and Air France are the only airlines allowed to provide service between West Berlin and other West German cities.

As to **transatlantic service,** Lufthansa offers more flights to and from North America than any other carrier, serving a total of 17 North American cities including 11 in the U.S.A. The majority of these land at Frankfurt; one of the largest, most modern, and busiest airports in the world. This is the hub of Lufthansa's world-wide service—where easy connections can be made to virtually all major cities in Europe and around the globe. The airline also has direct flights from North America to Düsseldorf, Munich, Hamburg, and Stuttgart.

While on the subject of air travel, passengers landing at Frankfurt or Düsseldorf may want to take advantage of the **Lufthansa Airport Express,** a luxurious high-speed train linking the Frankfurt and Düsseldorf airports with intermediate stops at Bonn, Cologne, Cologne-Deutz, and downtown Düsseldorf. The route follows the scenic banks of the Rhine for most of the distance, with complimentary meals and drinks served en route. An airline ticket and reservation are required. Full details are available from your travel agent or Lufthansa.

The Frankfurt airport has commuter train *(S-Bahn)* service to Frankfurt's main station as well as other points in the city. These run at very frequent intervals and take only 12 minutes for the ride. Departures are from a station located on the lower level of the terminal building, below the luggage claim area. Tickets should be purchased from the vending machines, which have instructions in English (see page 145 for details). Commuter trains to Mainz and Wiesbaden also leave from here, as do InterCity express trains to other cities in Germany and beyond. The railroad offers a handy baggage delivery service to and from other destinations in Germany. Those wishing to take a taxi to downtown Frankfurt will find the fares to be reasonable.

PACKAGE PLANS:

The cost of your German trip can be cut substantially by selecting one of the many attractive plans which combine transatlantic airfares with hotel accommodations, car rentals, or railpasses. A particularly wide choice is available in conjunction with Lufthansa flights, as well as with some other carriers. Since the offerings change frequently and advance purchase is necessary, you should consult with a travel agent well ahead of time.

HOLIDAYS:

Legal holidays *(Feiertage)* in West Germany are:

January 1 *(Neujahr)*
Good Friday *(Karfreitag)*
Easter Monday *(Ostermontag)*
May 1 (Labor Day) *(Tag der Arbeit)*
Ascension Day (40 days after Easter) *(Christi Himmelfahrt)*

Whit Monday (2nd Monday after Ascension) *(Pfingstmontag)*
June 17 (Unity Day) *(Tag der Deutschen Einheit)*
November 21 (Repentence Day) *(Busstag)*
Christmas *(1. Weihnachstag)*
December 26 *(2. Weihnachstag)*

A DRIVER'S GLOSSARY

Achtung . . . . Caution
Anfang . . . . Start, entrance
Anlieger Frei . . . . Local residents only
Ausfahrt Freihalten . . . . No parking in driveway
Ausgang . . . . Exit
Aussichtspunkt . . . . Look-out point
Autobahn . . . . High-speed limited-access highway,
                                       indicated by letter "A" preceding
                                       route number
Autovermietung . . . . Car rental
Baustelle . . . . Road construction
Benzin . . . . Gasoline (Petrol)
Blaue Zone . . . . Time-indicator disc required for parking
Bremsen . . . . Brakes
Brücke . . . . Bridge
Bundesstrasse . . . . Main road, indicated by letter "B"
                                       preceding route number
Durchfahrt Verboten . . . . No thoroughfare
Durchgangsverkehr . . . . Through traffic
Einbahnstrasse . . . . One-way street
Einordnen . . . . Follow in line
Ende . . . . End
Ende des Parkverbots . . . . End of no-parking zone
Engstelle . . . . Road narrows
Fähre . . . . Ferry
Freie Fahrt . . . . No speed limit
Führerschein . . . . Driver's license
Fussgänger . . . . Pedestrians
Gefahr . . . . Danger
Gefährliches Gefälle . . . . Dangerous descent
Gefährliche Steigung . . . . Steep hill
Gegenverkehr . . . . Two-way traffic
Geradeaus . . . . Straight ahead
Halt . . . . Stop
Kein Durchgang . . . . No thoroughfare
Kurzparkzone . . . . Short-term parking
Kurve . . . . Bend in road
Langsam . . . . Slow
Links . . . . Left
Links Fahren . . . . Keep to the left
LKW . . . . Truck
Mietwagen . . . . Rental car
Münztank . . . . Coin-operated gasoline pump
Nebel . . . . Fog
Öl . . . . Oil

Parken Verboten	. . . .	No parking
Parkplatz	. . . .	Parking place
PKW	. . . .	Private car
Rechts	. . . .	Right
Rechts Fahren	. . . .	Keep to the right
Reifen	. . . .	Tire
Sackgasse	. . . .	Dead-end steet (cul-de-sac)
Schlechte Fahrbahn	. . . .	Rough road surface
Schule	. . . .	School zone
Steinschlag	. . . .	Falling rocks
Stadtmitte	. . . .	Town center
Strasse	. . . .	Road
Strasse Gesperrt	. . . .	Road closed
Strassenarbeiten	. . . .	Road construction
Strassenkarte	. . . .	Road map
Tankstelle	. . . .	Gasoline (Petrol) station
Überholen Verboten	. . . .	No passing
Umleitung	. . . .	Detour (Diversion)
Unfall	. . . .	Accident
Verengte Fahrbahn	. . . .	Road narrows
Vorfahrt	. . . .	Priority
Vorsicht	. . . .	Attention
Wagen	. . . .	Automobile
Wasser	. . . .	Water
Zoll	. . . .	Customs

DAYS OF THE WEEK: SEASONS:

Montag	Monday		**Jahreszeit**	Season
Dienstag	Tuesday		**Frühling**	Spring
Mittwoch	Wednesday		**Sommer**	Summer
Donnerstag . . .	Thursday		**Herbst**	Autumn
Freitag	Friday		**Winter**	Winter
Samstag				
(Sonnabend)	Saturday			
Sonntag	Sunday			
Heute	Today			
Morgen	Tomorrow			
Feiertag	Holiday			

APPROXIMATE CONVERSIONS

1 Mile = 1.6 km   **1 U.S. Gallon** = 3.78 liters
1 KM = 0.6 miles   **1 Liter** = 0.26 U.S. gallons

Trains operate on holiday schedules on these days, and some attractions may be closed—see the "When to Go" section for each daytrip. Banks, of course, are closed—so make your change ahead of time. In addition, some of the states *(Länder)* have their own holidays.

FOOD AND DRINK:

Several choice restaurants are listed for each destination in this book. Most of these are long-time favorites of experienced travelers and serve classical German cuisine. Their approximate price range, based on the least expensive complete meal offered, is indicated as follows:

> $ — Inexpensive, but may have fancier dishes available.
>
> $$ — Reasonable. These establishments may also feature daily specials.
>
> $$$ — Luxurious and expensive.

Those who take their dining very seriously should consult an up-to-date restaurant and hotel guide such as the classic red-cover *Michelin Deutschland,* issued annually in February.

It is always wise to check the posted menu outside the restaurant before entering, paying particular attention to any daily specials listed on the *Tageskarte.* Fixed-price complete meals are indicated by the word *Gedeck,* while the regular menu is called a *Speisekarte.* The use of a pocket-sized translator book such as the *Marling Menu Master* will allow you to try unfamiliar dishes without anxiety.

Those in a hurry to get on with their sightseeing can save both time and money by eating at a *Schnellimbiss,* usually a stand-up counter where tasty sausages are dispensed along with beer and other beverages. American-style fast-food chains have invaded Germany with a vengeance, and can be found in just about every town along with the ubiquitous pizzerias. On the more elegant side, foreign cuisines such as French, Italian, and Chinese are becoming increasingly popular in the larger cities.

Beer remains the national beverage of Germany, and comes in a bewildering variety of tastes and local specialties. The most common of these are *Export*—the closest thing to an American brew—and *Pils,* which is considerably more bitter. Germany also produces—and drinks—large quantities of wine, some of which rank among the best in the world. Soft drinks, mineral water, and fruit juices are available everywhere.

WEATHER:

Current weather forecasts in English may be heard on the AFN radio stations, both AM and FM, operated throughout much of the country by the U.S. military forces. In the north a similar service is provided by the British military. German radio stations in some major cities have news and weather in English. Forecasts on German TV are usually graphic enough to understand without a command of the language. A simpler approach, however, is to just ask at the front desk of your hotel about the status of *das Wetter*—or to call ahead.

SUGGESTED TOURS:

The do-it-yourself walking tours in this book are relatively short and easy to follow. On the assumption that most readers will be traveling by train, they always begin at the local station. Those going by car can make a simple adjustment. Suggested routes are shown by heavy broken lines on the maps, while the circled numbers refer to major attractions or points of reference along the way, with corresponding numbers in the text.

Trying to see all the sights in a given town could easily become an exhausting marathon. You will certainly enjoy yourself more by being selective and passing up anything that doesn't catch your fancy in favor of a friendly *Bierstube*. God will forgive you if you don't visit *every* church.

TOURIST INFORMATION:

Virtually every town, or even *Dorf*, of any tourist interest in Germany has its own information office which can help you with specific questions or book local accommodations. Usually identified by the words *Verkehrsbüro, Verkehrsverein, Verkehrsamt, Kurverwaltung,* or simply by the letter "**i**," they almost invariably have English-speaking personnel on staff.

The location of these offices is shown on the town maps in this book by the word "**info.**," and repeated along with the phone number under the "Tourist Information" section for each trip. To phone ahead from another town in Germany you must first dial the area code, which always begins with 0 and is shown in parentheses, followed by the local number. Calling ahead is useful if the whole reason for your daytrip hinges on seeing a particular sight which might possibly be closed, or perhaps to check the weather. Pay phones—including those on IC trains—use coins. Just load up the slot with small denominations and any which are not used will be returned.

ADVANCE PLANNING INFORMATION:

The **German National Tourist Office** has branches throughout the world which will provide help in planning your trip. In North America these are located at:

747 Third Ave.,
New York, NY 10017
Phone (212) 308–3300

444 South Flower St.,
Los Angeles, CA 90071
Phone (213) 688–7332

P.O. Box 417, 2 Fundy
Place Bonaventure,
Montreal, P.Q., H5A 1B8
Canada
Phone (514) 878–9885

In England, they are at 61 Conduit Street, **London** W1R 0EN, phone (01) 734-26-00.

Bavaria

The enormous state, or *Land,* of Bavaria with its splendid capital of Munich did not really become a part of Germany until the last century, and then only with reluctance. It still fancies itself as an almost separate nation, a fact made abundantly clear by the border signs proudly proclaiming *Freistaat Bayern.* With customs, manners, traditions, and even a dialect that is alien to the rest of the Federal Republic, Bavarians are a race apart; genuinely friendly, open and warm-hearted to strangers—yet hide-bound conservatives at heart. This is the land of fantastic castles, snow-capped mountains, clear blue lakes, and magnificent cities. In the eyes of many tourists it is the very essence and soul of Germany.

You may want to start your Bavarian adventures with an exploration of Munich, for which two walking tours are described in the next few pages. Following that are twenty carefully selected destinations, all within easy daytrip range of the city. It is not actually necessary to stay in Munich itself to make these trips—many will prefer basing themselves in the outlying districts, which often are more charming and less expensive. Munich's superb *S-Bahn* commuter trains make this a highly attractive alternative.

A few of the destinations make good base cities in themselves, such as Garmisch-Partenkirchen for much of the Alps, or Würzburg for Franconia. These options are suggested in the text whenever practical.

Four of the daytrips from Munich can also be made from Frankfurt. These are Rothenburg, Würzburg, Nuremberg, and Bamberg. Two other Bavarian towns, Miltenberg and Aschaffenburg, are included in Section III as they are much closer to Frankfurt and The Rhineland than to Munich.

Munich Tour 1
The Old City

Everyone loves Munich. It is Germany's favorite good-time city, a place that is both elegant and sophisticated and yet seems to be perpetually drenched in a beery earthiness. Bavaria's capital lives in the best of two worlds—in some ways a southern city almost belonging to the Mediterranean, and in others an affluent northern metropolis. Many of its streets are reminiscent of Rome or Athens, but under those cobblestones runs a transit system of Teutonic efficiency. Buildings which appear to be from earlier centuries are often post-World War II reconstructions, built from the ashes of destruction and already imbued with the patina of age.

Not really old as German cities go, Munich was founded in 1158 as a place to collect taxes from the lucrative salt trade. Its site, next to a 9th-century Benedictine abbey, gave it the appellation *zu den Mönchen*—"Place of the Monks"—which easily corrupted into the present German name of *München*. A little child-monk, the *Münchner Kindl,* still adorns the city's coat of arms. By 1180 the new settlement came under the control of the Wittelsbach family, who as dukes, and later kings, made it their capital. From here they ruled Bavaria until 1918, a span of over seven hundred years. It was this unbroken dynasty of art-loving sovereigns which was responsible for the splendid city of today.

Munich is famous throughout the world for its once-a-year *Oktoberfest*—16 days of beer-sodden revelry beginning in late September. Equally exuberant is *Fasching,* a bizarre carnival held just before Lent. Both epitomize the meaning of that untranslatable word, *Gemütlichkeit,* which for many tourists neatly sums up the special magic that is Munich's.

You cannot possibly see all of the city in a single day, or a week for that matter. The tour which follows was designed to take you past most of the major sights which can easily be reached on foot. Which of these you decide to actually visit will depend on the time available and, of course, your particular interests. The tour can be cut short without sacrificing too much by skipping directly from Odeons Platz (7) to the nearby Hofgarten (14). Many will want to surrender to the lure of the Hofbräuhaus (15) and call it quits in that beer-lovers paradise.

GETTING AROUND:

Although the tour was intended for walking, you may prefer to use public transportation part of the way. The system consists of subways, buses, and streetcars. A map and instructions are available at information offices of the Munich Transit *(MVV)* or tourist offices.

The city has *two* subway systems; the **U-Bahn** which remains underground, and the **S-Bahn** which pops up to the surface once beyond the inner city and continues on as a suburban commuter rail network. The Eurailpass or GermanRail Tourist Card may be used on the S-Bahn, *but very definitely not on the U-Bahn, streetcars, or buses.* Before boarding these (or the S-Bahn if you have no pass), it is necessary to buy a ticket or 24-hour pass at one of the coin-operated ticket-vending machines in subway stations, by streetcar or bus stops, or on board those vehicles marked with a white letter "K". These are valid for the U- or S-Bahns, streetcars, or buses, or any combination going in a direct route to your destination. They must be cancelled *(entwerten)* at the time of use by inserting them in a small time-stamping machine (identified by a letter "E") at subway entrances or on board the streetcar or bus. Your trip must then be completed within two hours. Failure to do the above could result in a fine.

The system is divided into fare zones, as shown on the maps, but all or virtually all of your travels will probably be within the basic inner-city zone. Note that fares are different for adults *(Erwachsene)* and children *(Kinder)*, indicated by pictograms on the vending machines. Those using the S-Bahn should beware of boarding first-class cars with an ordinary ticket.

If all this sounds confusing, you can relax. There is an easy way out. All you have to do is purchase an economical 24-hour *(24-Stunden)* ticket from the machine, sign it below the word *unterschrift*, and cancel it. For the next 24 hours you can travel at will as long as you stay within the inner zone *(Innenraum)*.

System-wide 24-hour passes, allowing you to travel to the farthest reaches of the combined systems, are also available for a slightly higher price at U- or S-Bahn station ticket offices. These are a good deal for people staying in the suburbs who do not have railpasses.

WHEN TO GO:

Munich is a city for all seasons. It is best to avoid making this trip on a Monday or major holiday, when many of the important sights are closed.

FOOD AND DRINK:

Few cities in Europe can match the range of restaurants and cafés available in Munich. You should plan on having lunch between Karlsplatz (2) and the Residenz (6), after which the choices become very thin. Some of the better selections along the walking route, in the order you will pass them, are:

Mövenpick (Lenbachplatz 8, near Karlsplatz) Several dining rooms. $$ and $$$

Augustiner (Neuhauser Str. 16) $

Zum Pschorrbräu (Neuhauser Str. 11) $$

Bratwurstglöckl am Dom (by the rear of the Frauenkirche) An old favorite. $$

Ratskeller (in the Rathaus on Marienplatz) $$

Dallmayr (upstairs at Diener Str. 14) $$$

Spatenhaus (Residenz Str. 12, across from the Residenz) $$

And, of course, there is always the Hofbräuhaus (15), that venerable institution and major tourist attraction. Go there for fun and beer. The food is adequate and inexpensive.

TOURIST INFORMATION:

The tourist information office, phone (089) 239-12-56, is located opposite track 11 in the main train station. There is also a branch by Marienplatz, phone (089) 239-11.

SUGGESTED TOUR:

Some people will find it convenient to start their tour at the main train station, the **Hauptbahnhof** (1), where the city tourist office is located. From here it is only a short stroll down Schützenstrasse to the real beginning of the walk, **Karlsplatz** (2). Popularly known as "*Stachus*," this busy intersection should be crossed via the underground passageway.

Enter the old part of town through the 14th-century city gate, the Karlstor, and walk along Neuhauser Strasse to **St. Michael's Church** (3). Built in the 16th century along Italian lines, it is one of the finest examples of Renaissance architecture in all Germany. Be sure to visit the crypt, which contains the tombs of some thirty-odd members of the ruling Wittelsbach family, including that of King Ludwig II. Often called the "mad" king, whose extravagant fantasies nearly bankrupted the state, Ludwig was never really insane by any objective standards. His enigmatic life and tragic death in 1886 were full of mysteries; yet he left his country with an artistic heritage that continues to draw millions of visitors from all over the globe. As you travel throughout Bavaria you will frequently be exposed to his legacy, from the wildly romantic castles of Neuschwanstein, Linderhof, and Herrenchiemsee to the operas of Richard Wagner at Bayreuth.

Continue on past the Hunting Museum (*Jagdmuseum*), located in a former Augustinian church, and turn left to the **Frauenkirche** (4), which serves as Munich's cathedral. Its twin towers are regarded as

Marienplatz

the city's trademark and look, appropriately enough, like two gigantic
old-fashioned beer steins. One of these may be ascended—by elevator—for a good view of the city and even, on a clear day, of the Alps.

Built in the 15th century and badly damaged during the last war,
this strikingly austere cathedral has since been restored. The original
Gothic stained-glass windows had been put away for safekeeping before the bombs fell, and are now back in place along with other art
treasures. These include the 17th-century tomb of Emperor Ludwig
the Bavarian (1282–1347), by the south tower, and a crypt containing
the remains of several Wittelsbach princes.

Return to the main pedestrian mall, here called Kaufinger Strasse,
and turn left to **Marienplatz** (5). If you arrive by 11 a.m. you will be
treated to a free show, complete with glockenspiel and mechanical
figures, given daily on the façade of the **New Town Hall** *(Neues Rathaus)*. This richly decorated neo-Gothic structure was erected in the
late 19th century and forms the northern wall of one of the most attractive squares in Germany. Its tower, like that of the Frauenkirche,
may be ascended by elevator for a splendid view. In the center of the
platz stands the *Mariensäule,* a column dating from 1638 atop which
the Virgin Mary watches out over Munich.

To complete the scene with a romantic touch there is the turreted
15th-century **Old Town Hall** *(Altes Rathaus)* standing guard over the
eastern end. Now used for special exhibitions, it may be visited if

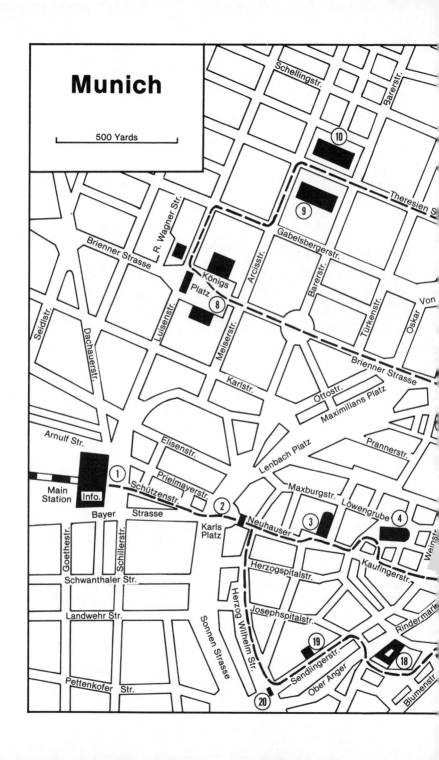

Munich

500 Yards

Schellingstr.

Barerstr.

R. Wagner Str.

Brienner Strasse

Theresien S

Gabelsbergerstr.

Arcisstr.

10

9

Königs
Platz

8

Seidlstr.

Dachauerstr.

Luisenstr.

Meiserstr.

Barerstr.

Türkenstr.

Oskar

Von

Brienner Strasse

Karlstr.

Ottostr.

Maximilians Platz

Arnulf Str.

Elisenstr.

Lenbach Platz

Prannerstr.

Prielmayerstr.

1

Schützenstr.

Maxburgstr.

Löwengrube

4

Main
Station

Info.

2

3

Bayer   Strasse

Neuhauser

Weinstr

Karls
Platz

Goethestr.

Schillerstr.

Schwanthaler Str.

Herzogspitalstr.

Kaufingerstr.

Landwehr Str.

Josephspitalstr.

Sonnen Strasse

Herzog Wilhelm Str.

Rindermark

19

Sendlingerstr.

18

Pettenkofer   Str.

Ober Anger

Blumenstr

20

open. **St. Peter's Church**, just south of the square, is the oldest in Munich and actually predates the founding of the town. Rebuilt many times over the centuries, it has a lovely interior which is well worth visiting. The tower, affectionately known as *Der Alter Peter*, may be climbed—on foot—for an unmatched view of the Marienplatz, Old Town, and possibly even the Alps.

From here, Diener Strasse and Residenz Strasse lead to Max-Joseph Platz, whose eastern end is dominated by the **National Theatre,** home of the Bavarian State Opera. First built in 1818, it was destroyed during the war and completely reconstructed to the original design in 1963.

The **Residenz** (6), fronting the north side of the square, was the royal palace of the Wittelsbach family from the 16th century until the end of the kingdom in 1918. It is a vast, incoherent complex of adjoining buildings in various styles; difficult to comprehend in a single visit, but well worth the effort if only for a tiny glimpse at the life to which royalty was accustomed. A visit to the Residenz is divided into three separate parts, each with its own admission.

First, there is the **Treasury** *(Schatzkammer)*, entered directly from Max-Joseph Platz. A dazzling collection of Wittelsbach heirlooms, some over a thousand years old, fills ten rooms with crowns, gold, crystal, rubies, diamonds, and just about everything else that glitters.

Following this you may want to visit the **Residenz Museum,** a long trek through about one hundred rooms, many restored to their original appearance and others used as art galleries. While it is possible to rush through this in an hour or so, it is better saved for a rainy day when enough time can be devoted to a proper digestion of the riches on display. The entrance is the same as for the Treasury, and both are open Tuesdays through Saturdays, 10 a.m. to 4:30 p.m., and on Sundays from 10 a.m. to 1 p.m. Both museums are closed on Mondays and some holidays.

The third attraction of the Residenz is the **Cuvilliés Theatre** *(Altes Residenztheater)*. Originally built by the famed architect François de Cuvilliés in 1753, it was dismantled in 1943, just before the firebombs fell, and later reassembled in its present location. Lavishly decorated in gold, this small but exquisite theatre is just about the ultimate in rococo décor. It is entered by way of a courtyard off Residenz Strasse, and is open weekdays from 2–5 p.m., and on Sundays from 10 a.m. to 5 p.m., but closed on some holidays.

Continue along Residenz Strasse to the **Theatinerkirche** (7), an Italian Baroque church from the 17th century with a later façade by Cuvilliés. Its name derives from a small order of monks called the Theatines, founded by St. Kajetan. The interior is especially beautiful and should not be missed.

Just opposite the church is the **Feldherrnhalle,** an open building with statues of Bavarian military leaders. From here the massive Odeonsplatz, scene of Hitler's abortive Beer Hall Putsch of 1923, opens the way to Munich's newer sections to the north.

Those who would like to make an extended tour should turn left onto Brienner Strasse; otherwise the walk can be cut short at this point by entering the Hofgarten (14) and continuing on from there.

The elegant and very fashionable Brienner Strasse leads to **Königsplatz** (8), a little bit of classical Greece in Munich. At the west end of the square stands the **Propyläen,** inspired by the entrance to the Acropolis in Athens. This and the surrounding pseudo-temples were all the doings of King Ludwig I (not to be confused with his grandson, Ludwig II), who had a peculiar passion for the Hellenic Age. Oddly enough, his second son, Otto, actually became king of Greece in 1832. The Grecian motif is continued on the north side by the **Glyptothek,** and on the south by the **Antikensammlungen.** Both are museums; the former specializing in Greek and Roman sculpture, the latter in small works of ancient art. Opposite the Glyptothek, on Arcis Strasse, there is a large and rather pompous building in which the ignominious Munich Agreement of 1938 was reached between Hitler, Mussolini, Britain's Chamberlain, and France's Daladier. It is now a music academy.

The charming **Villa Lenbach** on Luisen Strasse, to the right of the Propyläen, provides a welcome touch of relief from all that grandeur. Formerly the home of the fashionable 19th-century painter Franz von Lenbach, it is now a small museum *(Städtische Galerie)* specializing in turn-of-the-century art, particularly that of Kandinsky and the "Blue Rider" school. The museum is open Tuesdays through Sundays, from 10 a.m. to 6 p.m.

Follow the map to the **Alte Pinakothek** (9) on Theresienstrasse. This is one of the greatest art museums in the world, and by far the most famous in Munich. It houses the awesome collection of Old Masters put together over a period of centuries by the Wittelsbachs, including works by Rembrandt, Rubens, Dürer, Van Dyck, El Greco, and so on. Allow plenty of time for this or, better still, come back another day. The museum is open daily except Mondays; 9 a.m. to 4:30 p.m., and also from 7–9 p.m. in the evening on Tuesdays and Thursdays.

Directly across the street is the very modern **Neue Pinakothek** (10). This new art museum, opened in 1981, is a stunning addition to Munich's architecture. Its collections encompass the 18th and 19th centuries, with fine selections of Impressionist and *Jugendstil* works along with the German romantics. Again, it is worth several hours of your time and might better be combined with a re-visit to the Alte Pinako-

In the English Garden

thek. Opening hours are from 9 a.m. to 4:30 p.m., Tuesdays through Sundays; and also on Tuesday evenings from 7–9 p.m.

Continue down Theresienstrasse and turn left up Ludwigstrasse. Make a right on Veterinärstrasse just opposite the university and enter one of Europe's best city parks, the **English Garden** (11). Laid out in 1789 by an American with British sympathies, the enormous and very beautiful landscape is a favorite retreat for *Münchners* of all ages. Following the map will lead you to the Chinese Pagoda, surrounded by a popular beer garden. On the return stroll you will pass the Monopteros, a Grecian love temple atop a grassy knoll.

Leave the park at Prinzregenten Strasse. To the left is the **Bavarian National Museum** (12) with its gigantic collections of just about everything that could loosely be termed art—an entire cultural history of Bavaria from Roman times until the 19th century. Especially noteworthy is the Tilman Riemenschneider room, devoted to that great 15th-century sculptor from Würzburg. The museum is open every day except Mondays, from 9:30 a.m. to 5 p.m.

The **Haus der Kunst** (13) is yet another art gallery, this time erected not by the Wittelsbachs but by Adolf Hitler as a temple of official Nazi art. Somehow the bombs missed and it now houses a museum of contemporary art as well as temporary exhibitions. Visits can be made any day except on Mondays, from 9 a.m. to 4:30 p.m., and on Thursday evenings from 7–9 p.m.

In the Hofbräuhaus

Cross the busy intersection via the underground passageway and walk over to the **Hofgarten** (14), a formal garden from the 17th century. From here follow the map past the rear of the Residenz (6) to that tiny square so well known to generations of tourists, the Platzl. It was close to this spot that a brewery was set up for the royal court in 1589, expanding onto Platzl in 1644. When this was later moved, the space was filled by the world-famous **Hofbräuhaus** (15), built by the Wittelsbachs in 1896 to provide the poorer citizens of Munich with a place where they could drink cheaply, thus helping to avoid social revolutions. Today it is mostly visitors—millions of them a year—who guzzle down the one-liter mugs to the beat of an oom-pah band. Whether you like this sort of thing or not, it is at least an interesting phenomenon; one which may very well bring your walk to an end right there.

Those who have not succumbed to the Hofbräuhaus may want to carry on by following Orlandostrasse and a passageway through a building to Tal, a busy street leading to the **Isartor** (16). This 14th-century town gate, nicely restored, opens the way to the Deutsches Museum; which really requires an entire day in itself.

From here follow the map to the **Viktualien Markt** (17), a fabulous open-air market where all sorts of delicacies can be purchased. A few more steps will bring you to the **Municipal Museum** *(Stadtmuseum)* (18) on Sebastiansplatz. Those who venture inside will be amply re-

The Viktualien Markt

warded with a history of the city, a brewing museum, puppets and musical instruments, and a splendid exhibition of the history of photography and the cinema. Don't miss the 15th-century wooden carvings of the Moorish dancers on the ground floor. Entrance is through a courtyard, and the museum is open daily except on Mondays; from 9 a.m. to 4:30 p.m.

Wander over to Sendlinger Strasse and visit the **Asamkirche** (19), also known as the Church of St. John of Nepomuk. It was built by the Asam Brothers, Egid Quirin and Cosmas Damian, for their own use in the 18th century and is simply the most joyous riot of rococo décor to be found in Munich. The Asam Brothers' own house, next door at Number 61, is nearly as fanciful.

Continue down the street to the 14th-century **Sendlinger Tor** (20), another medieval town gate, and follow the map back to the starting point at Karlsplatz (2). Those whose feet have collapsed will be happy to know that there is a subway stop by the Sendlinger Tor, from which you can get home in minutes.

NEARBY SIGHTS:

Munich has several other interesting sights, mostly beyond walking distance of the center. One of these, Nymphenburg, is covered in the next chapter. Other suggestions for an extended stay include:

Deutsches Museum—probably the world's greatest museum of science and technology; where exhibits are presented in an enjoyable and easy-to-understand manner. Allow plenty of time. The museum is open daily from 9 a.m. to 5 p.m., but closes on certain holidays. Located on an island in the Isar, its closest subway stop is the S-Bahn at Isartor Platz (16).

Schleissheim—another fabulous baroque palace with great gardens, this one is nine miles north of Munich. Reach it on the S-1 line of the S-Bahn, getting off at Oberschleissheim. Open daily except Mondays and some holidays.

Theresienwiese—the site of the annual Oktoberfest, with a monstrous statue of "Bavaria." The nearest subway is at Goethe Platz on the U-3 and U-6 lines.

Schwabing—often compared to Greenwich Village or Chelsea, but really a very different place, is best seen at night. Take the U-Bahn, lines U-3 or U-6, to Münchener Freiheit station and wander around on foot.

Olympic Park—a modern sports complex built for the 1972 Olympics.There is the usual revolving restaurant on a high tower, a feature common to many German cities. Don't miss the nearby BMW Museum. The fastest way to get there is by subway, on the U-3 or U-8 lines, to Olympiazentrum station.

Dachau—a pretty suburban village noted for its infamous Nazi concentration camp, now a museum, which is open daily except for a few major holidays. Take the S-Bahn, line S-2, to Dachau station; then a bus to Dachau Ost.

Munich Tour 2
Nymphenburg

Another fascinating excursion to make while in Munich is a delightful half-day stroll through the Nymphenburg Palace and its surrounding park. This summer home of the Wittelsbachs is one of the most splendid royal palaces of Europe, in many ways outshining their downtown Residenz itself.

Begun in 1664 as a simple Italianate villa, Nymphenburg gradually expanded over the next century and a half as succeeding generations added their own ideas of how royalty should live. In much the same way as Versailles, the main palace is only part of the attraction. Hidden among the trees is an absolute jewel of a hunting lodge and several intriguing pavilions. The formal gardens are dazzling, while the carriage museum, botanical gardens, and royal porcelain factory all add their measure of interest.

GETTING THERE:

From the lower level of Munich's main train station take the **U-Bahn** (route U-1) to Rotkreuzplatz, the present end of the line. Here you change to streetcar #12 in the direction of Amalienburg Strasse, getting off at the Schloss Nymphenburg stop.

By car, follow Arnulfstrasse from the train station to Roman Platz, which is very close to the palace.

WHEN TO GO:

Schloss Nymphenburg is open every day except Monday, from 9 a.m. to 12:30 p.m. and 1:30–5 p.m. During the winter season the hours are reduced to 10 a.m. to 12:30 p.m. and 1:30–4 p.m.

FOOD AND DRINK:

There is a reasonably priced restaurant in the south wing of the palace, to the left of the carriage museum (9), as well as a café in the garden. Beyond that the choice is very limited.

TOURIST INFORMATION:

Check with the Munich tourist office listed on page 26.

Nymphenburg Palace

SUGGESTED TOUR:

From the **streetcar stop** (1) on Notburgastrasse there is a wonderful view of the palace complex. Walk along the ornamental canal to the central building and purchase a combined ticket for the *Schloss*, carriage museum, and the park pavilions.

Upon entering the **Palace** (2) you will first step into the **Great Hall** *(Steinerner Saal)*, a vast room of rococo splendor. The ceiling frescoes, full of allegorical references, are well worth a detailed examination. Stroll through the gorgeously decorated north wing, noting the gallery with the paintings of Nymphenburg as it appeared in the 1720s.

For most visitors, however, the south wing is more interesting. Here you will find King Ludwig I's famous **Gallery of Beauties**—36 paintings commissioned by the king of the most beautiful women of his time. Included in the group is the notorious Lola Montez, an Irish-born "Spanish" dancer who ultimately became his undoing. At the ripe old age of 60 the king took her as his latest mistress, an act which did not sit well with the conservative Bavarians, and which was partly responsible for his forced abdication in 1848. Poor Lola was sent into deepest exile—the far-off United States, where she entertained folks from New York to California. Today she lies buried in Brooklyn.

Close to this is the bedroom in which Ludwig II, the "mad" king, was born on August 25th, 1845. You will probably be meeting up with him, or at least his creations, several times during your Bavarian adventures.

Other particularly interesting rooms nearby include the south gallery, with its paintings of various Wittelsbach properties, and the Chinese lacquer room.

Leave the palace and walk out into the gardens. The part facing you, laid out in a formal manner, is called the **Large Parterre** (3). Statues of mythological gods adorn the paths leading to the fountain.

Follow the trail on the left to **Amalienburg** (4), an exquisite hunting lodge in the rococo style by Cuvilliés. Its exterior is rather restrained, but once inside you will be treated to a visual feast. The most sumptuously decorated room here is the circular Hall of Mirrors. The Pheasant Room, kitchen, and bedroom are also outstanding.

A path leads through the trees to the *Dörfchen*, a tiny group of cottages reminiscent of the *hameau* at Versailles. The nearby 18th-century pump house still works the big fountain in the parterre. Continue on to the **Badenburg** (5), an elegant bath house complete with a banquet hall and a luxurious indoor swimming pool. The trail now follows along the side of a lake in the Monopteros, a little love temple on the water's edge.

The elaborate **Cascade** (6) marks the beginning of the main canal. Stroll through the woods beyond to the **Pagodenburg** (7), an octagonal tea pavilion whose upper floor is decorated in Chinese motifs.

Returning in the direction of the palace brings you to the **Magdalenenklause** (8), also called the Hermitage. A refreshing change after all the splendor, this at first seems to be in a state of ruin. Don't be deceived—it was built that way in 1725 for the private meditations of the ruler; the appearance of poverty then being very fashionable. The interior contains a strange chapel in the form of a grotto, and unadorned rooms where the ceremonies of court life could be avoided.

Continue through the ornamental gardens and exit the grounds via a passageway under the palace. To the right, in the south wing, is the **Carriage Museum** *(Marstallmuseum)* (9). Here the state coaches and sleighs of the Wittelsbachs are on display, including the utterly fantastic ones used to transport Ludwig II on his nocturnal escapades.

The **New Botanical Gardens** (10), slightly to the north of Nymphenburg on Menzinger Strasse, provide a delightful end to this trip. Various climates of the world are skillfully re-created and planted with appropriate flora in this wonderful landscape of natural beauty.

On the way back to the streetcar stop (1) you may want to pause at the **Royal State Porcelain Factory** (11), where Nymphenburg porcelain is still made to traditional rococo designs.

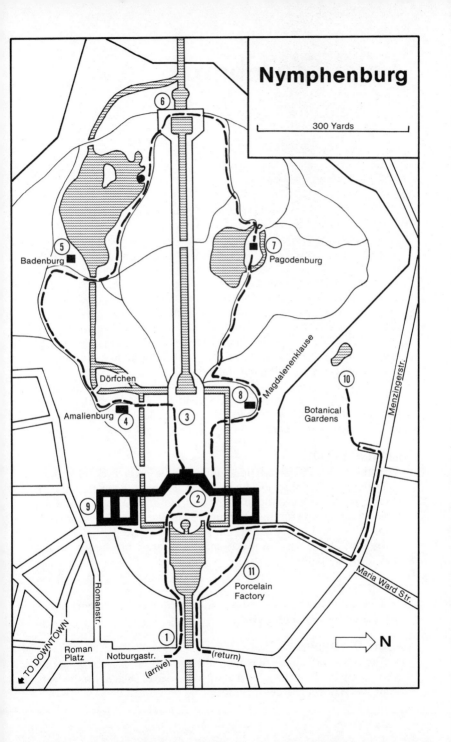

Nymphenburg

300 Yards

⑥

⑤ Badenburg ■

⑦ Pagodenburg ■

Dörfchen

Amalienburg ■ ④   ③   ⑧ ■

Magdalenenklause

⑩

Botanical Gardens

Menzingerstr.

⑨   ②

⑪ Porcelain Factory

Maria Ward Str.

⇨ N

Romanstr.

TO DOWNTOWN

Roman Platz   Notburgastr. ① (return)
(arrive)

Lake Starnberg

Long a popular playground for the people of Munich, Lake Starnberg is a delightful daytrip destination within sight of the Alps. Its particular attraction, beyond natural beauty, lies in the fact that it is so easy to reach. Only a half-hour ride from the city by commuter train or car, the lake has a good boat service which carries visitors onwards to lovely, secluded villages.

Royalty has been drawn to these shores for centuries. The castle at Berg, still a residence of the Wittelsbachs, was always a favorite of King Ludwig II. It was here, too, that his bizarre life ended in tragedy. The artistic collaboration between Ludwig and the composer Richard Wagner was first realized at Starnberg, with many later scenes in their strange relationship taking place nearby.

For travelers, the Lake Starnberg region offers a wonderful alternative to staying in Munich. A wide choice of accommodations, at prices often well below those in the city, is available through the local tourist office in Starnberg.

GETTING THERE:

Trains to Starnberg leave frequently from the lower level of Munich's main station. They may also be boarded at other S-Bahn stations, including those under Marienplatz or Karlsplatz. Take route S-6 in the direction of Tutzing for the half-hour ride to Starnberg. Those without railpasses should follow the ticketing instructions on page 25.

By car, Starnberg is some 16 miles southeast of Munich on the A-95 (E-6) Autobahn.

WHEN TO GO:

This trip is most pleasant on a fine, warm day in summer; and is well suited for weekend travel.

FOOD AND DRINK:

There is a wide range of restaurants and cafés in Starnberg, particularly along the lake shore, and in the other small villages on the lake. Some well-known choices include:

Lake Starnberg

Undosa (in Starnberg, on the Seepromenade) $$
Strandhotel Schloss Berg (in Berg, at Seestrasse 17) $$
Dorint Seehotel Leoni (in Berg-Leoni, at Assenbucher Str. 44) $$$
Café am See (in Tutzing, at Marienstr. 16) $$

TOURIST INFORMATION:
The tourist information office in Starnberg is at Kirchplatz 3, phone (08151) 132-74.

SUGGESTED TOUR:
Leave the **Starnberg train station** (1) and stroll over to the **pier,** just a few yards away. Study the posted boat schedule and decide whether to take a ride to Berg now, or see the town of Starnberg first. If you choose the latter, continue up Wittelsbacher Strasse to Kirchplatz, where the tourist office and parish church are located.

Cross Hauptstrasse and follow the map past the town hall, climbing uphill to the 16th-century **castle** (2) around which the town developed. This is now occupied by government offices, but you can poke your head in for a look. Just beyond the *Schloss* there is a beautiful garden with exceptionally fine views of the lake and the distant Alps.

Schlossbergstrasse leads over a boldly designed arch to the St. Josef Kirche, an enchanting 18th-century rococo church typical of Bavarian villages. Its interior is well worth a visit, especially for the high altar. Return to lakeside via the Günther Steig, Achheimstrasse, and Bahnhofstrasse. Turn right just before the railway to the local **Folk Museum** (Heimatmuseum) (3). This is located in a charming early-16th-century log-built house, one of the oldest structures of its kind in Germany. Visits may be made from Tuesdays through Sundays; 10 a.m. to noon and 2–5 p.m.

From here you can take a lovely stroll along the **lakeside promenade** (4). There are several outdoor cafés and restaurants along the way, as well as places where you can rent electric boats quite reasonably. This may be a more intriguing idea than the boat ride.

Walk back to the pier (1) and board the boat. The short round-trip cruise (Kurzrundfahrt) goes to Berg and Leoni before returning to Starnberg and takes about 45 minutes, not including stopovers. The longer round-trip (Rundfahrt) covers the entire 12-mile length of the lake, stopping at Berg, Leoni, Possenhofen, Tutzing, Ammerland, Bernried, Ambach, and Seeshaupt; and then makes the same halts on the way back. This takes a total of about three hours, again not counting any stopovers.

A highly recommended trip is to take the boat to Berg, walk a bit over a mile to Leoni, then either return to Starnberg or continue on the long cruise. If you do the latter you can get off at Possenhofen or Tutzing and catch an S-Bahn train back to Munich rather than return to Starnberg.

Disembarking at **Berg** (5), walk up Wittelsbacher Strasse past **Berg Castle,** a favorite residence of King Ludwig II. This is where he spent his last captive hours after being deposed in 1886. It is still occupied by the family and cannot be visited. From here a path, Am Hofgarten, leads through the woods to the **Votive Chapel** erected in his honor. At the water's edge a cross marks the spot where the young monarch's body was found along with that of his doctor. Both drowned under highly mysterious circumstances, possibly murder but more likely a struggle to escape followed by suicide. Completely out of touch with reality, Ludwig's dream world was shattered and he had nothing more to live for.

Following the path to **Leoni** (6), you can either take a boat back to Starnberg or continue on the long cruise. Suggestions for a stop along the way include **Possenhofen** (7), where Ludwig's distant cousin, the empress Elisabeth of Austria, spent much of her time. At one point he was engaged to her younger sister Sophie, but this was hastily terminated by the king as the actual date drew near.

From here the boat passes the Roseninsel, a tiny island where Ludwig had yet another castle, and where some of his affairs took place.

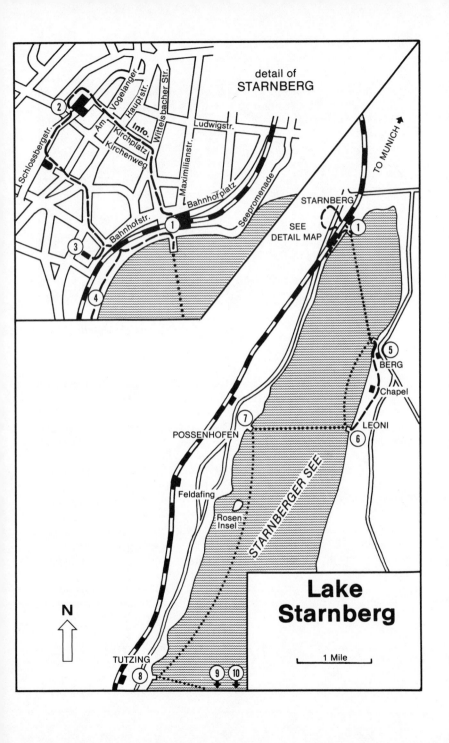

detail of
STARNBERG

Vogelanger
Hauptstr.
Wittelsbacher Str.
Schlossbergstr.
Am Kirchplatz
Info.
Kirchenweg
Ludwigstr.
Maximilianstr.
Bahnhofplatz
Seepromenade
Bahnhofstr.

STARNBERG
SEE DETAIL MAP
TO MUNICH

BERG
Chapel
LEONI

POSSENHOFEN

Feldafing

Rosen Insel

STARNBERGER SEE

N

TUTZING

Lake Starnberg

1 Mile

The Cross in the Water

Tutzing (8), a quiet resort, is the last stop on the lake to be served by S-Bahn commuter trains. Those venturing beyond will have to return by boat. Two other interesting halts are at **Ammerland** (9), an ancient fishing village with a castle; and **Seeshaupt** (10), the southern end of the lake, practically next door to the Alps.

The Ammersee

Another lovely lake within easy commuting distance of Munich is the Ammersee. More secluded than Lake Starnberg and virtually unknown to foreign tourists, it has the added attraction of a gorgeous rococo monastery at Andechs, which brews what some consider to be Germany's finest beer. This is the perfect daytrip for anyone who loves riding boats, walking quiet trails, seeing great art, and drinking fabulous brew in a convivial atmosphere.

Like Starnberg, the Ammersee region has fine hotels and guest houses which offer lower prices than those in Munich—a practical alternative to staying in the city.

GETTING THERE:

Trains on the S-Bahn commuter service leave frequently from the lower level of Munich's main station, after first making underground stops at Marienplatz, Karlsplatz, and other midtown stations. Take the S-5 line all the way to the last stop, Herrsching, a journey of about 45 minutes. Those without railpasses should follow the ticketing instructions on page 25.

By car, leave Munich on the A-96 Autobahn in the direction of Landsberg to the Oberpfaffenhofen exit, then follow local roads past Wessling and Seefeld to Herrsching. The total distance is about 25 miles. You can drive to Andechs instead of walking if you prefer.

WHEN TO GO:

The Ammersee should be visited on a fine day in the summer season. This is a good weekend trip, especially on Sundays.

FOOD AND DRINK:

There are several good cafés and restaurants in Herrsching, the most noted of which are:

    Alba Seehotel (near the boat landing) $$

    Piushof (on Schönbichlstrasse, near the trail to Andechs) $$

The town of Diessen also offers some fine choices. In Andechs, you—and about two thousand others—may quaff the monk's own beer along with good food at low prices.

TOURIST INFORMATION:

The tourist office, phone (08152) 34-49, is located in Herrsching's town hall on Bahnhofstrasse.

Andechs Monastery

SUGGESTED TOUR:

Leaving the **Herrsching train station** (1), stroll over to the **pier** (2) and check the schedule of boats to Diessen. If you have a wait before the next departure you may want to visit the **Kurpark** (3) with its picturesque little castle.

The boat ride to **Diessen** (4) takes a little over thirty minutes. Sights to see there include the sailing school and the abbey church *(Stiftskirche),* a masterpiece of the Bavarian rococo style.

Return to Herrsching by boat and follow the map to St. Martin's Church, where the woodland trail to Andechs begins as Kientalstrasse. The two-mile walk to the monastery takes you through a lovely ravine and alongside a little stream. At the end it climbs up the Holy Mountain, a place of pilgrimage for centuries.

The **Benedictine Monastery of Andechs** *(Kloster Andechs)* (5) overlooks the surrounding countryside from its lofty perch. Originally a castle dating from the 12th century, it was later rebuilt as an abbey due to the discovery of important relics in its chapel. The present church was first constructed in the 15th century. In the mid-1700s, however, it was completely redone in the rococo manner, with frescoes and stuccoes by the famous artist J. B. Zimmermann. The result is simply dazzling—one of the very best examples of that style anywhere.

From here it is only a few steps to the beer garden, where the second reward of your pilgrimage awaits. The golden brew of the Andechs monks is renowned all over the land. Join the queue for a one-liter stein and sit down at one of the indoor or outdoor tables for a rest before returning to Herrsching.

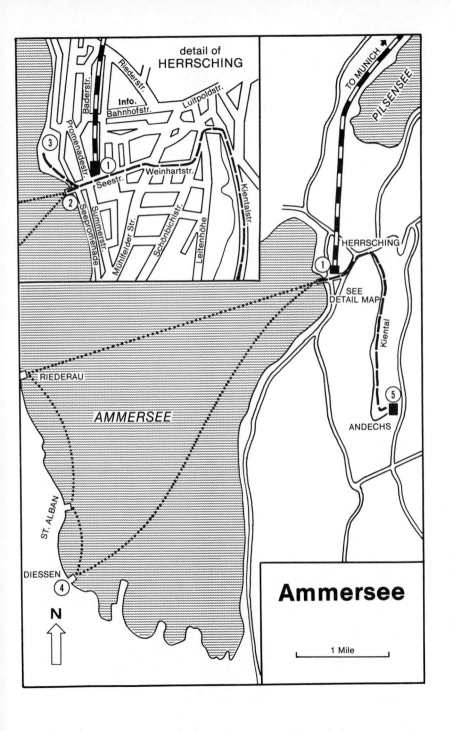

detail of HERRSCHING

Riederstr.
Baderstr.
Info.
Bahnhofstr.
Luitpoldstr.
Promenadestr.
③
①
Seestr.
Weinhartstr.
②
Seepromenade
Summerstr.
Mühlfelder Str.
Schönbichlstr.
Leitenhöhe
Kientalstr.

TO MUNICH
PILSENSEE
HERRSCHING
①
SEE DETAIL MAP
Kiental
⑤
ANDECHS

RIEDERAU

AMMERSEE

ST. ALBAN

DIESSEN
④

N

Ammersee

1 Mile

Oberammergau and Linderhof

Everyone has heard of the once-a-decade Passion Play of Oberammergau. What many may not realize, however, is that this ancient woodcarvers' village is equally as attractive during the nine out of ten years when its stage is empty. People come here in all seasons to enjoy the mountains, the quaint old houses, and the magnificent palace of King Ludwig II at Linderhof.

Easy to reach, Oberammergau makes an excellent daytrip from Munich. By staying overnight or longer it can also be used as a convenient base for one-day excursions by bus or car to nearby Garmisch-Partenkirchen, the Zugspitze, Füssen, or Mittenwald.

GETTING THERE:

Trains for Garmisch-Partenkirchen leave hourly in the morning from Munich's main station. Take one of these as far as Murnau and there change to the connecting local for Oberammergau. This last segment of the trip is extremely lovely as you slowly climb the mountain. The total journey from Munich takes less than two hours. Special one-day return fares are available for those without a railpass. Service back to Munich operates until early evening.

By car, leave Munich on the A-95 (E-6) Autobahn in the direction of Garmisch-Partenkirchen. Just north of that town, at Oberau, turn right on a local road that leads quickly to Oberammergau. The total distance is about 50 miles.

WHEN TO GO:

A fine day in warm weather will make this trip more enjoyable. Schloss Linderhof is open every day, although its grotto and Moorish pavilion are closed in winter. Anyone going to Oberammergau while the Passion Play is on should expect crowds.

View of Oberammergau

FOOD AND DRINK:
Being a major tourist attraction, Oberammergau has a wide range of restaurants and cafés. Some choices are:
Alois Lang (St. Lukas Str. 15) $$
Alte Post (Dorfstr. 19) $$
Wolf (Dorfstr. 1) $$
There is also a restaurant and café at Schloss Linderhof.

TOURIST INFORMATION:
The tourist office is located in the new Ammergauer Haus convention center on Eugen Papst Strasse. You can call them at (08822) 49-21.

SUGGESTED TOUR:
Upon arrival at the **Oberammergau train station** (1) you should check the posted schedule of buses to Linderhof. These may be boarded here or, more conveniently, in front of the town hall (5). Decide which bus you would like to take and how much time can be spent first in Oberammergau, allowing at least two hours to see Linderhof. Those with cars will, of course, be driving there instead.

The **Passion Play Theatre** (*Spielhaus*) (2) is easily reached by following the map across the Ammer River. As the whole world knows by now, this sometimes controversial play is held once a decade, from May through September, in the years ending in zero. Every day during that period this otherwise peaceful village is invaded by thousands of visitors. Tickets to the event are available only in combination with overnight accommodation, and are usually sold out well in advance.

The play itself, depicting the story of Christ's Passion, lasts about six hours and uses the talents of some one thousand local amateur performers, many of whom have taken a few months off from their erstwhile occupation of woodcarving. It was first performed during the 17th century as a result of a vow taken by surviving villagers after deliverance form the black plague. The theatre, seating about four thousand spectators, is a marvel of ingenious design. It is open to visitors, and guided tours of its interior may be taken.

Stroll over to the **Heimatmuseum** (3) for a look at some wonderful antique Christmas *crèches* and fine examples of the local woodcarvers' art. You may want to visit this on the way back to the station as it is usually open in the afternoons only.

Turn right at the square and walk down Dorfstrasse. This leads to the magnificent 18th-century **Parish Church** (*Pfarrkirche*) (4), well worth a visit for its marvelous rococo interior. Wandering around the nearby streets will reveal several examples of *Lüftmalerei,* the "air paintings" with which many of the houses are decorated.

The bus to Linderhof may be boarded in front of the **town hall** (*Rathaus*) (5) on Schnitzlergasse. Eurailpasses are accepted for this 25-minute ride; otherwise pay the driver. By car the distance is under ten miles. Leave town via Ettaler Strasse and bear right to Linderhof.

Schloss Linderhof (6) is the most satisfying of "mad" Ludwig's creations, and the only one where he actually spent much time. Built between 1870 and 1879, the palace is best understood as a stage set in which a deranged mind could act out its fantasies. An incredible amount of opulence is packed within this relatively small structure.

To see the interior, as well as the grotto and Moorish pavilion, you must join one of the very frequent guided tours which begin in front of the palace. Some of these are conducted in English. Tickets are sold at the park entrance, opposite the bus stop. A descriptive booklet in English is also available.

When the palace tour is finished you should be sure to climb uphill to the **Grotto,** an artificial cave entered by way of a hinged boulder. Here the inside of the Venus mountain from Wagner's *Tannhäuser* is re-created, complete with lake, waterfall, and a cockle-shell boat in which the king was transported more deeply into his dream world.

Sometimes these illusions took other shapes, as when Ludwig de-

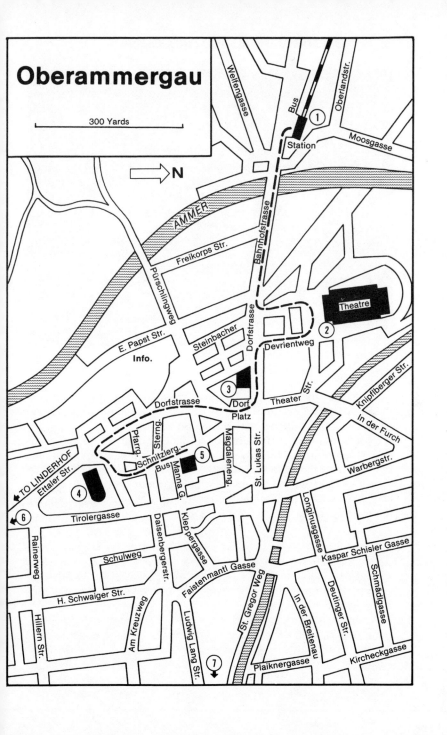

Linderhof Palace

cided to play the role of an Oriental potentate. For this, he erected the **Moorish Pavilion** on the path which leads back to the palace. Don't miss seeing this—the peacock throne is spectacular.

Finish your tour of Linderhof by strolling through the splendid gardens, then return to the bus stop and Oberammergau. An additional sight there, if time allows, is a cable car ride up the **Laber Mountain** for a superb view. The lower station (7) is about one mile from Dorf Platz by way of a path along the creek, just beyond the Wellenberg recreation center.

Garmisch-Partenkirchen

It was the Winter Olympics of 1936 which made Garmisch-Parten-kirchen famous. Formerly two separate resort towns, they were merged for that event and have shared the unwieldy name ever since. Neatly split down the middle by the Partnach stream, with Garmisch to the west and Partenkirchen—once the Roman settlement of *Parthanum*—to the east, the combined entity has become Germany's leading center for winter sports.

Mountains are what Garmisch-Partenkirchen is all about. The town lies in a broad, flat valley at the foot of the highest peak in Germany, the Zugspitze, and is surrounded on all sides by towering Alps, whose bases literally run right into the village streets. Despite immense popularity, Garmisch-Partenkirchen remains remarkably unspoiled in its easygoing Bavarian manner.

By getting off to a very early start and cutting the tour short it is possible to combine this trip in the same day with one to the Zugspitze, covered in the next chapter. With its wide range of accommodations, the town also makes an excellent base for daytrips to Oberammergau, Mittenwald, or Füssen; all served by local buses.

GETTING THERE:

Trains depart Munich's station hourly for the 90-minute trip to Garmisch-Partenkirchen. Return service operates until early evening. Special one-day round-trip tickets are available.

By car, Garmisch-Partenkirchen is 55 miles south of Munich via the A-95 (E-6) Autobahn.

WHEN TO GO:

The resort is active all year round, but the Partnachklamm may be closed after a heavy snow or spring melt. Those making this walk should be prepared to get a little wet, and need suitable shoes. The mountains can be chilly, even in summer.

FOOD AND DRINK:

This international resort has a broad selection of restaurants and cafés in all price ranges. Some suggestions, in the order you will pass them, are:

Trail to the Partnachklamm

Reindl Grill of the Partenkirchner Hof (Bahnhofstr. 15) $$$
Forsthaus Graseck (near the Partnachklamm, at the top of the cable car) $$
Post Hotel Partenkirchen (Ludwigstr. 49) $$
Berggasthof Panorama (near the Church of St. Anton) $$
Clausings Post Hotel (Marienplatz 12, near the casino) $$
There is also a pleasant café at the top of the Wank, and several inexpensive places going into the Partnachklamm.

TOURIST INFORMATION:
The tourist office, phone (08821) 530-55, is at Bahnhofstrasse 34, near the train station.

SUGGESTED TOUR:
Start at the **train station** (1) and follow the map along the Partnach stream to the **Olympic Ski Stadium** (2). Accommodating about 100,000 spectators, this gigantic outdoor structure was built by the Nazi regime as a showcase. Removing the swastikas did little to improve the architecture, but functionally it is still excellent and remains in use every winter. Entry is free.

A fascinating and easy walk into the mountains can be made by following the road to the right. In about one mile, level all the way, you will come to the tiny **Graseckbahn cable car** (3). Ride this to its

In the Partnachklamm

upper station at the Frosthaus Graseck, a wonderful alpine inn and a great place for lunch.

Cross the hotel terrace and continue along a trail with spectacular views to the upper end of the **Partnachklamm** (4). This wildly romantic gorge, only a few feet wide and very deep, is filled with torrents of rushing white water. A narrow footpath with guardrails has been carved from the sheer rock sides, at times tunneling through impossible passages. You'll get a little wet, but that's a small price to pay for such a breathtaking experience. There is a modest admission charge, payable at the exit.

Leaving the gorge will put you back on the road to the Olympic Ski Stadium. Return there and either walk or take a bus to the **Werdenfels Folk Museum** *(Heimatmuseum)* (5) on Ludwigstrasse, a fascinating exhibition of mountain life in olden times. The museum is open Tuesdays through Fridays, 10 a.m. to 1 p.m. and 3–6 p.m.; and on Saturdays and Sundays from 10 a.m. to 1 p.m.

Now follow the map to the 18th-century **Pilgrimage Church of St. Anton** (6), going past some remarkable Stations of the Cross along the hilly path. The interior of this chapel is truly extraordinary, and well worth the climb. On the way in you will pass a touching display of plaques, some with photographs, in memory of local sons who never returned from the last two wars.

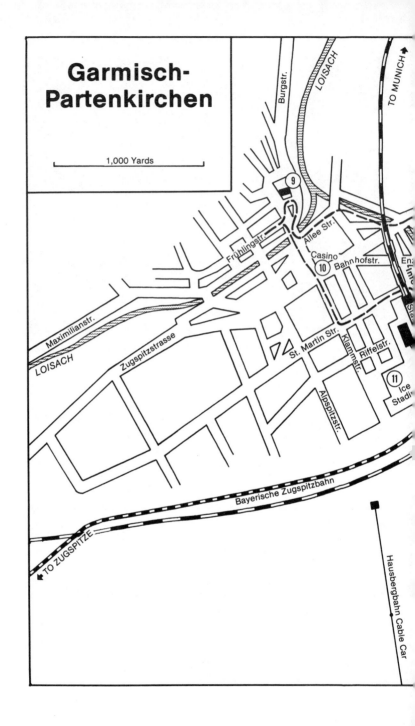

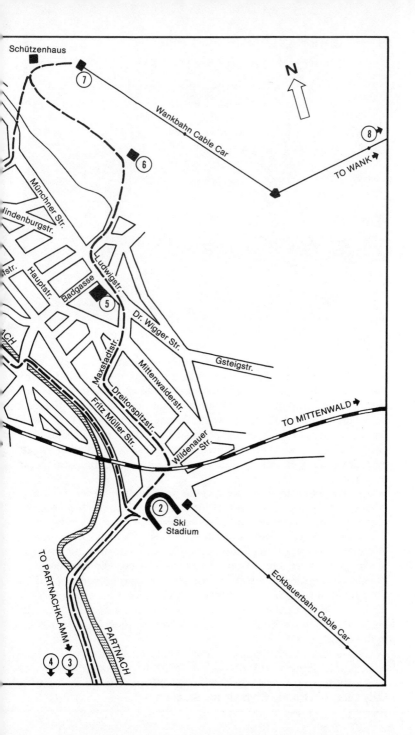

View from the Wank Summit

The Philosophenweg, a trail with stunning views of the Alps, leads to the Schützenhaus. From there take a steep but short footpath to the lower station of the **Wankbahn cable car** (7). Board one of the small cabins for a lift up the mountain, but don't get off at the first stop. Stay on all the way to the **Wank Summit** (8) for the most glorious panorama possible of the Zugspitze and the Wetterstein range towering over a toy-like Garmisch-Partenkirchen, safely nestled in its valley below. There is a sunny outdoor café to help you enjoy the scene even more.

At 5,850 feet, the summit is a center for the thrilling sport of hang gliding. This is a fast way down for some brave souls, but you will probably prefer to return on the cable car.

Leave the lower station and follow the map through Partenkirchen and into Garmisch. A path along the Partnach stream brings you to the Kurpark, from which it is a short stroll to the **Old Church** *(Alte Kirche)* (9). Located in a picturesque district, its origins may predate the spread of Christianity into this area. Or at least according to local tradition. Some of the mural paintings date as far back as the 13th century. The church itself was originally Romanesque, but later rebuilt in the Gothic style.

Take a look down Frühlingstrasse, a colorful street of quaint chalets, then begin a short walk back to the station. Along the way you may want to stop at the new **Casino** *(Spielbank)* (10) for a fling with Lady Luck, or visit the **Olympic Ice Stadium** (11).

The Zugspitze

One of the classic daytrips in Bavaria is an excursion to the top of the Zugspitze. At nearly ten thousand feet, Germany's highest peak offers a fantastic panoramic view extending across four nations. At one time only mountain climbers could enjoy this spectacle, but today an ingenious network of cable cars and a rack railway make the ascent fast, easy, and safe.

There are several possible ways up the mountain. The route suggested here is the most common and could be done in reverse if desired. People who become queasy at the thought of a cable-car ride can go both ways by rail instead.

Germany shares its peak with Austria, which has its own cable-car system as well as a café and restaurant at the top. Be sure to bring your passport for crossing this lofty frontier.

This excursion can be combined in the same day with an abbreviated version of the Garmisch-Partenkirchen trip by getting off to a very early start, but only during the summer when the hours of sunlight are longer.

GETTING THERE:

Trains from Munich's main station leave hourly for Garmisch-Partenkirchen, a ride of about 90 minutes. From the station there walk over to the adjacent Zugspitz Bahnhof and take one of the hourly trains operated by the Bayerische Zugspitzbahn, a private company. Eurailpasses or the GermanRail Tourist Card are not valid for this rack railway; however, holders of the Eurailpass do get a discount. Those without railpasses will be happy to know that a bargain one-day excursion ticket, going all the way from Munich or Augsburg to the highest peak and back, including cable cars, is available.

By car, leave Munich on the A-95 (E-6) Autobahn and drive 55 miles south to Garmisch-Partenkirchen, parking there at the Zugspitz Bahnhof. Take the rack railway as above. It is also possible to drive to the Eibsee and pick up the trip from there, a small savings of time and money.

WHEN TO GO:

The ascent of the Zugspitze may be made all year round, but clear weather is necessary to enjoy the sights. Should the skies cloud over en route you might consider making either the Garmisch-Partenkirchen or Oberammergau trip instead. Remember, however, that the weather atop the Zugspitze is often clear when the valley is socked in. Ask at the Zugspitz Bahnhof if in doubt. You may want to bring a sweater or jacket, even in summer.

FOOD AND DRINK:

A meal at the **Schneefernerhaus** ($$) near the top of the Zugspitze is an unforgettable experience. Along with the main dining room overlooking the Alps, there is also an inexpensive cafeteria opening onto a terrace.

The café and restaurant on the Austrian side of the peak is also quite good and accepts German money.

There are several restaurants and cafés at the Eibsee and, of course, a superb selection in Garmisch-Partenkirchen.

TOURIST INFORMATION:

The tourist office in Garmisch-Partenkirchen, phone (08821) 530-55, is at Bahnhofstrasse 34, near the train station. You can phone the Bayerische Zugspitzbahn at (08821) 580-58.

SUGGESTED TOUR:

Leave the **Garmisch-Partenkirchen train station** (1) and walk over to the **Zugspitz Bahnhof** (2), a separate station for the privately owned rack railway going up the mountain. Purchase a round-trip tour ticket *(Rundreise)*, which includes the rack railway, summit cable car, and the Eibsee cable car. Departures are hourly from 7:35 a.m. to 3:35 p.m., with some seasonal variations.

The train first travels along a relatively level route, then begins the climb to the **Eibsee** (3), a lovely lake near the foot of the mountain, reached in about 40 minutes. Those with cars can drive this far and board the train here. This is also the lower station of the Eibsee cable car, going all the way to the very top, on which you will be returning.

Shortly after this the train plunges into a long tunnel, winding its way like a corkscrew through the inside of the Zugspitze, and reaches the **Schneefernerhaus** (4) about 75 minutes after leaving Garmisch-Partenkirchen. Walk out to the terrace for a view from the heights. At 8,100 feet above sea level, this is one of the loftiest hotels in the world, offering almost year-round skiing, overnight accommodations, and good food.

From here you may want to take a little side trip to the **Zug-spitzplatt** (5), a glacier ski area reached by the Gletscherbahn cable

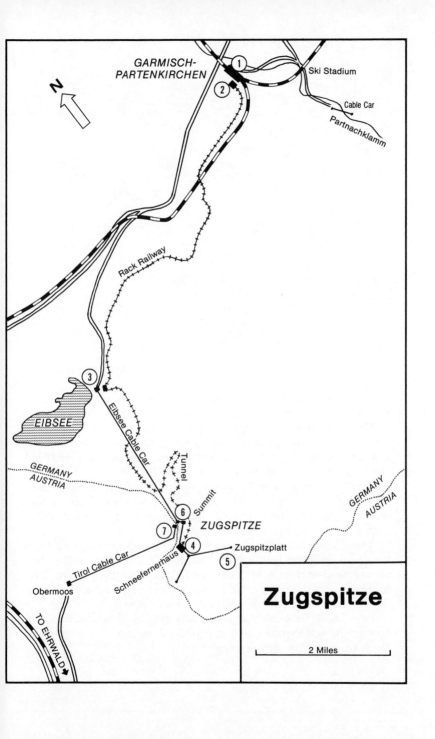

GARMISCH-PARTENKIRCHEN

Ski Stadium

Cable Car

Partnachklamm

N

① ②

Rack Railway

③

EIBSEE

Eibsee Cable Car

GERMANY
AUSTRIA

GERMANY
AUSTRIA

Tunnel

Summit

⑥

⑦ *ZUGSPITZE*

④ → Zugspitzplatt

⑤

Tirol Cable Car

Schneefernerhaus

Obermoos

TO EHRWALD

Zugspitze

2 Miles

Cable Car to the Summit

car, for which there is a small additional charge. Some of the trains now go through a new tunnel extension directly to the Zugspitzplatt.

This is still not the top of the Zugspitze. To get there, take an elevator in the Schneefernerhaus hotel up to the lower station of the summit cable car *(Gipfel Seilbahn),* which runs at least every half-hour and takes only four minutes to reach the peak.

Finally at the **very top** *(Zugspitzgipfel)* (6), stroll out onto the sunny terrace and survey the world far below. It is possible to cross the **border** (7) to Austrian soil—or snow. Snacks and drinks are available on both sides, as well as a restaurant in Austria.

The return journey begins on the German side of the peak. From here take the large Eibsee cable car *(Seilbahn)* for the thrilling ten-minute descent directly to the Eibsee (3). Alternatively, you could return by way of the small cable car to the Schneefernerhaus and then ride the train back, although this way is much slower.

From the Eibsee continue on by rack railway or bus back to Garmisch-Partenkirchen, where you board the regular train to Munich. These operate until early evening.

Mittenwald

If you were asked to design a stage set for an alpine romance you could hardly do better than to copy Mittenwald. This dreamy resort on the Austrian border has everything—a rugged mountain peak rising vertically from its own back yard, colorfully painted houses lining the peaceful streets, and the sound of a thousand violins filling the air.

The latter is Mittenwald's chief industry, next to tourism. Once a prosperous trading post on the Venice-to-Augsburg road, its economy fell to ruin as traffic moved to other passes. Then, in the 17th century, an unlikely miracle happened. A local lad named Matthias Klotz had moved to Cremona, where he learned the art of violin making from the legendary Nicolo Amati. On his return in 1684 he founded the trade which today exports Mittenwald string instruments to the entire world.

With its extraordinary selection of hotels and inns, Mittenwald makes a good base for daytrips to Garmisch-Partenkirchen, the Zugspitze, and Oberammergau.

GETTING THERE:

Trains to Mittenwald leave Munich's main station about once an hour each morning. The trip takes a little under two hours. Be sure to get on a car marked for Mittenwald as some are dropped off en route. Return trains run until early evening.

By car, Mittenwald is 68 miles south of Munich. Take the A-95 Autobahn to Garmisch-Partenkirchen, then continue on the B-2 highway. There is also a slightly shorter scenic route via the B-11 from Munich, passing many small towns en route.

WHEN TO GO:

Mittenwald is a year-round resort. Good weather is necessary to really enjoy this trip. The local museum is open daily from May through October, and late December to Easter.

FOOD AND DRINK:

The town has many restaurants and cafés in all price ranges. Among the most noted are:
   Hotel Post (Obermarkt 9) $$
   Hotel Rieger (Dekan-Karl Platz) $$

Obermarkt

Post Keller (Innsbrucker Strasse 13) $$
Arnspitze (Innsbrucker Strasse 68) $$$

TOURIST INFORMATION:
The tourist office, phone (08823) 10-51, is in the town hall at Dammkarstrasse 3.

SUGGESTED TOUR:
Leave the **train station** (1) and follow Bahnhofstrasse to the **Town Hall** *(Rathaus)* (2), which houses the tourist office. From here it is a short stroll to the stunning baroque **Parish Church** (3). Built in the 18th century by the famous architect Josef Schmuzer, its beautifully frescoed tower and richly decorated interior are symbols of the town's prosperity. In front of it stands a statue of Matthias Klotz making a violin.

A few steps down Ballenhausgasse brings you to the violin-making and folk-life **museum** *(Geigenbau und Heimatmuseum)* (4). Step inside to view the process of making stringed instruments in a traditional workshop. The museum is open Mondays through Fridays from 10–11:45 a.m. and from 2–4:45 p.m.; and on weekends from 10–11:45 a.m. only. It is closed between Easter and the beginning of May and from November through late December.

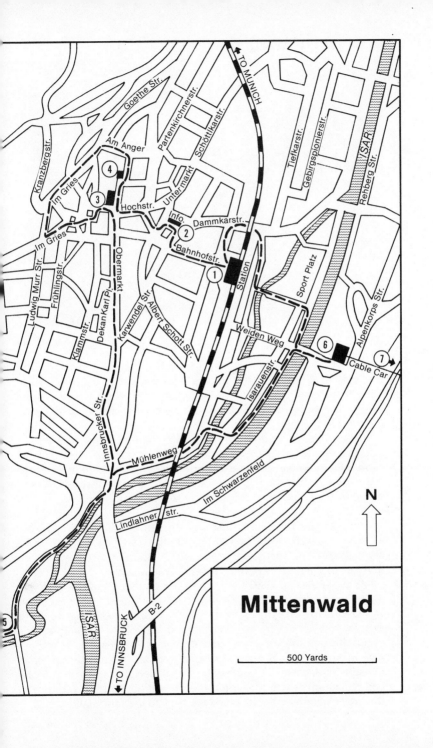

TO MUNICH

Goethe Str.
Kranzbergstr.
Partenkirchnerstr.
Schottlkarstr.
Tiefkarstr.
Gebirgspionierstr.
Rehberg Str.
ISAR

Am Anger
Im Gries
④
③
Hochstr.
Untermarkt
Im Gries
Info.
Dammkarstr.
②
Bahnhofstr.
①
Station
Obermarkt
Karwendel Str.
Albert Schott Str.
Weiden Weg
Sport Platz
⑥
Cable Car
⑦
Alpenkorps Str.
Ludwig Murr Str.
Frühlingstr.
Klammstr.
Dekan Karl Pl.
Isarauenstr.

Innsbrucker Str.
Mühlenweg
Im Schwarzenfeld
Lindlahner str.

ISAR

⑤

TO INNSBRUCK
B-2

N

Mittenwald

500 Yards

Atop the Karwendel

From here follow the map past some charming painted houses and return to the church. Obermarkt, the main street, is lined with wonderfully frescoed structures. Walk along it to the edge of town, where it becomes Innsbrucker Strasse. Just before the first bridge a path leads off to the right.

Follow the country trail a short distance to the **Leutaschklamm** (5), a very narrow gorge filled with rushing water. Actually in Austrian territory, the mountain ravine has a wooden gangway suspended above the torrent, which takes you to a spectacular 82-foot waterfall. The gorge may be entered in the summer season, or in winter if it is very cold.

Return to Innsbrucker Strasse and stroll down Mühlen Weg. Cross a bridge and walk along the Isar River to the lower station of the **Karwendelbahn** (6), a large cable car which transports you within ten minutes to the heights of the Karwendel mountain.

At an altitude of 7,362 feet, the **upper station** (7) of the cable car looks nearly straight down on Mittenwald and offers fabulous views across the Alps. Like the Zugspitze, the Karwendel peak is shared with Austria, but here there is no customs post. Follow the trail leading uphill through the snow and pass the *Freistaat Bayern* sign. You are now in Austria for the second time in one day. When you tire of all the sunshine, clean air, and marvelous scenery you can visit the café and restaurant adjacent to the cable car station. After this, return to the lower station and follow the map back to the train station.

Füssen and Neuschwanstein

The most instantly recognized symbol of Germany is undoubtedly Neuschwanstein, which graces the covers of numerous guidebooks, brochures, and travel posters. Everything a fairy-tale castle should be, "mad" King Ludwig II's most spectacular creation has even served as a model for Disneyland.

While countless tourists trek through it every year, relatively few visit the neighboring castle of Hohenschwangau—in which Ludwig was actually raised—and only a small minority venture down the road to the delightful frontier town of Füssen. This trip combines all three for an exciting day filled with memorable sights.

Füssen and its surrounding area also makes a good base for day-trips to Oberammergau, Garmisch-Partenkirchen, and the Zugspitze.

GETTING THERE:
   Trains depart Munich's main station between about 7 and 9 a.m. for either Kaufbeuren or Buchloe, where you change to a local for Füssen. Be sure to check the schedules at the Munich rail information office to determine at which town the change must be made. At the same time carefully note the return schedule. The journey takes about two hours each way, but the lovely scenery beyond Kaufbeuren makes it all worthwhile.
   By car, leave Munich on the B-12 road, going west to Landsberg, then turn south on the B-17 to Hohenschwangau and Füssen. The distance is a little over 70 miles. Another route is via Starnberg and Weilheim.

WHEN TO GO:
   The castles are open all year round, but are more crowded on weekends during the tourist season.

FOOD AND DRINK:
   There are many good restaurants and cafés in Füssen and at Hohenschwangau. Among the best, in trip sequence, are:

Hirsch (in Füssen, at Augsburger Torplatz, near the tourist office) $$

Kapuziner (in Füssen, at Schwangauer Str. 20, on the far side of the Lech River) $

Müller (in Hohenschwangau, at Alpstr. 14) $$

Lisl und Jägerhaus (im Hohenschwangau, at Neuschwanstein Str. 1) $$

There is also a restaurant and café near the entrance to Neuschwanstein Castle.

TOURIST INFORMATION:

The tourist office in Füssen is near the train station at Augsburger Torplatz. You can call them at (08362) 70-77.

SUGGESTED TOUR:

Leave the **Füssen train station** (1) and walk over to the bus stop across the street. Check the posted schedule of service to Hohenschwangau, also called *Königsschlösser* or Royal Castles. From this you can determine the amount of time available for exploring Füssen, allowing at least three hours for Neuschwanstein and Hohenschwangau castles.

Stroll down Bahnhofstrasse to Augsburger Torplatz, where the tourist information office is located. From here turn right on Reichenstrasse, a charming pedestrians-only street lined with outdoor cafés, which leads to **Kloster St. Mang** (2). This former Benedictine abbey was founded in the 8th century and rebuilt during the 18th. It now serves as the town hall and contains a small museum. In the courtyard you will find the Chapel of St. Anne, noted for its unusual *Totentanz* painting from 1602, and the parish church with its ancient 9th-century crypt. Both are worth a visit.

Climb uphill to the **Castle** *(Hohes Schloss)* (3), once a residence of the bishops of Augsburg. The present structure, curiously painted, dates from the 13th and 16th centuries. Long before that, in the 3rd century A.D., the Romans had a castle on the same site to protect their military road.

Now follow the map to the **Lech Waterfall** (4), a very beautiful spot just yards from the Austrian border. Cross the Maxsteg footbridge over the cascade and return via Tiroler Strasse. Once across the main bridge bear right onto Brotmarkt and Brunnengasse, then return to the bus stop.

Board the bus to Hohenschwangau *(Königsschlösser)*, a distance of about two miles. You could, of course, walk or drive there instead. Check the posted return schedule upon arrival.

From the **Hohenschwangau bus stop** (5) it is a fairly steep climb

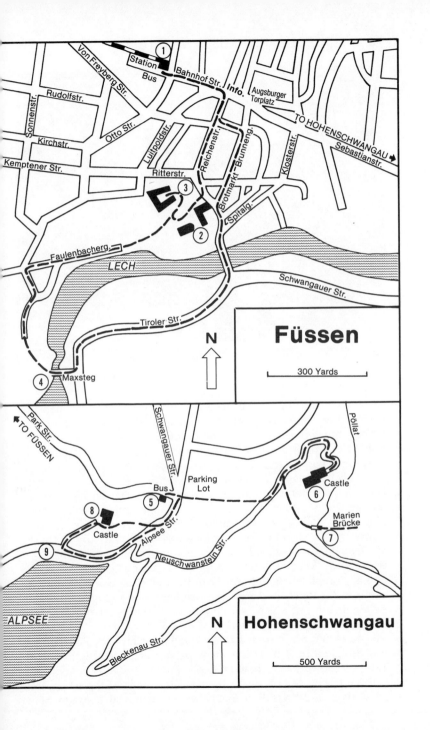

Reichenstrasse in Füssen

via a woodland trail to Neuschwanstein Castle, with park benches provided en route. This can be avoided by taking one of the rather touristy horse-drawn carriages, or a special bus (still requiring a little uphill trek), both of which start from a point opposite the bus stop, next to the parking lot.

Neuschwanstein Castle (6) is pure fantasy. By comparison, King Ludwig II's other creations of Linderhof and Herrenchiemsee, although wildly extravagant, have at least some basis in reality—other kings have built lavish palaces for themselves before. For this one, however, there is no model, except possibly the Wartburg in Thuringia. Ludwig was obsessed with strange notions of a transfigured past whose gods, knights, and swans form the hazy bedrock of Wagnerian opera. Completely withdrawn from the industrial world of the 19th century, this lonely monarch wrapped himself in a cloud of long-forgotten dreams, of which Neuschwanstein is simply the most spectacular manifestation.

The castle, rising from a rocky crag high above the Pöllat gorge, was designed by a theatrical scene-painter employed by the court. This was Ludwig's first creation, begun in 1869, but it remained unfinished at the time of his death 17 years later. He lived there for a total of 102 days, and it was there that he was taken into custody after being

Neuschwanstein Castle

declared insane. The young king's life ended tragically in the waters of Lake Starnberg the very next day.

Enter the castle and join one of the very frequent guided tours, many of which are in English. Unlike the rococo fantasies of his later structures, Neuschwanstein is heavily Teutonic, with wall murals depicting those heroic sagas so dear to the hearts of Wagnerians.

After the tour you may want to take a short but invigorating walk to the **Marienbrücke** (7) for some truly splendid views.

Return to the bottom of the hill and visit **Hohenschwangau Castle** (8). Despite its excessive decoration, this *Schloss* has a homely, lived-in feel about it. Dating from the 12th century, it was heavily reconstructed by Ludwig's father, Maximilian II. The future king spent much of his youth here and was undoubtedly influenced by its dreamy, romantic atmosphere.

From here, stroll down to the **Pindarplatz** (9) for another gorgeous view across the Alpsee, then return to the bus stop (5) and Füssen.

Lindau

Smiling, sunny Lindau, the beautiful and elegant old resort town on an island in Lake Constance, makes a delightful destination for a daytrip from Munich. Although inhabited since the ninth century and possessing many fine medieval buildings, its character is really shaped by the nearby Alps and the warm, placid lake that joins three nations together. There is just enough to see here to leave most of the day free for relaxing in the sunshine, sitting at outdoor cafés, or sailing across the shimmering waters. A day in Lindau is really a day reserved for pleasure.

Lake Constance, known to Germans as the *Bodensee*, is the third-largest lake in central Europe. It is actually a part of the Rhine, whose waters, flowing north from the Swiss Alps, are trapped in an old glacial basin before continuing their long passage to the sea. This area has been settled since prehistoric times. For centuries it formed an important link in joining the economies of northern Europe with those south of the Alps. Today the lake is a playground for the people of Germany, Austria, and Switzerland.

GETTING THERE:

Trains leave Munich's main station between 7 and 9 a.m. for Lindau, taking about two and a half hours for the journey. The last return train departs Lindau at about 6:20 p.m.

By car, Lindau is approximately 110 miles from Munich following the B-12 and B-18 roads via Landsberg and Memmingen. You are probably better off parking on the mainland and walking across the bridge.

WHEN TO GO:

A sunny day in warm weather will make Lindau an unforgettable experience, but be prepared for crowds on weekends and holidays.

FOOD AND DRINK:

This old resort has plenty of restaurants and cafés. A list of the best would include:

Bayerischer Hof (Seepromenade) $$$
Seegarten (Seepromenade) $$
Helvetia (Seepromenade) $$

Lindau Harbor

Lindauer Hof (Seepromenade) $$
Spielbank Restaurant (in the casino) $$$
Weinstube Frey (Maximilianstr. 15) $$
Zum Sünfzen (Maximilianstr. 1) $$

TOURIST INFORMATION:
Located just opposite the train station, the tourist office can be phoned at (08382) 50-22.

SUGGESTED TOUR:
Begin your walk at the **train station** (1). It was the coming of the railway in the late 19th century which radically changed the character of this former Free Imperial City. For centuries before that Lindau was a prosperous trading center—a port from which goods were exchanged across the lake. This business died as the tracks continued on to Austria and Switzerland. But the trains provided an easy way for vacationers to reach these sunny shores, and the old warehouses were soon torn down to make way for grand hotels.

A stroll along the Seepromenade will take you past these. Stop at one of the **piers** (2) to ask about departure times for a round-trip **sightseeing cruise** *(Rundfahrt)* on the lake. A wonderful way to spend an hour or so, the cruises usually take you by Bregenz in Austria and Rorschach in Switzerland. The size of the lake is astonishing. It is easy to see why it played such an important part in the early days of aviation. Both the Zeppelins, whose home base was always in Friedrichshafen, just twelve miles away, and the Dornier flying boats were developed on these waters.

Back on land, continue along the Seepromenade to the **Mangturm**, an old lighthouse erected in the 13th century as part of the defensive fortifications. Beyond this lies the **Römerschanze** (3), once a separate island and now a terrace offering good views across the harbor. A large statue of the Bavarian Lion proudly stands guard at the end of the quay.

Stroll back along the harbor and into Reichsplatz. The beautifully frescoed **Old Town Hall** (*Altes Rathaus*) (4), whose façade has both a sundial and a clock, was first built in 1422 and later modified in the Renaissance style. Once the meeting place of a 15th-century Imperial Diet, it now serves as the town library and may be visited.

Turn right, passing the Fountain of Lindavia, onto the picturesque Ludwigstrasse. This leads past the ancient Stadttheater and into Fischergasse. Along here you will find a little passageway on the right which winds its way around old houses to the **Gerberschanze** (5), a charming spot on the water.

Return to Fischergasse and make a right into a narrow alleyway called Kickengässele. In a few steps you will come to Hintere Fischergasse, a relic of olden times. A left on this quaint street puts you back on Fischergasse, which continues to the **Heathens' Wall** (*Heidenmauer*), the remains of a defensive bastion probably dating from Roman days. To the right are the public gardens and the **gambling casino** (*Spielbank*) (6).

Stroll through the gardens and turn right on Schmidgasse. The Protestant **St. Stephen's Church** (*Stefanskirche*) (7) was built in 1180 and later reconstructed in the baroque style. Next to it is the Roman Catholic **St. Mary's Church** (*Stiftskirche*) (8), formerly part of a convent, with its rococo interior. Both are worth seeing.

Cross the market square and visit the **Haus zum Cavazzen** (9). This grand old patrician mansion now houses the Municipal Museum (*Städtische Kunstsammlungen*). You can easily spend an hour here looking at the old room settings, folk art, armaments, and paintings ranging from medieval to Art Nouveau (*Jugendstil*). The museum is open Tuesdays through Saturdays, from 9 a.m. to noon and 2–5 p.m.; and on Sundays and holidays from 10 a.m. to noon. It closes from January to March.

Now follow the map along Cramergasse to the pedestrians-only Maximilian Strasse, a particularly inviting main street lined with beautifully restored old houses and sidewalk cafés.

Continue on to the **Thieves' Tower** (*Diebsturm*) (10), whose tur-

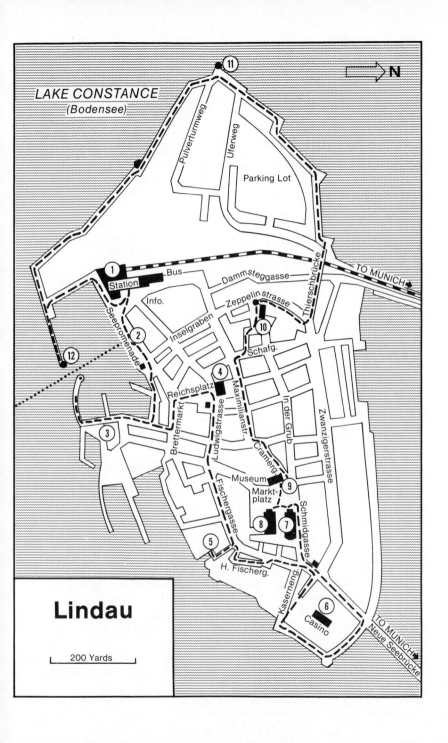

LAKE CONSTANCE
(Bodensee)

N

Pulverturmweg
Uferweg
Parking Lot

① Station — Bus
Dammsteggasse
Thierschbrücke
TO MUNICH

Info.
Zeppelinstrasse
Seepromenade
Inselgraben
②
⑩
Schafg.

④

⑫
Reichsplatz
Brettermarkt
Maximilianstr.
Ludwigstr.
In der Grub
Zwanzigerstrasse

③
Cramerg.
Museum
Markt-platz
⑨
Schmidgasse

Fischergasse
⑧ ⑦

⑤
H. Fischerg.
Kaserneng.

⑥
Casino
TO MUNICH
Neue Seebrücke

Lindau

200 Yards

The Old Town Hall

reted spire, a landmark of Lindau, evokes a vision right out of the Middle Ages. Built in 1420, this was once both a watch tower and a prison. Directly adjacent to it is the former **St. Peter's Church**, reputed to be the oldest building on Lake Constance. Now a war memorial, it dates from about the year 1000 and contains what are probably the only surviving frescoes by the Swabian artist Hans Holbein the Elder.

Walk along the top of the old town walls following Zeppelin Strasse and turn left across a bridge. Follow the path by the water's edge to the **Gun Powder Tower** *(Pulverturm)* (11), another medieval defensive work. From here continue back to the harbor where you can go out on the breakwater to the **New Lighthouse** (12). A climb to the top reveals a spectacular view of Lindau and the distant peaks in Austria, Liechtenstein, and Switzerland. After this it is only a few steps back to the train station.

Augsburg

Although it was founded by the Romans as far back as 15 B.C., Augsburg is really a city of the Renaissance. At that time its medieval merchant dynasties made this the richest place in Europe, a magnet to which great talent was naturally attracted. Much of that heritage remains intact today, and can be seen in the form of magnificent architecture and some truly outstanding museums. This is a city for serious travelers; those who come in search of history, art, and culture rather than natural splendor or foot-stomping merriment.

Because of its proximity to Munich and its location at the junction of major rail lines, Augsburg makes an excellent alternative base for daytrips to nearly all of Bavaria. A visit here could also be combined in the same day with one to Ulm by cutting both tours short.

GETTING THERE:

Trains to Augsburg depart Munich's main station at very frequent intervals. The fastest of these—those of the IC class—take less than thirty minutes for the run. Return service operates until nearly midnight.

By car, Augsburg is 42 miles northwest of Munich. Take the A-8 (E-11) Autobahn to the Augsburg-Ost exit and park as close to Königsplatz as possible.

WHEN TO GO:

Avoid going to Augsburg on a Monday, when most of the major museums are closed. Any other time is fine. Good weather is not essential for this trip.

FOOD AND DRINK:

There is a fairly wide selection of restaurants and cafés in every price range. Among the best choices are:

Sieben Schwaben Stuben (Bürgermeister Fischer Str. 12) Swabian specialties. $$

Fuggerkeller (Maximilian Str. 38) $$

Fuggerei-Stube (Jakoberstr. 26) $$

Ratskeller (Rathausplatz 2) $

Ecke-Stuben (Elias Holl Platz 2, near the Rathaus) In business since 1492. $$

TOURIST INFORMATION:
The tourist office, phone (0821) 360-24, is conveniently located at Bahnhofstrasse 7, near the train station.

SUGGESTED TOUR:
Leave the **train station** (1) and follow Bahnhofstrasse past the tourist information office to Königsplatz. Continue along Bürgermeister Fischer Strasse and turn right onto Maximilianstrasse. This very elegant old street was once part of the *Via Claudia Augusta*, an ancient Roman road leading north from Verona. At that time Augsburg, named after the emperor Augustus, was the capital of the province of Rhaetia. Today this broad thoroughfare is part of the famous Romantic Road, a heavily promoted tourist route from Würzburg to Füssen going by way of Rothenburg and Augsburg.

The early-16th-century **Fugger House** (2) was the town residence of one of the wealthiest families on earth. Jakob Fugger the Rich, financier of emperors and a man of incredible power, lived here until his death in 1525. Be sure to see the inner courtyards, particularly the *Damenhof* with its curiously Florentine appearance.

Now follow the map to the **Roman Museum** (3), located in a former Dominican church. Many valuable relics from Augsburg's Roman era are displayed in this magnificent setting, including a superb gilded horse's head from the second century A.D.

Return to Maximilianstrasse and visit the **Schaezler Palace** (4), facing the Hercules Fountain of 1602. The building itself features a stunning rococo festival hall, and houses the city's two major art museums. The first of these, nearest the entrance, is the **German Baroque Gallery**, which is interesting enough. But the real treasures are in the **State Gallery** *(Staatsgalerie)*, reached via a connecting passage through the festival hall. The well-known portrait of *Jakob Fugger the Rich* by Albrecht Dürer is here, along with many great masterpieces of the Renaissance. On the way out you may also want to stop at the Graphic Exhibition, a display of prints from the 15th to the 20th centuries. These museums, along with the Roman and some others, have a free entrance policy and are open every day except Mondays, from 10 a.m. to 4 p.m.

At the far end of Maximilianstrasse are the two adjoining **Churches of St. Ulrich** (5), the larger one Roman Catholic and the other Protestant. Together they symbolize the spirit of the Peace of Augsburg, an agreement of 1555 which brought religious freedom to the peers of the realm, although not to their subjects. Both are worth visiting, with the Catholic church being the more interesting.

Continue on to the **Red Gate** *(Rotes Tor)* (6), a fortified bastion first built in 1544. Next to this is a large open-air theatre in which opera

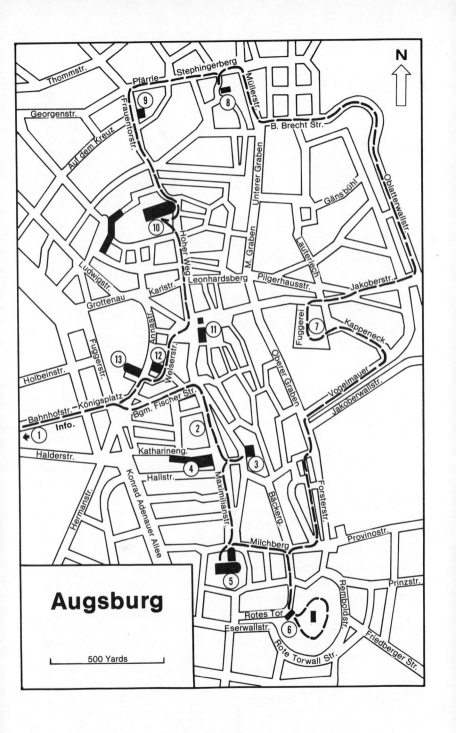

Augsburg

500 Yards

Maximilianstrasse

performances are given during July and August. A stroll through the gate leads into a peaceful park, with access to the old town walls. While there, you may want to visit the **Handwerker Museum** of crafts, open Mondays through Fridays from 2–6 p.m., and on Sundays from 10 a.m. to 6 p.m.

Return and follow the map past the Vogeltor, a defensive tower from 1445 with an old watermill, to what is probably the most famous sight in Augsburg. The **Fuggerei** (7) is hardly where Jakob Fugger the Rich lived. It is, however, where he shrewdly took out insurance on his soul, buying eternal salvation through an act of charity. For the unbelievably low rent of 1.72 marks a year, poor elderly families may live out their days in comfort and dignity in this, the world's first public housing development. The payment, equal to one Rhenish Guilder, has remained unchanged since its founding in 1519. In addition, they must also promise to pray every day for the souls of the Fuggers.

The Fuggerei is actually a rather attractive town-within-a-town, complete with its own walls and gates, which are closed at night for security. Although the houses appear to be quite old, most are post-war reconstructions with modern facilities. One of the few originals to survive is now a **museum**, furnished as it was during the 17th to 18th centuries. It may be visited any day from March through November, between 9 a.m. and 6 p.m.

A further walk along the fortifications will bring you to the little **Chapel of St. Gallus** (8), Augsburg's oldest church, which dates from 1051. Just behind this there is a hole in the town wall through which Martin Luther escaped in 1518, fearing certain arrest after refusing to recant his theological position.

Continue on a short distance to the **Mozart House** (9). Wolfgang Amadeus, of course, was born in Salzburg, but his father Leopold was raised here, and the house is now an interesting museum of Mozart memorabilia. Incidentally, Mozart's great-grandfather, Franz, lived in poverty at the Fuggerei. Entrance is free, and it is closed on Tuesdays.

Frauentorstrasse leads to the **High Cathedral** *(Hoher Dom)* (10), begun in the 9th century but rebuilt in the Gothic style during the 14th. To the left of its main entrance, on the south side, there is a fascinating bronze door decorated with strange reliefs depicting both mythology and the Old Testament. This dates from the 11th century. Equally ancient are the stained-glass windows of the prophets, said to be the oldest of their kind in the world. There are some fine altar paintings by Hans Holbein the Elder, and other interesting works of art.

Leave the cathedral and stroll down Hoher Weg to the **Town Hall** *(Rathaus)* (11). This splendid Renaissance structure is considered by many to be the finest in Germany, and is noted for its spectacular Golden Hall. The doors are open every day, except on weekends and holidays. Standing next to it is the Perlach Tower, which may be climbed for a bird's eye view between April and October. The open square in front contains a 16th-century fountain with a figure of the emperor Augustus.

Walk down Philippine Welser Strasse past the former residence of the Welser family at Number 13. Like the Fuggers, this dynasty was incredibly rich and at one time actually owned most of Venezuela. Unfortunately, they left little behind and have since fallen into obscurity. Visit the **Maximilian Museum** (12) for a look at some outstanding souvenirs of Augsburg's history. Its opening times are the same as those of the Schaezler Palace (4).

St. Anne's Church (13) is entered through a side door to the left in the Annahof. In 1518 Martin Luther found sanctuary in this former Carmelite monastery, which has been Protestant since the Reformation. Inside, there is a remarkable burial chapel of the Fuggers, and the famous portrait of Luther by Lucas Cranach the Elder. From here it is a relatively short walk back to the train station.

Ulm

The ancient city of Ulm has a lot to offer today's travelers. Admittedly, not too many foreign tourists come this way, but that's their loss. For starters, Ulm's cathedral easily ranks among the greatest on earth—and is reason enough for the journey. Then there is the medieval fishermen's quarter, oozing with quaintness; and one of the most splendid small art museums to be found anywhere. But the real attraction of this city lies in its atmosphere, an intangible element at once both captivating and refreshing.

Spiritually, Ulm is a part of Bavaria, although in fact the bulk of it lies just within the *Land* of Baden-Württemberg, whose capital is Stuttgart. Its situation at the confluence of the Danube, Iller, and Blau rivers as well as major land routes made it an important trading center as early as the 9th century. In 1164 the growing town received its municipal charter from Frederick Barbarossa, and in 1274 became a Free Imperial City. One of the first democratic constitutions was granted to its various trade guilds in 1397. The Thirty Years War brought a decline from which Ulm did not recover until the late 19th century. It was badly devastated during World War II and later rebuilt along mostly modern lines, although much of the city's medieval heritage either survived or has since been reconstructed.

By getting off to an early start, a trip to Ulm could be combined in the same day with one to Augsburg. This would, of course, require cutting both tours short.

GETTING THERE:

Trains leave Munich's main station at least hourly for Ulm, making the journey in less than 90 minutes. Return service operates until late evening.

By car, Ulm is 86 miles from Munich by way of the A-8 (E-11) Autobahn. Get off at the Ulm-Ost exit and park as close as possible to the train station.

WHEN TO GO:

A prerequisite for a trip to Ulm is good weather, as very little time will be spent indoors. Avoid coming on a Monday, when the art museum is closed.

The Crooked House

FOOD AND DRINK:

Ulm has a wide range of restaurants and cafés all over town. Some suggestions are:

Ratskeller (Marktplatz 1) $$
Zum Pflugmerzler (Pfluggasse 6, behind the cathedral) $$$
Zur Forelle (Fischergasse 25) $$
Zunfthaus der Schiffleute (Fischergasse 31) $$
Schwarzer Adler (Frauenstr. 20, 2 blocks NE of museum) $

TOURIST INFORMATION:

Located in a pavilion in front of the cathedral, the very helpful tourist office may be phoned at (0731) 641-61.

SUGGESTED TOUR:

Leave the **train station** (1) by way of the underground passage to reach Bahnhofstrasse. From here follow the pedestrians-only Hirschstrasse, a main shopping street, to Münsterplatz, where you will find the tourist information office.

Ulm Cathedral *(Münster)* (2) is the second-largest Gothic church in Germany and has the tallest steeple on the face of this earth. It was begun in 1377 but not completed until 1890, when its spire was at last raised to pierce the heavens.

The cathedral's interior is awe-inspiring, with a ceiling nearly one hundred feet above the central nave. There is no transept, but the four aisles contribute to a feeling of immense spaciousness. Note in particular the magnificent 15th-century carving on the **choir stalls**, the work of Jörg Syrlin the Elder—probably the best example of this sort of art anywhere. If you are lucky enough to come during an organ recital you will have the opportunity to experience the effect which near-perfect acoustics have on the sounds produced by eight thousand pipes. The pulpit, dating from 1500, has above it a splendid sounding board and a second pulpit for the Holy Ghost.

Before leaving the cathedral you will have to decide on whether to climb the 530-foot **tower**. Bear in mind that you can always turn around if it gets to be too much. The first part is relatively easy and offers glorious views. As you approach the top, however, the staircase becomes virtually open and quite narrow—an almost terrifying experience for the faint-hearted. The reward, of course, is the magnificent panorama which on a clear day extends all the way to the Swiss Alps.

Return from the fringes of heaven and stroll over to the **Ulmer Museum** (3). Occupying several old patrician houses, the museum specializes in the arts and crafts of Ulm and Upper Swabia from the Middle Ages to the present. The various collections, exceptionally well displayed on four floors, rival those of much larger and more famous institutions. Opening hours are from 10 a.m. to noon and 2–5 p.m., Tuesdays through Sundays. From July through September the museum is open from 10 a.m. to 5 p.m. It is closed on Mondays.

In front of the museum is the exquisite Dolphin Fountain, dating in part from 1585. The Marktplatz is only a few steps from here. It too has a notable fountain, the *Fischkasten*, built by Syrlin in 1482. This square is dominated by the elegant 14th-century **Town Hall** *(Rathaus)* (4). Although badly damaged in the last war, the building has been restored to its former Late Gothic and Renaissance splendor. The astronomical clock on its east façade is fascinating.

Walk down Herdbruckerstrasse and turn right onto the bridge. To your left you can see the Adler Bastei, the scene of one of man's earliest attempts to fly. It was in 1811 that one Albrecht Ludwig Berblinger, the "Tailor of Ulm," tried to soar across the Danube on a giant pair of cloth wings. Poor Albrecht's hopes were dashed as he plunged into the river, wiser but wetter.

Reaching the opposite bank, you are now in Neu Ulm, the part of town which belongs to Bavaria. Turn right and go down the steps onto

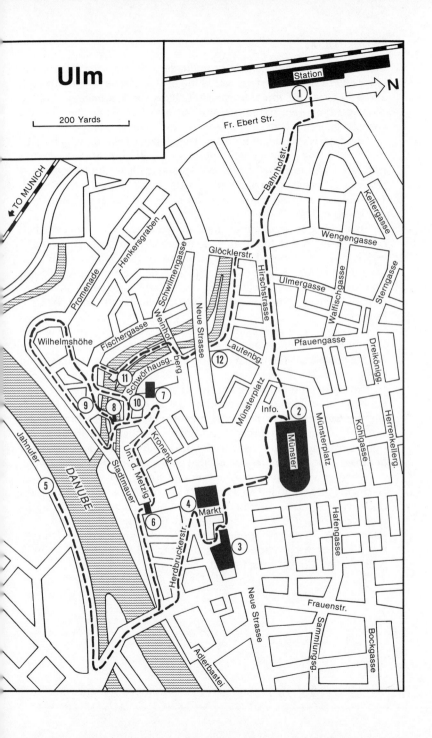

the **Jahnufer** (5), a waterside promenade with nice views of the old city. Now retrace your steps across the bridge. At the far end turn left and walk along the top of the ancient **city walls** (Stadtmauer), built in 1480 as a defensive bastion. These failed in 1805 when the Austrian garrison guarding Ulm surrendered to Napoleon at this spot.

Ulm has its own leaning tower, the **Metzgerturm** (6), which dates from 1345. This former prison tilts over six feet out of vertical. Pass through it and turn left. Unter der Metzig leads to the **Schwörhaus** (7), from whose balcony the city's constitution is annually reaffirmed. The building itself is a reconstruction of the 1613 original, which was destroyed in 1944.

Stroll down to the picturesque **Crooked House** (Schiefes Haus) (8) on the banks of the tiny Blau stream. Leaning precariously over the water, this half-timbered dwelling from about 1500 still fulfills its original purpose. Across the cobbled square is the ancient municipal mint. You are now in the medieval fishermen's and tanners' quarter, a peaceful district of narrow passageways, small canals, and venerable houses.

From here you may want to follow the map along the river and around the Wilhelmshöhe, or save a climb and continue straight to the **Fischerplätzle** (9), which has some very appealing restaurants and cafés.

Cross the little footbridge to the right, again passing the Crooked House, and turn left onto Schwörhausgasse. Along this street you will see the **Staufenmauer** (10), a 12th-century wall. In one block again turn left, crossing a narrow stone bridge. Fischergasse leads to the right. Go along it a short way to the next bridge and cross this to **Auf der Insel** (11). This entire area is filled with a quiet Gothic charm.

When you come to the Weinhofberg bridge turn right and, once across the stream, make an immediate left onto a passage which goes under Neue Strasse. To your right is the huge **Neuer Bau** (12), a former warehouse from the 16th century. Continue along the water's edge to Glöcklerstrasse, noticing how the Blau stream is divided into two different levels before flowing down to the Danube. From here it is only a few blocks to the train station.

Rothenburg

Rothenburg is almost too good to be true. This once-prosperous medieval town went to sleep after the Thirty Years War and didn't wake up until centuries later, when hordes of tourists began knocking at the gates. By that time its dreamy antiquity had become a gold mine, and its citizens happily vowed to keep the town just as it was in the Middle Ages.

There was a castle at this strategic and easily defended spot high above the Tauber valley a thousand years ago. This was extended in the 12th century and around it a town developed. As the population increased the original ramparts became too confining, so that new walls—which are still completely intact—had to be built beginning in the 13th century.

During the Reformation the town turned Protestant and as a result suffered terribly in the Thirty Years War of the 17th century. Stripped of its wealth and much too poor to afford new buildings, Rothenburg sank into obscurity. Its revival began with the late-19th-century romantics, who had discovered in the midst of their rapidly industrializing nation a true miracle in the form of this long-forgotten and perfectly preserved medieval town.

The only problem with Rothenburg is that everyone knows about it. The mobs of tourists who come here in summer will thin out considerably once you get away from the town hall area, and you may even have some parts of town to yourself.

Rothenburg also makes an excellent daytrip from Frankfurt, or from smaller bases such as Würzburg, Nuremberg, or Heidelberg. The very best way to visit the town, however, is to make an overnight stop en route between Munich and Frankfurt, or vice versa.

GETTING THERE:

One well-known way to reach Rothenburg, aside from driving, is via the **Romantic Road Bus**, operated by the railroad between Munich, Würzburg, Frankfurt, and Wiesbaden. This is free to railpass holders. To use the bus you should first check the schedule and then make reservations. There are drawbacks, however. Unless you are staying overnight it will not allow enough time to see Rothenburg properly. Contrary to popular belief, it actually is practical to get there by train from either Munich or Frankfurt (and very easy from Würzburg) without too much trouble.

Trains from Munich require an early start and a change at Steinach. Be sure to check the schedules both ways carefully. The ride takes a bit over three hours each way. You can also go via Würzburg, which is longer but possibly faster.

Trains from Frankfurt also call for an early start. Changes must be made at both Würzburg and Steinach. With good connections the total trip should take about two and a half hours. Check the schedules carefully.

By car from Munich, take the A-8 (E-11) Autobahn to the Augsburg-West exit, then the B-2 north to Donauworth, and finally the B-25 road via Nördlingen and Dinkelsbühl into Rothenburg. The total distance is 130 miles. Try to park outside the walls.

By car from Frankfurt, take the A-3 (E-5) Autobahn to Würzburg, then head south on the A-7 to the Rothenburg exit. The distance is about 115 miles. Again, park outside the walls.

WHEN TO GO:

Rothenburg can be visited at any time, but is loveliest in winter after a fresh snowfall. For your own sanity, avoid weekends and holidays during the summer.

FOOD AND DRINK:

This popular tourist attraction abounds in quaint old restaurants. Among the best are:

Bayerischer Hof (Ansbacher Str. 21, near the station) $
Hotel Markusturm (Rödergasse 1) $$
Ratsstube (Marktplatz 6) $$
Hotel Eisenhut (Herrngasse 3) $$$
Baumeisterhaus (Obere Schmiedgasse 3) $$
Goldener Hirsch (Untere Schmiedgasse 16) $$
Klosterstüble (Heringsbronnengasse 5, near the Franciscan Church) $

TOURIST INFORMATION:

The tourist office, phone (09861) 20-38, is on the Marktplatz, by the Town Hall.

SUGGESTED TOUR:

Leave the **train station** (1) and follow the map to the Old Town, which begins at the **Rödertor** (2). This 17th-century bastion leads through the medieval walls and onto Rödergasse. Walk straight ahead past the Markusturm—a surviving part of the oldest ramparts—and into the very center of Rothenburg, the Marktplatz.

The Town Hall

The imposing **Town Hall** (Rathaus) (3) reflects the former wealth of this small town. It consists of two adjoining structures, one in the 16th-century Renaissance style facing the market place and the other a Gothic building completed in the 14th century, which opens onto Herrngasse. You may explore the interior by using the entrance on Marktplatz. The Imperial Hall is interesting, but the main attraction is to climb the 165-foot **tower** for a fabulous view of medieval Rothenburg. This is reached by a difficult staircase which gets progressively narrower. Be warned in advance that some minor acrobatics are required to get out on the platform.

On the north side of the Marktplatz is the 15th-century *Ratstrinkstube*, a former tavern for the city councillors. Above this there is a **clock** with mechanical figures which act out the story of the *Meistertrunk* at 11 a.m., noon, and 1, 2, 3, 9, and 10 p.m. daily. The legend dates from the Thirty Years War, when Protestant Rothenburg was captured by the Catholic General Tilly, who ordered widespread destruction and executions. Pleas for mercy fell on deaf ears until Tilly was offered a cup of the local wine. Impressed, he agreed to spare the town if one of the councillors could drink the entire 3¼-liter bumper in one mighty draught. An ex-mayor named Nusch performed the feat, then slept for three days and nights and lived on for another 37 years before dying at the age of 80. It's a nice story. The tourist office, by the way, is in the same building.

Stroll over to **St. James' Church** *(St. Jakobs Kirche)* (4), begun in the early 14th century and consecrated in the late 15th. Its Altar of the Twelve Apostles, at the east end, is beautifully carved and merits a careful examination, as do the stained-glass windows. The main attraction, however, is in the west gallery, up a flight of stairs. This is the **Altarpiece of the Holy Blood**, a major work by the renowned sculptor Tilman Riemenschneider, completed in 1504. Its depiction of the Last Supper is simply fantastic.

Now follow the map to the **Klingentor** (5), a 14th-century town gate attached to the very curious fortified Church of St. Wolfgang. The latter dates from the late 15th century and has windows on the south side only. To the north it is a fortress, whose casemates and subterranean passages may be explored via an entrance near the high altar.

Continue along the walls to the **Castle Gate** *(Burg Tor)* (6), leading into a park built on the site of the original 10th-century castle. All that remains of its 12th-century successor is the Chapel of St. Blasius, now a war memorial. There is a marvelous view from the gardens, extending across the Tauber valley and encompassing the tiny and rather odd Toppler Castle, just below, and the medieval fortified Double Bridge to the left.

Leave the gardens and walk around to the **Franciscan Church** (7), the oldest in town, which dates from the 13th century. An unusual feature is the wooden screen separating the nave from the choir. It also contains some fine tombs. From here the elegant and wide Herrngasse, lined with stately homes of the gentry, leads back to the town hall.

Turn right on Obere Schmiedgasse, passing several beautiful patrician houses. The most notable of these is the Renaissance-style Baumeister House at Number 3, with statues of the seven virtues and the seven deadly sins adorning its upper façade. In a few steps you will come to the **Crime Museum** (8), a large and fascinating display of medieval life and justice. The collections occupy four floors of an ancient building, and every item is thoroughly explained in both German and English. Don't miss seeing this.

The most famous spot in Rothenburg is the **Plönlein** (9), the subject of countless travel pictures. Formed by the intersection of two cobbled streets, each with a tower, and framed by half-timbered houses, this little square is almost unbearably picturesque. Continue straight ahead through Siebers Tower and turn left to the walls.

From here you can walk along the top of the **ramparts**, remarkably unchanged since the 14th century. At the Rödertor (2) it is possible to

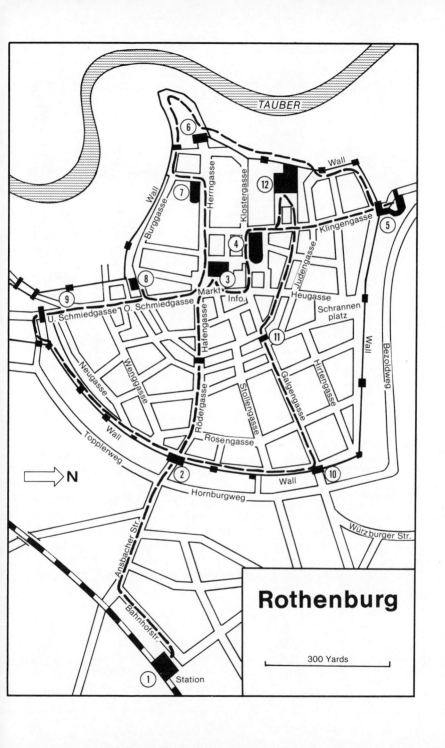

TAUBER

Wall

Burggasse

Herrngasse

Klostergasse

Wall

Klingengasse

Judengasse

Heugasse

Schrannen platz

Markt

Info.

Hafengasse

O. Schmiedgasse

U. Schmiedgasse

Neugasse

Wenggasse

Rödergasse

Stollengasse

Rosengasse

Topplerweg

Wall

Galgengasse

Hirtengasse

Wall

Bezoldweg

Hornburgweg

Würzburger Str.

Ansbacher Str.

Bahnhofstr.

→ N

① ② ③ ④ ⑤ ⑥ ⑦ ⑧ ⑨ ⑩ ⑪ ⑫

Station

Rothenburg

300 Yards

The Plönlein

climb up into the tower for an even better view. Stay on the walls as far as the **Gallows Gate** *(Galgentor)* (10), then descend and follow the map past the 12th-century **White Tower** *(Weisser Turm)* (11), another part of the earliest town walls.

A series of narrow streets lead to the **Imperial City Museum** *(Reichsstadtmuseum)* (12), located in a former Dominican convent. Here you will find the whole history of Rothenburg displayed in surviving artifacts, including the famous wine tankard used by the ex-mayor Nusch to perform his heroic feat. Now walk over to the nearby Marktplatz, from which you can retrace your steps back to the train station.

Würzburg

Although situated on the Main River, Würzburg really belongs to the south of Germany. This "Town of the Madonnas" is famous for its splendid Residenz and other triumphs of the baroque style, as well as for its delicious wines. Curiously enough, and despite its central location, Würzburg is often overlooked by foreign tourists as they scurry from Heidelberg to Rothenburg and Munich. That's a pity, for this lovely old town at the northern end of the famed "Romantic Road" has a lot to offer the traveler.

Würzburg dates from at least the seventh century, and its history is filled with the comings and goings of saints, kings, and emperors; including the likes of Charlemagne and Frederick Barbarossa. The noted sculptor Tilman Riemenschneider worked here most of his life, was elected mayor, and in 1525 led a peasant revolt for which he was imprisoned.

Würzburg's greatest era, however, was the 18th century. It was then that the ruling prince-bishops moved down from their fortress on the Marienberg and into the magnificent new Residenz, where they set a style of unparalled opulence. By the early 19th century the grandeur subsided as the town became a part of Bavaria. The vast destruction of World War II led to a near-total restoration, so that the Würzburg you see today looks very much as it did in centuries past.

This trip may also be taken from Frankfurt, which is considerably closer than Munich. Würzburg makes a good alternative base for day-trips in Franconia and along the Main valley, or as a stopover between Munich and Frankfurt.

GETTING THERE:

Trains from Munich's main station leave at one-hour intervals for the two-and-a-half-hour run to Würzburg. Return service operates until mid-evening.

Trains from Frankfurt's main station depart at hourly intervals, arriving in Würzburg about 80 minutes later. There is return service until mid-evening.

By car from Munich, take the A-9 (E-6) Autobahn to Nürnberg, then the A-3 (E-5) to Würzburg. The distance is 173 miles.

By car from Frankfurt, it is 73 miles to Würzburg via the A-3 (E-5) Autobahn.

The Residenz

WHEN TO GO:
Würzburg may be visited in any season, but avoid coming on a Monday, when virtually all major sights are closed.

FOOD AND DRINK:
The local Franconian wines, in their characteristic *Bocksbeutel* flask, are superb, as is the local beer. Some good restaurant choices are:
Bürgerspital-Weinstuben (Theaterstr. 19) $
Zur Stadt Mainz (Semmelstr. 39) $$
Hotel Rebstock (Neubaustr. 7) $$
Ratskeller (Langgasse 1) $$
Juliusspital (Juliuspromenade 19) $$

TOURIST INFORMATION:
Tourist information offices are located in front of the train station, phone (0931) 374-36; and on the Marktplatz, phone (0931) 522-77.

SUGGESTED TOUR:
Leave the **train station** (1) and pass the tourist office located just outside. From here follow the map to Würzburg's main attraction, the **Residenz** (2). Primarily the work of the renowned architect Balthazar

Marktplatz

Neumann, this magnificent baroque palace was built between 1720 and 1744 as a residence for the prince-bishops of Würzburg, who had previously lived in the Marienberg fortress.

Inside, the most spectacular sight is the **grand staircase**. As you approach the first landing you become aware of a dazzling ceiling depicting the four continents known at that time. This fresco, one of the largest on earth, is regarded as the supreme achievement of the Venetian master Giambattista Tiepolo. The **White Hall**, an elegant monochromatic masterpiece of pure rococo, provides visual relief before continuing on to the **Imperial Hall**. Again, Tiepolo outdid himself on the frescoes and, together with the architect Neumann and the sculptor Antonio Bossi, created one of the most splendid interior spaces in Germany. There are other wonderful rooms to see before leaving the palace, especially the **Garden Room** on the ground floor. The Residenz is open daily except on Mondays, from 9 a.m. to 5 p.m., and from 10 a.m. to 4 p.m. between October and March.

The **Court Chapel** *(Hofkirche),* another part of the complex, is entered from the outside. This breathtaking accomplishment by the same team is in every way equal to what you've seen in the palace proper. A gate next to this leads into the delightful **gardens**, which deserve to be explored thoroughly.

Stroll down Hofstrasse to the **Cathedral** *(Dom)* (3). Begun in the 11th century on the site of an earlier cathedral, it has been greatly modified in the years since, including some modern work installed as part of a postwar restoration. There are several fine sculptures by Tilman Riemenschneider, particularly the tombs of the prince-bishops Rudolf von Scherenberg and Lorenz von Bibra. Also noteworthy is the outstanding Schönborn Chapel, designed by Balthazar Neumann, in the north transept.

The **Neumünster Church** (4), just a few steps away, has a fine baroque façade at its west end. Much of this church dates from the 11th and 13th centuries and was built on the burial site of the Irish monk St. Kilian, who was murdered here in A.D. 689. Again, the rich interior has several excellent sculptures by Riemenschneider. There is a small garden on the north side, called the Lusamgärtlein, in which the famous 13th-century minnesinger Walther von der Vogelweide is supposed to be buried.

From here follow the map to the **Marktplatz** (5). There are two remarkable structures on its north side. One of these is the Haus zum Falken, a former inn with a fabulous rococo façade which now houses the main tourist office. The other is the late-Gothic St. Mary's Chapel *(Marienkapelle)*. Enter through the north portal and take a look at the tombstone of Konrad von Schaumberg—another marvelous carving by Riemenschneider—and the tomb of Balthazar Neumann, the architect who brought so much splendor to Würzburg.

Walk around to the **Town Hall** *(Rathaus)* (6), a picturesque complex of buildings from different eras, one of which dates from the 13th century. Step inside and visit the Wenzelsaal, named for King Wenceslas, who dined here in 1397. You can do the same, but only downstairs in the Ratskeller.

The **Old Bridge** *(Alte Mainbrücke)* (7) still carries traffic over the Main, as it has since the 15th century. This medieval span is beautifully adorned with statues of saints. Stroll across it and climb up to the **Marienberg Fortress** *(Festung Marienberg)* (8), home to the prince-bishops from the 13th to the 18th century. There is, of course, a great view of the town from here. Defensive fortifications of some sort have existed on this hill since about 1000 B.C., but the earliest part now remaining is **St. Mary's Church** *(Marienkirche)* in the courtyard, consecrated in A.D. 706. You may tour the various sections of the fortress any day except Monday, from 9 a.m. to 5 p.m., April through September, or 10 a.m. to 4 p.m. in the winter season.

Be sure to see the **Franconian Museum** *(Mainfränkisches Museum)* (9), located in the former arsenal *(Zeughaus)* of the fortress. A showcase for the arts and artifacts of historic Würzburg, it contains an entire gallery of sculptures by Tilman Riemenschneider as well as works

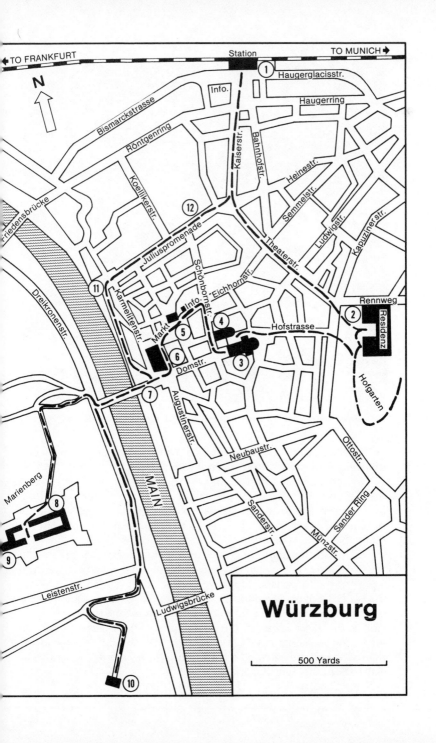

Marienburg Fortress from the Old Bridge

by Tiepolo and others. The displays of wine-making are especially interesting as this hill is itself covered with vineyards.

Now return to the bridge. Before crossing it you may want to visit the **Käppele** (10), a baroque pilgrimage church on a nearby hill. Built by Balthazar Neumann in the 18th century, it has some wonderful frescoes by Matthias Günther, and a truly fabulous view of both the Marienberg and Würzburg.

Recross the ancient bridge and walk along the bank of the river to the **Old Crane** (11), an 18th-century reminder that Würzburg was also a port town. There is an attractive outdoor beer garden overlooking the water's edge adjacent to this; just the place to relax after a hard day's sightseeing. Those who would rather sample the local wine might stop at the *Weinstuben* of the **Juliusspital** (12), an atmospheric old institution founded in 1576. While there you should also ask to see the rococo apothecary and the gardens. From here it is only a short way back to the train station.

Nuremberg
(Nürnberg)

Often regarded as the most German of German cities, Nuremberg makes a fascinating daytrip destination whose very name recalls a contradiction of images. It is at once the perfect medieval city, the toy capital of the world, the setting for Wagner's incomparable opera *"Die Meistersinger,"* and a charming center of intellect and culture. Yet Nuremberg was the place chosen by Hitler for the infamous Nazi rallies of the thirties, and the city which lent its proud name to the despicable laws of racial purity. In retribution, it was practically leveled during World War II, and is still best known for the war crime trials held there after the collapse of the Third Reich.

Not really old as medieval cities go, Nuremberg was founded about 1040 as a military stronghold by Emperor Henry III. With the downfall of the Imperial House of Hohenstaufen in the 13th century it became a free city, fortunately located at the junction of several important trade routes which favored its growth as a commercial center. During this period of prosperity the arts flourished with such local talents as Albrecht Dürer and Hans Sachs. This all came to an end during the Thirty Years War, when Nuremberg's population and wealth declined greatly. It was not until the Industrial Revolution of the 19th century that the city, by now a part of Bavaria, regained its prominent position in German affairs.

This daytrip may be taken from Frankfurt as well as from Munich. Nuremberg is also a good base for excursions to Würzburg, Bamberg, Bayreuth, Regensburg, or even Rothenburg.

GETTING THERE:
Trains depart Munich's main station at least hourly for Nuremberg, about one hour and forty minutes away by IC express. Return service operates until about 9:45 p.m.

Trains leave Frankfurt's main station at least hourly for Nuremberg. Most of these take about two and a half hours for the journey, with some requiring a cross-platform change at Würzburg. Return trains run until about 8 p.m.

By car from Munich, it is 103 miles to Nuremberg via the A-9 (E-6) Autobahn.

By car from Frankfurt, take the A-3 (E-5) Autobahn all the way, a distance of 138 miles.

WHEN TO GO:

Nuremberg may be visited at any time. Much of the trip will be spent indoors, so even an overcast day will do. Most of the museums are closed on Mondays.

FOOD AND DRINK:

The local specialty is Bratwurst. These little sausages are better here than anywhere else. Nuremberg is also noted for its Lebkuchen cookies, excellent Franconian wines, and superb beer. Among the choice restaurants, in trip sequence, are:

> **Historische Bratwurstküche** (in the Handwerkerhof) $
> **Nassauer Keller** (Karolinenstr. 2, opposite St. Lorenz) $$
> **Ḥeilig-Geist Spital** (Spitalgasse 12) $$
> **Bratwurst Häusle** (Rathausplatz 1) $
> **Goldenes Posthorn** (Glöckleinsgasse 2) $$$
> **Zum Waffenschmied** (Ob. Schmiedgasse 22) $$$

TOURIST INFORMATION:

The tourist office is located in the train station, phone (0911) 23-36-32. There is also a branch in the Hauptmarkt, phone (0911) 23-36-35.

SUGGESTED TOUR:

Begin your walk at the **main train station** (1), where the tourist office is located. From here use the underground passageway to reach the **Königstor** (2), a part of the massive old fortifications. These walls, constructed over a period of centuries, remain practically intact today and give Nuremberg a medieval appearance largely missing from other major German cities.

Stroll along Königstrasse to **St. Lawrence's Church** *(St. Lorenz Kirche)* (3). Built between the 13th and 15th centuries, this is the city's largest house of worship. It contains some truly remarkable works of art, including the 16th-century *"Annunciation"* by Veit Stoss which hangs suspended in the choir. Other pieces to look for are the tabernacle by Adam Kraft, to the left of the high altar, and the wonderful stained-glass windows in the choir.

Opposite the front of the church is the tower-like **Nassauer Haus**, parts of which date from the early 13th century. It is reputed to be the oldest dwelling in town, and now houses a delightful restaurant. Continue along Königstrasse, here reserved for pedestrians, to the Mu-

The Heilig Geist Spital

seum Bridge. To your right is one of those wonderful scenes so typical of Nuremberg. The **Heilig Geist Spital** (4), a 14th-century almshouse spanning the Pegnitz River, still serves its original purpose and also contains a very popular *Weinstube* and restaurant.

You are now only a few steps from the **main market** *(Hauptmarkt)* (5), an open area usually filled with farmers' stalls. The traditional *Christkindlesmarkt* is held here each December for the sale of toys and ornaments. Facing the east side of the square is the 14th-century **Church of Our Lady** *(Frauenkirche)*, which provides a free show to spectators every day at noon in the form of mechanical figures acting out the story of the Golden Bull of 1356. Step inside to see the famous Tucher altarpiece from 1440 and other splendid works of art.

One of the best-known sights in Nuremberg is the **Beautiful Fountain** *(Schöner Brunnen)* in the northwest corner of the square. Dating from the 14th century, it is decorated with forty sculptured figures arranged in four tiers, and surrounded by a 16th-century wrought-iron grille. Now walk up to the **Old Town Hall** *(Altes Rathaus)* (6), where you can take a tour through medieval dungeons and the torture chamber.

St. Sebald's Church (7) was begun in 1225 and makes the transition from Romanesque to Gothic. On the outside of its choir, facing the old town hall, is the magnificent Schreyer-Landauer tomb of 1492 by Adam Kraft. Enter through the north portal and visit the **Shrine of**

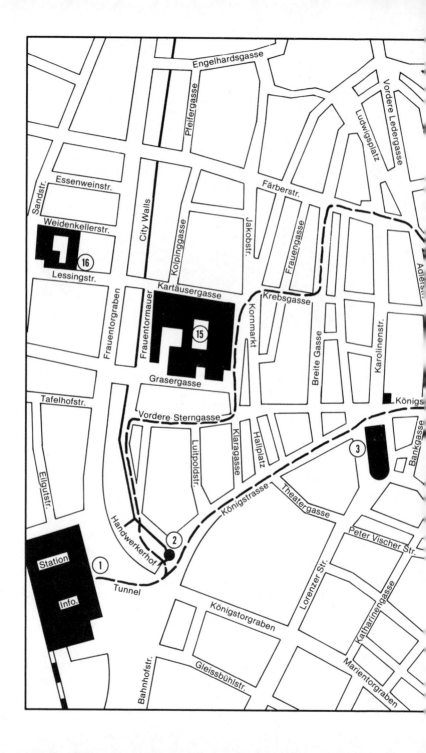

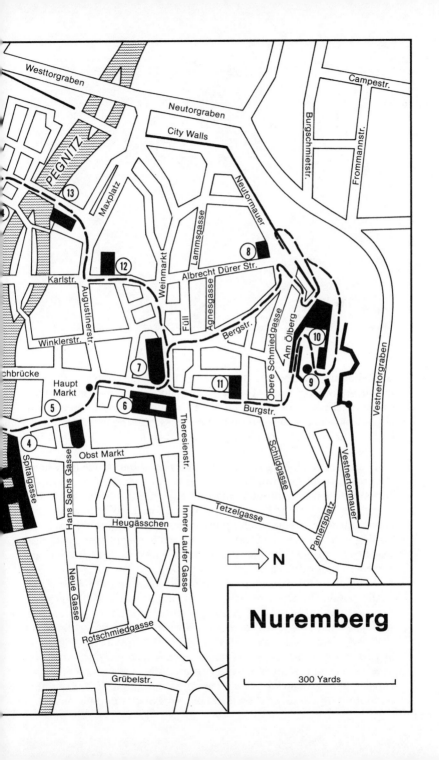

Westtorgraben
Neutorgraben
City Walls
Campestr.
Burgschmietstr.
Frommannstr.
PEGNITZ
⑬
Maxplatz
Neutormauer
⑫
Lammsgasse
⑧
Karlstr.
Weinmarkt
Albrecht Dürer Str.
Augustinerstr.
Füll
Agnesgasse
Bergstr.
Am Ölberg
Obere Schmiedgasse
⑩
Winklerstr.
⑦
⑨
chbrücke
Haupt Markt
⑪
Vestnertorgraben
⑤
⑥
Burgstr.
④
Spitalgasse
Hans Sachs Gasse
Obst Markt
Theresienstr.
Schildgasse
Panierplatz
Vestnertormauer
Heugässchen
Tetzelgasse
Innere Laufer Gasse
Neue Gasse
→ N
Rotschmiedgasse
Grübelstr.

Nuremberg

300 Yards

Detail of the Schöner Brunnen

St. Sebaldus, a wonderful 16th-century bronze sculpture containing the silver coffin of Nuremberg's patron saint. There are several other exceptional works of art, including a sunburst Madonna on a north aisle pillar, a Crucifixion group by Veit Stoss near the main altar, and, in the south aisle, a stone sculpture by Adam Kraft of Christ bearing the cross.

From here climb Bergstrasse to the **Albrecht Dürer House** (8), where the great artist lived from 1509 until his death in 1528. The first three floors are open as a museum and give a good impression of the surroundings in which he lived and worked. Of particular interest is the original kitchen, a replica of his printing press, and copies of his works. Visiting hours are from 10 a.m. to 5 p.m., daily except Mondays, with seasonal variations. The picturesque square next to this has some attractive outdoor cafés and restaurants.

Now follow the map uphill and through a garden to an opening in the town wall. From here you will have a marvelous view of the square—a scene right out of the Middle Ages. Return through the garden and stroll past the **Pentagonal Tower** *(Fünfeckiger Turm),* which dates from 1040 and is regarded as the oldest structure in Nuremberg. Adjoining this are the Imperial Stables, currently used as a youth hostel. You are now within the precincts of **Nuremberg Castle**, a residence of all acknowledged German kings and emperors from 1050 to 1571. Continue on to the 13th-century **Sinwellturm** (9), a massive round tower which

The Square by the Dürer House

may be climbed for the best panoramic view of the city possible. Close to this is the deep well *(Tiefer Brunnen)*, a source of water since the earliest days. This, too, may be visited.

The major part of the castle, the **Kaiserburg** (10), was begun in the 12th century, although most of what you see today dates from the 15th and 16th. There are frequent guided tours through its Gothic interior, which are worth taking if you can spare an hour. These include the interesting 12th-century **chapel**, a double-deck affair where emperors worshipped above the heads of lesser folk. The castle is open daily from 9 a.m. to noon and 12:45-5 p.m., April through September; and 9:30 a.m. to noon and 12:45-4 p.m. the rest of the year.

Walk down and turn right on Burgstrasse. This leads to the **Fembo Haus** (11), a marvelous museum of life in old Nuremberg, located in a well-preserved Renaissance mansion. Be sure to see the large model of the Old City on the fourth floor.

From here follow the map past St. Sebald's Church to the **Toy Museum** *(Spielzeug Museum)* (12) on Karlstrasse. A wealth of delightful playthings from all over the world is on display, ranging from simple dolls to elaborate model railway setups. Toys have been a major Nuremberg industry for centuries, making a visit here particularly appropriate. The museum is open daily except Mondays, from 10 a.m. to 5 p.m.

Continue on to the **Maxbrücke** (13), which offers stunning views up and down the Pegnitz River. The large half-timbered structure to your left, the Weinstadel, was built in 1446 as a home for lepers. Later used for wine storage, it is now a residence for university students. Adjacent to this is the Wasserturm, a part of the older 14th-century fortifications. From here the Pegnitz is spanned by a covered wooden footbridge called the **Henkersteg**, or hangman's bridge, to whose solitary dwelling it led. To the right, the view of the medieval walls arched over the river is equally charming.

The route now takes you past the 15th-century **Unschlitthaus** (14), a former granary, and through a more modern part of town to the **Germanic National Museum** (15). Dedicated to the many aspects of German art and culture from prehistoric times to the 20th century, this vast treasure house requires several hours to see properly and should really be saved for another day. It is open from 9 a.m. to 5 p.m., Tuesdays through Sundays; and also from 8-9:30 p.m. on Thursdays.

Return to the station via the route on the map. Just before the Königstor (2) you will come to the **Handwerkerhof**, a courtyard of small shops where present-day craftsmen carry on in the medieval tradition. This is a good place to try the local bratwurst if you have not already done so.

One other attraction which may interest you is the **Transport Museum** *(Verkehrsmuseum)* (16), located outside the city walls not far from the station. Its collection of old trains features the *Adler*, the first locomotive to operate in Germany, and "mad" King Ludwig II's incredible private cars. The museum is open daily from 10 a.m. to 5 p.m., closing an hour earlier on Sundays and in winter.

Bamberg

Of all the medieval cities in Germany, Bamberg stands out as perhaps the one least touched by the ravages of war. Well over a thousand years of history enrich this ancient ecclesiastical and commercial center in Upper Franconia. It is a place filled with picturesque corners, charming waterfront houses and narrow, winding streets, as well as magnificent churches whose spires cap the seven hills on which it is built.

Although this area has been settled since the late Stone Age, the earliest documented reference to *Castrum Babenberg,* as it was then called, dates from A.D. 902. Bamberg was well established as a center of learning before the 12th century. Despite occupation by the Swedes during the Thirty Years War, the town was spared the destruction of the Reformation and remained true to the Catholic faith. It was not until 1802 that it was secularized and made a part of Bavaria. Industrialization began in the late 19th century, but this took place at the eastern end of town, well away from its ancient core. Bamberg survived World War II virtually unscathed, and today offers visitors a chance to experience a city whose fabric has remained intact for centuries.

This trip can be made from Frankfurt as well as Munich, or from other bases such as Nuremberg or Würzburg.

GETTING THERE:

Trains leave Munich's main station in the morning for the three-hour trip to Bamberg. A change at Nuremberg *(Nürnberg)* may be necessary. Return connections run until early evening.

Trains depart Frankfurt's main station in the morning for Würzburg, where you change for Bamberg. The total trip takes under three hours. Return service operates until early evening.

By car from Munich, take the A-9 (E-6) Autobahn to Nuremberg, then the A-73 to Bamberg. The total distance is 143 miles.

By car from Frankfurt, it is 130 miles to Bamberg. Take the A-3 (E-5) Autobahn past Würzburg, then head north on the B-505.

WHEN TO GO:

Bamberg is compact and can be comfortably explored in any season. Some sights are closed on holidays.

FOOD AND DRINK:

Bamberg is famous for its unique *Rauchbier* (smoked beer), an acquired taste definitely worth trying. Its regular beers are superb, and its citizens probably quaff more of the suds than any other people on earth. Some recommended restaurants are:

Wilde Rose (Kesslerstr. 7, near Obst Markt) $
Rauchbierstube zum Schlenkerla (Dominikanerstr. 6) *The* place for Rauchbier. $
Würzburger Weinstube (Zinkenwörth 6, near Schillerplatz) $$
Theaterrose (Schillerplatz 7) $$
Weinhaus Messerschmitt (Lange Str. 41) $$$
Böttingerhaus (Judenstr. 14) $$$

TOURIST INFORMATION:

The tourist office, phone (0951) 264-01, is at Hauptwachstrasse 16, just across the river.

SUGGESTED TOUR:

Leave the **train station** (1) and follow the map to the Kettenbrücke, a bridge spanning the Regnitz. You will probably see barge traffic on the river, as Bamberg is a major inland port. Cross the bridge and continue on Hauptwachstrasse, passing the tourist office on the left.

Walk straight ahead past Maximiliansplatz, with its "new" town hall and market place, and into the delightful **Grüner Markt** (2). This large open square, dominated by the baroque St. Martin's Church and the 17th-century Neptune Fountain, is reserved for pedestrians.

Obstmarkt leads to the Untere Brücke, a bridge over the left arm of the Regnitz. In the center of this stands the **Altes Rathaus** (3), easily the most remarkable old town hall in Germany. Its extraordinary position in the middle of the river was determined by the local politics of the Middle Ages. At that time it had to administer both the ecclesiastical and civic halves of the city without showing preference for either, hence the truly mid-stream stance. Originally built in the 15th century, it was heavily reconstructed in the rococo style during the 18th. Looking downstream, you will have a good view of the colorful fishermen's houses along the Regnitz, an area known as **Little Venice** (*Klein Venedig*).

After crossing the river, make the first left and then another left onto the Obere Brücke, which goes through the old town hall, allowing a more detailed examination. Return to the left bank and stroll to

The Old Town Hall

a small footbridge from which you will have the best possible view of the Altes Rathaus and the 17th-century half-timbered building curiously attached to it.

On the other side make a right at Geyerswörth Castle, built in 1585 as the town residence of the prince-bishop. Continue along to the next bridge and turn right. Midway across this you can stroll out on Untere Mühlbrücke for a wonderful view.

Now follow the map through the Old Town to Domplatz, one of the most attractive public squares in Germany. The **Cathedral** *(Dom)* (4), first consecrated in 1012 by Emperor Heinrich II, was rebuilt in its present form during the 13th century after two fires destroyed the original structure. It contains the only tomb of a pope in Germany, that of Clement II, who died in 1047 and is buried in the west chancel. The cathedral is exceptionally rich in works of art, the most renowned of which is the **Bamberger Rider**, a 13th-century equestrian statue of a king by an unknown sculptor. Just to the right of this is the elaborate sarcophagus of Emperor Heinrich II and his wife Kunigunda, carved in 1513 by Tilman Riemenschneider. Another masterpiece, on the west wall of the south transept, is the Maria Altar by Veit Stoss. The **Dioc-**

esan Museum, adjacent to the cathedral, contains many more treasures, including the imperial cloak of Heinrich II and the robes of Pope Clement II.

Walk across the square to the **New Residence** (5), a massive baroque structure erected between 1697 and 1703 for the very wealthy Prince-Bishop Franz von Schönborn. Step inside for a look at the magnificent **Emperor's Room** *(Kaisersaal)* and the luxurious apartments of the prince-bishops. There is also a splendid art gallery with pictures ranging from the Middle Ages to the 18th century. The New Residence is open every day except some holidays, from 9 a.m. to noon, and from 1:30-5 p.m. It closes an hour earlier in the winter season. While there, be sure to go out into the **rose garden** for a superb view of the town.

The 16th-century gabled Ratsstube, across the square, is now the home of the **Bamberg History Museum**. Although small, it has several fascinating exhibits well worth seeing. Next to this is the Reiche Tor, a richly ornamented gate leading into the **Old Imperial Court** *(Alte Hofhaltung)* (6), one of the most enchanting sights in Bamberg. The grandiose, quiet inner courtyard is surrounded by half-timbered buildings and the remains of the old Diet Hall, which was used as the seat of local government for over 500 years after 1085.

A gate at the rear of the courtyard opens into Domstrasse. From here follow the map to **St. Michael's Church** (7), part of a former Benedictine abbey originally founded in the 11th century. Inside, there are several interesting things to see, particularly the tomb of St. Otto behind the high altar. Crawling through the hole in this is, according to local tradition, a sure cure for lumbago. The ceiling is also unusual, featuring paintings of over 600 different medicinal herbs. As you leave the church, turn right and walk out to the terrace, which offers a wonderful view of the surrounding countryside.

The route back to the Old Town takes you by the 14th-century **Upper Parish Church** *(Obere Pfarrkirche)* (8), considered by many to be Bamberg's finest Gothic structure. Turn right on Judenstrasse and take a look at the **Böttinger House** (9), one of the finest examples of a private mansion in the baroque style. Built in 1713, it was the winter residence of the court privy councillor Böttinger, who thought of himself as the supreme ruler of Bamberg—although Prince-Bishop von Schönborn entertained similar notions. Böttinger also had another mansion, this one for summer use, just a stone's throw away on the Regnitz.

Walk along the narrow Concordiastrasse for a block, then turn left and cross the tiny footbridge. In this area there are several old mills which have been converted to homes. An alleyway on the other side leads to the Mühlwörth, with an interesting view of Böttinger's other

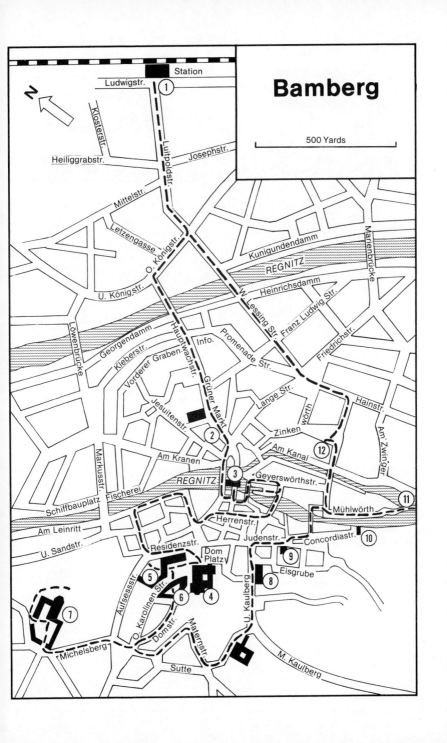

The Old Imperial Court

palace, the **Concordia House** (10) on the water's edge. Continue on past the locks of the former **Ludwig Canal** (11) for a short distance, then return and cross the Nonnenbrücke. Along the water, to the left, you can see two interesting old cranes.

The very narrow **E.T.A. Hoffmann House** (12) on Schillerplatz was the home of that great romantic writer from 1809 to 1813. It was his stories which formed the basis for Offenbach's opera *"The Tales of Hoffmann."* The house may be visited from April through October, between 4:30 and 5:30 p.m. on weekday afternoons, and from 9:30-10:30 a.m. on weekends and holidays. Now follow the map back to the train station.

Bayreuth

For admirers of Wagnerian opera, a daytrip to Bayreuth is a delightful pilgrimage—perhaps the highlight of their entire visit to Germany. Others may find this to be a day largely wasted in the boondocks of Franconia. How much joy you get out of this trip is determined by your musical tastes, and only you can know the answer to that.

There was a town here long before Wagner was ever born, of course. During the 18th century this was a minor cultural oasis under the influence of Princess Wilhelmina, the very talented sister of Frederick the Great, king of Prussia. She was married to the margrave of Bayreuth and was responsible for what few treasures Bayreuth has to offer aside from those associated with the composer.

The annual Bayreuth Festival, which had its premiere on August 13th, 1876, has since turned this provincial Bavarian town into a world-class mecca for music lovers. Organized by Richard Wagner for the express purpose of performing his own operas in his own theatre, it helped revolutionize the status of composers from glorified servants of the nobility to entrepreneurs. More than that, it began the entire concept of annual music festivals, now held all over the world.

Bayreuth is a bit difficult to reach from Munich, but dedicated fans will find it well worth the effort. It may also be visited from other Franconian bases, such as Nuremberg.

GETTING THERE:
Trains leave Munich's main station between about 6 and 7:30 a.m. for Nuremberg *(Nürnberg)*, where you connect to a local for Bayreuth. The entire journey takes about three hours. Return trains (and buses) leave until early evening, again changing at Nuremberg.

By car, it's the A-9 (E-6) Autobahn all the way from Munich to Bayreuth, a distance of 142 miles.

WHEN TO GO:
Unless you really love crowds, you should avoid coming during festival time, which lasts from the end of July until the end of August. Some of the major sights are closed on Mondays.

113

FOOD AND DRINK:
Bayreuth has several good restaurants catering to an international clientele, as well as the usual run of establishments. A few choices are:

> **Bayerischer Hof** (Bahnhofstr. 14, by the station) $$
> **Königshof** (Bahnhofstr. 23, by the station) $$
> **Postei** (Friedrichstr. 15, near Neues Schloss) $$
> **Wolffenzacher** (Badstr. 1, behind the old opera) $

TOURIST INFORMATION:
The tourist office is located at Luitpoldplatz 9, a few blocks south of the train station. You can call them at (0921) 220-15.

SUGGESTED TOUR:
Leave the **train station** (1) and walk down Bahnhofstrasse to the tourist office on Luitpoldplatz. Across the square is the 17th-century **Old Palace** (2), home of the ruling margraves until 1754. Destroyed in 1945, it was later rebuilt and now houses government offices. Walk through its courtyard and visit the Palace Church, which contains the tombs of Margrave Friedrich and his wife Wilhelmina. From here you can take an interesting stroll through the oldest part of town, perhaps stopping at the 15th-century Town Church on Kirchplatz before continuing on to the first major attraction.

Richard Wagner built **Haus Wahnfried** (3) in 1873 as his first, and last, permanent home. Born in Leipzig in 1813, he had always been a wanderer, fleeing both creditors and the police until his strange relationship with the mentally unbalanced King Ludwig II began in 1864. This solved his persistent money problems—he had always lived lavishly on a precarious income—but the composer's political manipulations and loose morals quickly gained him enemies, and he was forced into exile. Eventually, Wagner's ego required that he have his very own opera house, where his works would not be contaminated by those of other composers. Thus the move to Bayreuth, a place so remote and yet within the confines of Ludwig's Bavaria that his adoring public would have to come to *him*.

Haus Wahnfried remained in the possession of Wagner's descendants until 1973, when it was deeded to the town. It has since been restored and is now open as a fascinating museum of the composer's life; one which explores his creative genius without overlooking the blemishes. Visitors may relax in the drawing room and listen to recorded concerts of the operas. Allow plenty of time for this small but intriguing museum, which is open every day, except certain holidays, from 9 a.m. to 5 p.m.

Wagner, who died in 1883, lies buried along with his wife Cosima

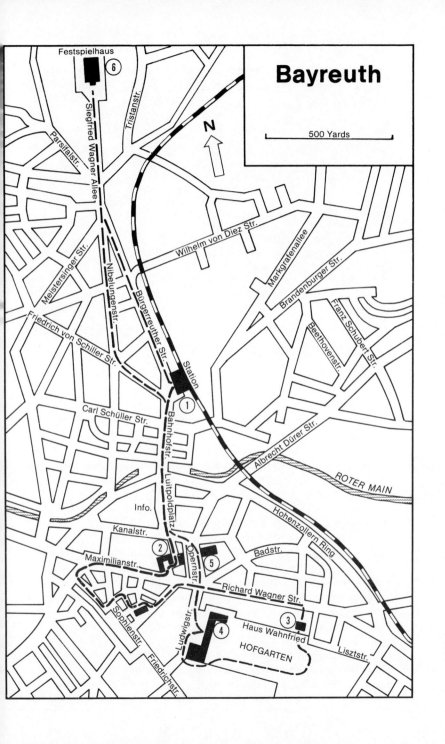

Haus Wahnfried

in a simple grave at the rear of the house. Continue past this and wander around the lovely Hofgarten to the **New Palace** *(Neues Schloss)* (4). Begun in 1753, this late rococo structure reflects the refined tastes of Princes Wilhelmina, who lived here until her death in 1758. Its many charming rooms, filled with period furniture, may be seen on guided tours given frequently every day except Mondays, from 10-11:30 a.m. and 1-4:30 p.m.

Now follow Ludwigstrasse to Wilhelmina's great masterpiece, the **Margrave's Opera House** *(Markgräfliches Opernhaus)* (5). First opened in 1748, it is an absolutely delightful jewel, right up there in the same class with Munich's Cuvilliés Theatre. Frequent guided tours are given daily, except on Mondays or during performances. Richard Wagner was originally attracted to Bayreuth by the thought of using this elegant theatre for his festival. Alas, its stage proved much too small for both Siegfried *and* the dragon, let alone all those Valkyries. In the end, of course, he built his own opera house, which you should visit next.

Return to the train station and take the route on the map to Wagner's **Festival Theatre** *(Festspielhaus)* (6), the most famous sight in Bayreuth. Set atop a small hill overlooking the town, this curiously nondescript structure was begun in 1872. Wagner was hardly able to

Bust of Wagner near the Festival Theatre

raise the money for a cornerstone, to say nothing of an entire opera house, so in the end he had to appeal once again to Ludwig. The king, somewhat peeved at the choice of Bayreuth and by now short of cash as a result of his lavish castles, came up with just enough for this unadorned building. Plans to add an elaborate façade at a later date never materialized.

Inside, however, it is a marvel of technical ingenuity. The acoustics, achieved at the expense of audience comfort, are world renowned. Singers can be heard over the roar of the orchestra, which is buried in a deep pit. The huge and highly mechanized stage was decades ahead of its time, as was the lighting. Guided tours are held daily except Mondays, from 10-11:30 a.m. and 1:30-3 p.m. These are naturally suspended when the theatre is in use. Tickets for performances are almost invariably sold out long in advance. From here it is an easy downhill walk back to the train station.

Regensburg

Nearly two thousand years of history have left their mark on unspoiled Regensburg, one of the most ancient cities in Germany. Its location in eastern Bavaria puts it somewhat off the usual tourist circuit, but those who do come this way are in for a treat.

Way back in A.D. 179 the Roman emperor Marcus Aurelius established a stronghold at the northernmost point of the Danube and called it *Castra Regina*. This was the real founding of the town, although the Celts had a settlement known as *Radasbona* on the site as early as 500 B.C.

In the centuries which followed the collapse of the Roman Empire, Regensburg continued to prosper, first as a bishopric and later as a residence of the Carolingian rulers. It was the capital of Bavaria until the 13th century, when it became a free imperial city. By the 16th century, however, its period of greatness declined as other cities such as Augsburg and Nuremberg eclipsed it in trade.

From the end of the Thirty Years War until 1806 the city regained some of its prominence as the seat of Germany's first real parliament, the Permanent Imperial Diet, but this was lost when the Holy Roman Empire of the German Nation ceased to exist. After that, Regensburg became a backwater place which slept through the Industrial Revolution and was largely untouched by World War II. Although prosperity has now returned in the form of modern industries, its center is extremely well preserved and offers tourists a remarkable variety of sights, some dating as far back as the Roman era.

GETTING THERE:
Trains leave Munich's main station several times in the morning for the approximately one-and-a-half-hour ride to Regensburg. Return service operates until mid-evening.

By car, leave Munich on the A-9 (E-6) Autobahn, then switch to the A-90 and local roads into Regensburg. The total distance is about 75 miles.

WHEN TO GO:
Regensburg may be visited in any season, but avoid coming on a Monday or holiday, when the major museum is closed.

View from the Stone Bridge

FOOD AND DRINK:

The gastronomic experience most visitors to Regensburg head for first is the ancient *Historische Wurstküche* along the river bank at the foot of the old bridge. There is little choice here—mostly sausage, sauerkraut, potato soup, and beer; but it is wonderfully atmospheric and quite inexpensive. Just stop by the kitchen and order, then take a seat and the food will find its way to you. Some fancier choices are:

Kaiserhof am Dom (Kramgasse 10, near the cathedral) $$
Ratskeller (Rathausplatz 1) $$
Obermünster Stiftskeller (Obermünsterplatz 7, near the Schloss Thurn und Taxis) $$

TOURIST INFORMATION:

The tourist office, phone (0941) 507-21-41, is in the Old Town Hall (8).

SUGGESTED TOUR:

Leave the **train station** (1) and walk down Maximilianstrasse to the **Alter Kornmarkt** (2), which continues to serve as a market place. On its western side there are two very old structures joined by an archway. One of these is the Roman Tower *(Römerturm)*, mainly dating from the Carolingian period but partially of Roman construction. To the left of it is the Ducal Court *(Herzogshof)*, built around 1200 as a palace for the local dukes.

Stroll under the archway and visit **St. Peter's Cathedral** *(Dom)* (3), often considered to be the finest Gothic structure in Bavaria. It was begun in 1275 and completed in the 16th century, although the steeples were not added until the 1860s. The western façade is graced with an unusual triangular porch. Go inside and look at the 14th-century stained-glass windows in the choir, then at the famous statues of **Regensburger Angel** and the Madonna on the western pillars of the transept.

There is a **treasury** containing some splendid works in gold along with medieval vestments just off the north aisle. Stroll into the cloister, which largely predates the cathedral, and visit its 10th-century Church of St. Stephan and the very lovely Romanesque **All Saints' Chapel.** If you happen to be in the cathedral at the right time, you may be treated to a concert by its renowned boys' choir, called the *"Domspatzen."*

Now walk through the Domgarten to the **Niedermünster** (4), a parish church where excavations have revealed parts of structures from the Roman *Castra Regina*. Continue on to the **Porta Praetoria** (5), the 2nd-century north gate of the original Roman fortifications. Some segments of this, incorporated into a later structure, are remarkably well preserved.

The Danube is only a block away. You may be interested in taking one of the boat rides offered along the quay, or in having a marvelous lunch at the **Historische Wurstküche** (6), one of the oldest eating establishments in Germany. No one seems to know just how long it has been serving those delicious and inexpensive sausages, but legend has it that the restaurant began as a kitchen for workers building the bridge—and that was in the 12th century!

Walk around the ancient salt warehouse and through the Brückturm gateway to the **Stone Bridge** *(Steinerne Brücke)* (7), a triumph of medieval engineering skills. Although constructed between 1135 and 1146, it still carries vehicular traffic and is indeed the oldest stone bridge in the country.

Cross the bridge for a wonderful view, then return and follow the map past the Fischmarkt to the **Old Town Hall** *(Altes Rathaus)* (8), which houses the tourist information office. Most of this imposing complex of structures dates from the 14th through the 16th centuries. Guided tours are conducted through its **Imperial Hall** *(Reichssaal)*—where the Permanent Imperial Diet met on and off between 1663 and 1806—and the sinister torture chamber, preserved in all its original hideousness.

From here you can stroll through the adjacent Kohlenmarkt for a look at two 13th-century **patrician towers** (9), built in the style of the

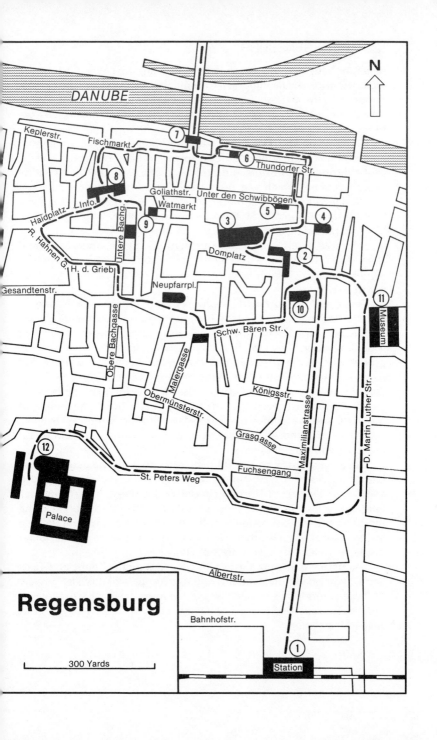

N

DANUBE

Keplerstr.
Fischmarkt
⑦
⑥
Thundorfer Str.
⑧
Goliathstr. Unter den Schwibbögen
Watmarkt ⑤
Info. ③
Haidplatz ⑨ ④
R. Hahnen G. H. d. Grieb
Domplatz ②
Gesandtenstr.
Neupfarrpl.
⑪
Museum
⑩
Schw. Bären Str.
Obere Bachgasse
Malergasse
Königsstr.
Maximilianstrasse
Obermünsterstr.
Grasgasse
D. Martin Luther Str.
⑫
Fuchsengang
St. Peters Weg
Palace
Albertstr.

Regensburg

Bahnhofstr.

300 Yards

①

Station

Italian nobility and unique to Regensburg among cities north of the Alps. These are the Baumburger Tower in the Watmarkt and the Golden Tower on Wahlenstrasse. Return to Kohlenmarkt and follow Neue Waag Gasse to Haidplatz, a colorful old square with several historic structures.

Continue on Rote Hahnen Gasse and Hinter der Grieb, a delightful medieval lane with more patrician tower-houses. The map shows a route through interesting old streets, going past the 16th-century Neupfarrkirche, which was built on the site of a former synagogue after the Jews were expelled from town in 1519. Just beyond this is the Romanesque Church of St. Cassian, documented as long ago as A.D. 885, and remodelled in the rococo style during the 18th century.

Schwarze Bären Strasse and Kapellengasse lead to the **Old Chapel** *(Alte Kapelle)* (10). More than a thousand years old, it too was given a sumptuous rococo interior during the 18th century, and is very well worth a visit.

Cross the Alter Kornmarkt and walk over to the **Municipal Museum** (11), housed in a former 13th-century monastery. Allow plenty of time for this as it explores two thousand years of history in over a hundred rooms. You don't have to see it all, of course, but once inside you will probably be so intrigued by the Roman relics, Renaissance art, period room settings, and other treasures that time will just seem to fly by. The one item which should not be missed is the foundation plaque of *Castra Regina*, which clearly establishes Regensburg's beginning in A.D. 179. The museum is open Tuesdays through Saturdays, from 10 a.m. to 4 p.m.; and on Sundays from 10 a.m. to 1 p.m. It is closed on Mondays and major holidays.

On the way back to the train station you may want to make an interesting side trip to **St. Emmeram's Church** and the adjacent **Thurn and Taxis Palace** (12). The church, one of the oldest in Germany, was built over a long period of time beginning in the 8th century. During the 18th century it was magnificently redecorated in the baroque style by the famous Asam Brothers of Munich. There is some wonderful art inside, as well as three very ancient crypts.

The palace adjoining this is still occupied by the Thurn und Taxis family, who made their money running Europe's first postal service. Its lavish interior may be seen on guided tours given daily except Saturdays. There is also a large coach museum. From here it is a short walk to the station.

The Chiemsee

The enchanting Chiemsee, Bavaria's largest lake, lies just north of the Alps within easy reach of Munich. It was on an island in these idyllic waters that Ludwig II, the unbalanced "Dream King," built a Teutonic version of Versailles as his final castle. He was not the first to appreciate the lonely beauty of this spot, however. As far back as A.D. 782 a Benedictine convent was founded on a neighboring island; its 15th-century replacement remains there to this day, as does an old fishing community which is now becoming an artists' colony. Between the nearby town of Prien and the ferry dock a 19th-century narrow-gauge steam train shuttles enthusiastic visitors out for a day of fun, sun, and exploration. Travelers staying in Munich or the Berchtesgaden area can easily join them and share in the *Gemütlichkeit*.

GETTING THERE:

Trains depart Munich's main station almost hourly for the approximately one-hour ride to Prien, the starting point of this trip. An early start is recommended. Return service operates until mid-evening. A bargain one-day round-trip ticket is available.

By car, the Chiemsee is reached from Munich via the A-8 (E-11) Autobahn in the direction of Salzburg. Use the Bernau exit and follow signs for Prien, parking at the ferry dock. The total distance is about 60 miles.

WHEN TO GO:

The best time to visit the Chiemsee is between late May and late September, when boats are frequent and the steam train operates. The castle is open daily all year round, except for a few major holidays. Some boats operate during the off-season. A lovely day will greatly enhance this trip.

FOOD AND DRINK:

There are several moderately priced restaurants near the ferry dock at Stock-Hafen with both indoor and outdoor tables. The island of Herreninsel has an exceptionally pleasant restaurant and café at the Altes Schloss with an outdoor terrace. Fraueninsel also has a good choice of eating places, particularly the one by the abbey. Two selections at Stock-Hafen are:

Reinhart (Seestr. 117) $$

Seehotel Feldhütter (Seestr. 101) $

TOURIST INFORMATION:

The tourist office in Prien, phone (08051) 30-31, is at Rathausstrasse 11, just west of the station.

SUGGESTED TOUR;

Immediately upon arrival at the **Prien train station** (1) take the underground passage to the adjacent Chiemsee Bahn, a 19th-century steam train which goes to the ferry landing. If a departure is imminent, buy a combination round-trip ticket *(Hin und Zurück)* which includes the train and ferry *(Schiff)* to Herreninsel and Fraueninsel, then board the train. If there is a long wait, however, you can either take a bus from the front of the station or just follow the map and walk there. The distance is about one mile. Tickets for the ferry are also available at the dock.

When you get to the **Stock-Hafen pier** (2) you will have a choice of getting on the next boat to Herreninsel or having lunch at one of the nearby restaurants.

The Chiemsee *(pronounced keem-zay)* covers an area of over 31 square miles and has three islands, one of which, Krautinsel, is uninhabited. Of the other two, Herreninsel *(Men's Island)* has had a monastery since 764 and Fraueninsel *(Ladies' Island)* a nunnery since 782. According to legend, Krautinsel *(Vegetable Island)* was the spot where the monks and nuns got together, at least to grow vegetables.

The boat ride to Herreninsel takes only 15 minutes. Upon arrival at its **landing stage** (3), walk uphill to the 17th-century **Altes Schloss** (4), once the home of Augustinian canons. There is a pretty outdoor café and restaurant in its precincts. From here a path leads through the woods, suddenly opening to reveal the palace in all its splendor.

King Ludwig II of Bavaria was just about the strangest monarch ever to rule a European country. Born centuries too late, he lived in a sheltered dream world of his own making. In the end, events swept him aside and he died tragically at the age of 40. The legacy he left behind, from the operas of Richard Wagner to the fantastic castles dotting the Bavarian landscape, has, however, greatly enriched all of western civilization.

Rising before you, the **Palace of Herrenchiemsee** (5) was Ludwig's final paean to an age which vanished long before he was born. Ludwig purchased the island, a religious center until 1803, as the site for his Teutonic Versailles. Louis XIV of France had long been his idol, and

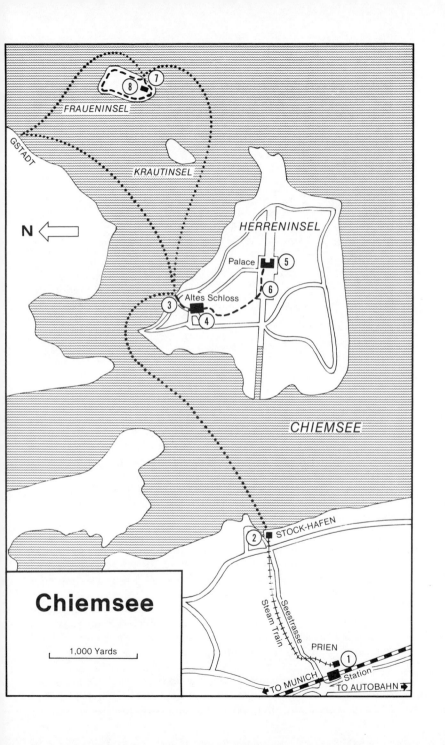

Chiemsee

FRAUENINSEL

GSTADT

KRAUTINSEL

N

HERRENINSEL

Palace

Altes Schloss

CHIEMSEE

STOCK-HAFEN

Steam Train

Seestrasse

PRIEN

Station

TO MUNICH

TO AUTOBAHN

1,000 Yards

Herrenchiemsee Palace

he made two visits to Paris to study the palace of the "Sun King." The similarity between the two buildings, while striking, is only superficial—most of the interior decoration at Herrenchiemsee is distinctly German. Construction began in 1878 and continued until 1885, when funds gave out. Ludwig occupied the unfinished *Schloss* on only one occasion, and then for only ten days. This was in the fall of 1885. Less than a year later he was deposed and afterwards found drowned in Lake Starnberg.

The interior of the palace is simply incredible. To see it you will have to join one of the very frequent guided tours, some of which are in English. An illustrated booklet describing the entire palace is available at the entrance, where there is also a small museum devoted to Ludwig's life.

Leaving the palace, walk straight ahead to the **Latona Fountain** (6), which erupts into jets of water at frequent intervals. From here stroll back to the landing stage and board the next boat for Fraueninsel. Ask to make sure that you are on the right boat, as some go to other points on the lake.

Arriving at the **Fraueninsel landing stage** (7), re-check the posted schedule to determine just how much time can be spent here. Turn left and walk around the Benedictine nunnery, founded in 782 and

View from Fraueninsel

rebuilt several times. Its **Abbey Church** (8), dating from the 13th and 15th centuries and combining Romanesque, Gothic, and baroque elements, is very well worth a visit.

Besides the convent, Fraueninsel is essentially a fishing village, albeit one which is rapidly being taken over by vacationers. A circular stroll around its perimeter reveals a charming oasis of quiet beauty embellished by a panorama of towering mountains to the south. With any amount of luck, you will have enough time before the return boat to sit down at an outdoor café and soak up the atmosphere.

Board the ferry to Stock-Hafen and, upon arrival, take either the steam train or the bus back to the Prien station.

Bad Reichenhall

Those who have already been to the more famous alpine resorts of Bavaria will find that Bad Reichenhall makes an interesting change of pace. In many ways the most elegant spa in the entire *Freistaat*, it still retains much of the atmosphere of an Edwardian watering place. Germans flock there by the thousands to relax in beautiful surroundings and take the curative treatments for a wide variety of ailments, real or imagined. Casual tourists will be more attracted to its mountains, the marvelous old salt works, the fashionable life style, or even the gambling casino.

It was the presence of salt in the nearby mountains which brought prosperity to Reichenhall as early as Celtic times. The local springs contain saline concentrations ranging up to 24%, the highest in Europe. These were exploited by the Romans, who shipped the salt throughout their empire. In the Middle Ages the trade continued to flourish and was largely responsible for the settlement of Munich during the 12th century. For the past hundred years, however, the springs have been used primarily for curative purposes.

GETTING THERE:

Trains leave Munich's main station around 7 and 9 a.m. for the two-hour-and-ten-minute trip to Bad Reichenhall. Be sure to get on a car marked for Berchtesgaden as some are dropped off at Freilassing. Return trains operate until early evening. A change at Freilassing may be necessary.

By car, leave Munich on the A-8 (E-11) Autobahn in the direction of Salzburg and get off at the Bad Reichenhall exit. The total distance is 85 miles.

WHEN TO GO:

Bad Reichenhall is a year-round resort, but daytrippers will find it more attractive in the summer. The salt works are open daily between April 1st and October 31st.

FOOD AND DRINK:

The town has an excellent selection of restaurants, some of which are quite luxurious. Choice establishments include:

> **Hotel Axelmannstein** (Salzburgerstr. 4, by the Kurpark) Two
> dining rooms: Park Restaurant $$$, and Axel Stüberl $$

Along Ludwigstrasse

Kurhotel Luisenbad (Ludwigstr. 33) $$$
Café Reber (Ludwigstr. 10) $$
Brauerei Bürgerbräu (Rathausplatz) $$
Deutsches Haus (Poststr. 32, near the Heimat Museum) $

TOURIST INFORMATION:
The tourist office, phone (08651) 14-67, is by the train station.

SUGGESTED TOUR:
Leaving the **train station** (1), walk past the tourist office and follow Bahnhofstrasse to the **Kurgarten** (2), a delightful park containing the casino, music pavilion, drinking hall, and other features. The most unusual of these is the *Gradierwerk*, a strange structure near the entrance in which salt water is filtered through twigs for evaporation.

Continue along the pedestrians-only Salzburger Strasse and Ludwigstrasse to **Rathaus Platz** (3), a market square in front of the beautifully frescoed old town hall.

The major sight in Bad Reichenhall is the **Old Salt Works** *(Alte Saline)* (4), just a few steps away. Built in 1834 by King Ludwig I, it has some utterly fantastic 19th-century machinery for pumping the salt water up from the springs below. Unlike nearby Berchtesgaden (and Hallein in Austria), where salt deposits are removed by flooding the sink works with clear water, the brine here comes directly from the earth in natural form. Conducted tours through the tunnels and caves

Rathaus Platz

are given every day between the beginning of April and the end of October, from 10-11:30 a.m. and 2-4 p.m. During the remainder of the year they are held on Tuesday and Thursday afternoons only, at 2 p.m.

From here follow the map uphill to **Schloss Gruttenstein** (5), a 13th- to 17th-century castle which offers great views of the town and surrounding mountains. Although it is now used for private housing, you can enter the courtyard and look around. Another path leads down to Obere Lindenplatz in the old part of town.

Cross the bridge over the Saalach River and turn left to the lower station of the **Predigtstuhl Bahn** (6). This cable car runs at least hourly and takes you to the top of the highest mountain in the vicinity for a marvelous panorama across the Alps. There is a restaurant near the summit, and several trails which can be walked.

Return to the town and stroll down Poststrasse to the **Heimat Museum** (7). Open from 2-6 p.m., Tuesdays through Fridays only, it has an interesting collection of local crafts and historical relics reflecting the region's long history.

Now follow the map to the **Church of St. Zeno** (8). Originally built in the 12th century, it was reconstructed in the Gothic style in 1520 and later given baroque features. The carved altarpiece, containing some splendid 16th-century sculpture, is particularly attractive. From here it is only a few blocks back to the train station.

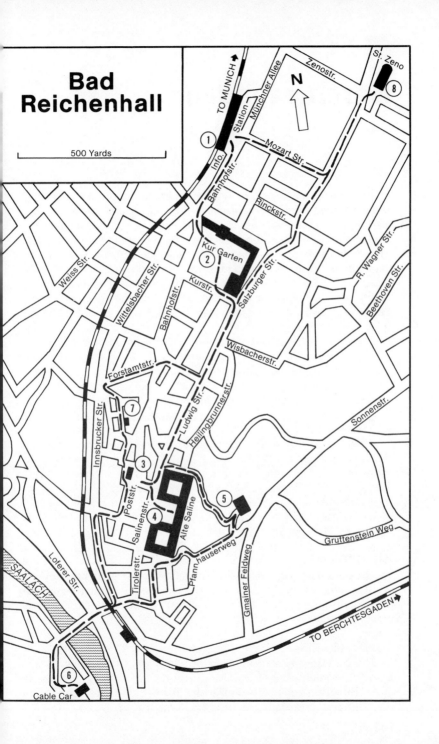

Bad Reichenhall

500 Yards

TO MUNICH

N

St. Zeno

Zenostr.

Münchner Allee

Info.

Station

Mozart Str.

Bahnhofstr.

Rinckstr.

Kur Garten

Salzburger Str.

Kurstr.

Weiss Str.

Wittelsbacher Str.

Bahnhofstr.

R. Wagner Str.

Beethoven Str.

Wisbacherstr.

Forstamtstr.

Innsbrucker Str.

Ludwig Str.

Heilingbrunnerstr.

Sonnenstr.

Poststr.

Salinenstr.

Alte Saline

Gruttenstein Weg

Tirolerstr.

Loferer Str.

SAALACH

Pfann hauserweg

Gmainer Feldweg

TO BERCHTESGADEN

Cable Car

Berchtesgaden

Berchtesgaden is one of the most popular resorts in Germany, and with good reason. Few places in the country offer such spectacular mountain scenery, and none have anything that equals the sublime beauty of its lake, the Königssee. Then there is the town itself, whose old castle and fascinating salt mines are certainly worth more than a detour. But, ironically, to many people the area is known only for its association with Adolf Hitler and his gang, who held court here during the short span of the Third Reich. That dreadful era is long since over, and Berchtesgaden has survived with all of its natural splendors intact.

The only problem with a daytrip to Berchtesgaden is that it requires some hard choices—you can't possibly see everything in the time available. The best solution, of course, is to stay overnight or longer, remembering that the town makes an excellent base for excursions to Bad Reichenhall, the Chiemsee, or Salzburg in Austria.

GETTING THERE:

Trains depart Munich's main station around 7 and 9 a.m. for the nearly three-hour ride to Berchtesgaden. Be sure to get on the right car as some are dropped off en route. Return service operates until early evening. A change at Freilassing may be necessary.

By car, leave Munich on the A-8 (E-11) Autobahn in the direction of Salzburg and get off at the Bad Reichenhall exit, then take the B-20 road into Berchtesgaden. The total distance is 96 miles.

WHEN TO GO:

The period between mid-May and mid-October is the best time to visit Berchtesgaden. Good weather will make the trip much more enjoyable. Be sure to check the opening times of each attraction before making your plans.

FOOD AND DRINK:

There are several restaurants in town in all price categories. Particularly recommended are:

> **Hubertusstuben** (Maximilianstr. 20, behind the station) $$
> **Post** (Maximilianstr. 2, near the Kurgarten) $$

Schlossplatz

Königssee offers a wide selection of places to eat between the bus stop and the lake, as well as one with a good view on the footpath to Malerwinkel.

Those going up to the Eagle's Nest can have a reasonably priced meal or drinks, complete with a fabulous view, right in Hitler's own hideaway, the **Kehlsteinhaus** $$. Also recommended is **Zum Türken**, near the Obersalzberg-Hintereck parking lot, $.

TOURIST INFORMATION:

The tourist office, phone (08652) 50-11, is just across the bridge from the train station.

SUGGESTED TOUR:

The three do-it-yourself tours described here all begin at the centrally located train station (1). You will only have time to do two of these in one single day.

THE TOWN:

Leave the **train station** (1) and follow the map uphill to the **Kurgarten** (2), a delightful little park with lovely views. Continue on through a colorful pedestrians-only area, passing the old market place, and walk under a passageway into Schlossplatz. This picturesque square is lined on its western side with 16th-century arcades.

The **Abbey Church**, on the eastern side, dates from 1122 and is well worth a visit for its fine works of art. Directly adjacent to it is the **Castle** *(Schloss)* (3), originally built as an Augustinian monastery. In 1810 this was secularized and used as a summer residence for Bavaria's ruling family, the Wittelsbachs. One of their descendants, Crown Prince Rupert, who had a tenuous claim to the British throne through his maternal Stuart ancestors, lived here until his death in 1955. Its marvelous interiors are now open to the public, who can view the sumptuous collection of art and furnishings on guided tours lasting about one hour. These are given daily except Saturdays and major holidays, starting at 10 a.m. to noon and 2-4 p.m. Between October 1st and Easter it is also closed on Sundays.

A highlight of any trip to Berchtesgaden is a tour through the **Salt Mines** *(Salzbergwerk)* (4), which can be reached on foot via Bräuhausstrasse and Bergwerkstrasse. In operation since 1517, the mines were the original source of wealth for the priory, and are still in active use today. Visitors are loaned traditional miners' clothes for protection against the cold and damp environment; then loaded aboard a motorized cart for the dark, eerie, half-mile-long journey into the bowels of the earth. Different parts of the subterranean excavations are reached via exciting downhill slides and a boat ride across an underground lake. About an hour later you will return to the outer world on another little tram. This fascinating tour is operated every day from May 1st to October 15th, 8 a.m. to 5 p.m.; and during the rest of the year daily except Sundays and holidays, from 12:30-3:30 p.m. From here it is a little over a mile back to the station.

KÖNIGSSEE:

Buses to the Königssee leave frequently from the front of the **train station** (1). Those with cars will, of course, drive the two-and-a-half-mile distance, while for the truly ambitious who would rather walk there is a footpath following the stream.

Many people consider the **Königssee** (5) to be the most enchanting lake in Germany, if not in all of Europe. It can be explored on one of the silent electric boat tours or by walking out to the Malerwinkel. Ideally, you should do both. From the bus stop or parking lot it is only a short stroll to the village, which is rather touristy but well hidden from the main part of the lake.

A path from here leads to the left and follows the lake's contours to the **Painters' Corner** *(Malerwinkel)* (6), a tranquil spot of astonishing beauty. About one-half mile from the village, it is the end of the trail—beyond which the mountains plunge vertically into the dark and mysterious waters.

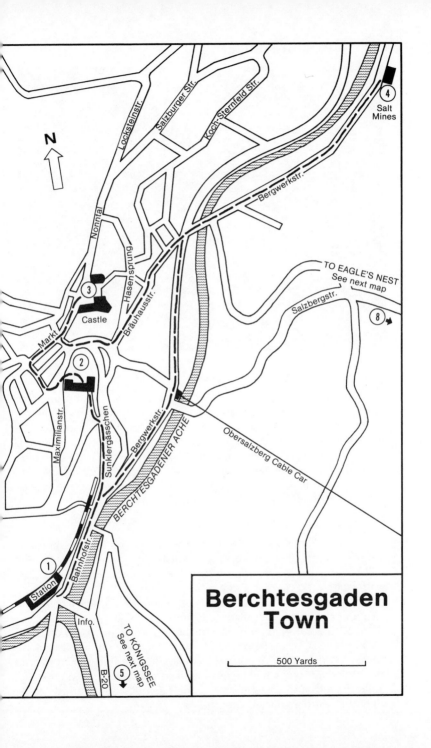

N

④ Salt Mines

Salzburger Str.

Locksteinstr.

Koch-Sternfeld Str.

Bergwerkstr.

TO EAGLE'S NEST
See next map

Nonntal

Hasensprung

Salzbergstr.

⑧ →

③

Castle

Bräuhausstr.

Markt

②

Maximilianstr.

Sunklergässchen

Bergwerkstr.

BERCHTESGADENER ACHE

Obersalzberg Cable Car

①

Station

Bahnhofstr.

Info.

TO KÖNIGSSEE
See next map

B-20

⑤ ↓

Berchtesgaden Town

500 Yards

The Königssee from Malerwinkel

Boats leave frequently from the village for the two-hour round-trip ride to St. Bartholomä and beyond. Those making the longer trip should get off at the end and take a ten-minute walk to the Obersee, once a part of the Königssee that was cut off by an avalanche eight centuries ago. The **Chapel of St. Bartholomä** (7), at the foot of the Watzmann, Germany's second-highest peak, is a scene right out of a fairy tale. When you've had your fill of natural splendor, return to the village and take the bus back to the Berchtesgaden station.

EAGLE'S NEST:

A visit to Hitler's alpine aerie begins by taking a bus to Obersalzberg-Hintereck, or by driving there—a distance of two and a half steep miles. Buses can be boarded in front of the post office next to the **train station** (1). There is also a cable car from the Bergwerkstrasse in Berchtesgaden, but this involves a walk of about a mile and a half from its upper station to Obersalzberg-Hintereck.

Adolf Hitler lived on the **Obersalzberg plateau** (8) on and off from 1923 until 1933, when he began construction there on his permanent home, the Berghof. Other Nazi leaders followed suit, and by World War II the area was a highly developed complex of party and military buildings linked by underground tunnels. For obvious reasons, nearly all of this was demolished after the war.

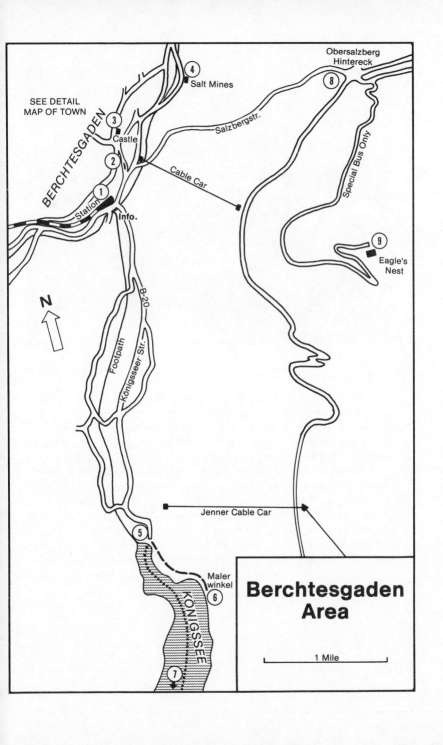

SEE DETAIL
MAP OF TOWN

Obersalzberg
Hintereck

Salt Mines ④

BERCHTESGADEN

③
Castle

②

① Salzbergstr.

Station

Info.

Cable Car

⑧

Special Bus Only

⑨
Eagle's
Nest

N

Footpath

B-20

Königsseer Str.

Jenner Cable Car

⑤

Maler
winkel
⑥

KÖNIGSSEE

**Berchtesgaden
Area**

1 Mile

⑦

The Eagle's Nest

One famous structure that does remain, however, is Hitler's hide-away, the **Eagle's Nest** *(Kehlsteinhaus)* (9). Located on a rocky crag high above the compound, it can only be reached by a special bus which departs frequently from the Obersalzberg-Hintereck parking lot. Other vehicles are not allowed to use the steep and dangerous road. Upon arrival you should make return reservations, then enter a tunnel and take the elevator at its end to the Eagle's Nest.

Seldom used by the *Führer,* this retreat was allowed to survive and is now a restaurant. Stroll out to the crest beyond for a fabulous view of the Alps. The Eagle's Nest can be visited daily between mid-May and mid-October, but is closed the rest of the year because of weather. From here retrace your route back to the Berchtesgaden train station.

The Wendelstein

The Wendelstein is not the highest peak in the Bavarian Alps, but it does provide the focus for a very enjoyable daytrip. *Münchners* have been reveling in the view from its summit ever since Germany's first alpine rack railway was built there in 1912. A cable car down its other side has been added in recent years, making possible an exciting circular tour. Add to this the charming small resort of Bayrischzell and you have the makings of a fun-filled day in the mountains.

GETTING THERE:

Trains leave Munich's main station around 7:45 and 9:30 a.m. for the one-and-a-half-hour ride direct to Bayrischzell. Those making the full circular trip will be returning via Brannenburg, from which trains to Munich run until early evening. Some of these require a change at Rosenheim. If you decide against making the full circuit you can return from Osterhofen as late as early evening. Be sure to check the schedules carefully.

By car, leave Munich on the A-8 (E-11) Autobahn in the direction of Salzburg. Get off at the Irschenberg exit and head south on local roads past Schliersee to Bayrischzell. It is not very practical to make the full circular tour by car, although there is infrequent bus service from Brannenburg back to Osterhofen.

WHEN TO GO:

Good weather is absolutely essential for this trip since it involves a few miles of pleasant country walking, except for those who are driving. The cable car and rack railway are in operation all year round.

FOOD AND DRINK:

Bayrischzell and the Wendelstein offer an excellent choice of places to eat or drink. Some of these are:

In Bayrischzell:

Schönbrunn (Sudelfeldstr. 23) $$
Hotel Wendelstein (Ursprungstr. 1) $
Zur Post (Schulstr. 3) $$

Outdoor Café in Bayrischzell

In Osterhofen:
Alpenhof (Osterhofen 1) $$
Atop the Wendelstein:
Berghotel Wendelstein $$

TOURIST INFORMATION:
The tourist office *(Kuramt)* is at Kirchplatz 7 in Bayrischzell. You can call them at (08023) 648.

SUGGESTED TOUR:
Begin your tour at the **Bayrischzell train station** (1). Tourist information is available at the Kur office near the church to the left. It would be a good idea to pick up a large-scale map *(Wanderkarte)* of the area before setting out. The pretty village is small enough to explore in a half-hour or so, and has a wide selection of restaurants.

From Bayrischzell you can walk along a lovely trail *(sign-posted as route K5)* just north of the railway line to the cable car station in **Osterhofen** (2). The distance is a little less than two miles. It is also possible to get there by train, bus, taxi, or car.

Those making the circular tour should purchase a combination ticket for the cable car and rack railway to Brannenburg. If you would rather return to Munich from Osterhofen you can get a round-trip cable car

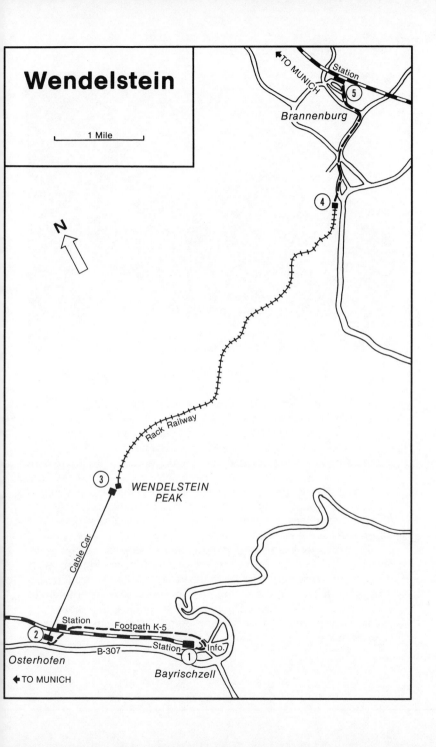

Wendelstein

1 Mile

N

TO MUNICH

Station

⑤

Brannenburg

④

Rack Railway

③

WENDELSTEIN PEAK

Cable Car

Station

Footpath K-5

②

Station

Info.

①

B-307

Osterhofen

← TO MUNICH

Bayrischzell

Atop the Wendelstein

ticket *(Berg und Talfahrt)* instead. Board the cable car *(Seilbahn)* for the six-minute ride to the top.

From the **upper station** (3) you can stroll out on the terrace for a fabulous view of the Alps and the Chiemsee far below. Food and drinks are offered at Bavaria's oldest mountain inn, built in 1883. There is an attractive chapel nearby, the highest in Germany, which dates from 1718. Just below this is the entrance to the 600-foot-long cave *(Höhle)*, giving you a chance to explore the insides of the mountain. Trails lead in several directions, the most interesting of which climbs to the solar observatory at the summit.

The rack railway *(Zahnradbahn)* to Brannenburg leaves from a station near the hotel. Those making the circular trip should board it for the delightful one-hour descent to the **valley station** (4). From here it is possible to get one of the infrequent buses back to Osterhofen, or walk a little less than two miles to the **Brannenburg train station** (5) and take a train from there to Munich. Some of these require a change at Rosenheim.

Section III

The Rhineland

If Bavaria is the very soul of Germany, then the Rhineland must be its heart. This large and loosely defined area offers travelers a tremendously wide variety of destinations. Such diverse experiences as a village in the Black Forest, the greatest Roman ruins north of the Alps, glittering cities and quiet university towns, elegant spas, river cruises, and wine tasting all lie within easy daytrip range of its center.

The hub of the Rhineland is Frankfurt—for many tourists the starting point of their German adventures. This is where most overseas flights to the Federal Republic terminate, and a place from which rail lines and highways reach out in all directions. Before embarking on any trips, however, it may be a good idea to devote at least half a day to exploring the city itself—the subject of the next chapter.

While all of the excursions described in this section can be made from Frankfurt, for some you may prefer alternative bases such as Mainz, Wiesbaden, Koblenz, Cologne, Darmstadt, or Heidelberg. These options are mentioned in the text whenever they are practical.

Four of the daytrips outlined in the previous section on Bavaria can also be taken from Frankfurt, namely Rothenburg (see page 87), Würzburg (page 93), Nuremberg (page 99), and Bamberg (page 107). Details concerning transportation from Frankfurt are given for each.

Frankfurt Tour

Thousands of travelers pass through Frankfurt's international airport every day, most of them en route to somewhere else. For many, this bustling metropolis on the Main is just the beginning—or the end—of their journey, not a destination in itself. The city has an undeserved reputation of being cold and impersonal, and of offering little in the way of tourist interest. True, Frankfurt is hardly picturesque, nor does it project the style of a Munich or a Düsseldorf. But it does have a tremendous vitality, a sheer creative drive that makes a visit here essential to understanding what modern Germany is all about.

Frankfurt has been a trading place since prehistoric times, a fact made inevitable by its location at a point where the Main River could be forded. The Romans had a fort here until they were driven out by a succession of tribes. Around A.D. 500, this was captured by the Franks, after which it became known as the Franks' Ford.

The growing town assumed real importance as early as the 8th century, when Charlemagne held court here. Between 1562 and 1806 Frankfurt was the coronation city of the Holy Roman emperors. The long tradition of trade fairs dates from the early 13th century, and was responsible for the rise of the banking interests which dominate the city's life today.

Nearly bombed out of existence during World War II, Frankfurt was quickly rebuilt in the modern mold, its skyline dotted with high-rise office towers. In recent years a determined effort has been made to restore what little remains of the past, and the sterility of its new architecture is gradually being relieved by attractive pedestrian zones.

Frankfurt is the hub of a vast transportation network, making it the ideal base for daytrips into central Germany. Those who prefer a less hectic atmosphere, but would still like to take advantage of its unrivalled travel facilities, may want to consider staying in the easily reached suburbs, such as Bad Homburg, or in other nearby cities, including Wiesbaden, Mainz, and Darmstadt.

GETTING AROUND:

While the suggested walking tour is rather short, you may want to use public transportation at some point. The system consists of subways, buses, and streetcars. A map and instructions are available at information offices of Frankfurt transit *(FVV)* or at tourist offices.

Frankfurt, like Munich and Hamburg, has *two* subway systems; the **U-Bahn** which remains underground, and the **S-Bahn** which surfaces once beyond the main station and continues on as a suburban commuter rail network. The Eurailpass or GermanRail Tourist Card may be used on the S-Bahn, *but very definitely not on the U-Bahn, streetcars, or buses.* Just before boarding these (or the S-Bahn if you have no pass) it is necessary to buy a ticket from one of the automatic coin-operated vending machines, labeled *Fahrscheine,* located in subway stations or by streetcar or bus stops. These are valid for any combination of modes going in a direct route to your destination. The time of purchase is stamped on the ticket, and the fares automatically increased during rush hours. Failure to have a valid ticket could result in a fine.

The system is divided into fare zones, as shown on the maps, but most of your travels will probably be within the basic inner-city zone. Note that fares are different for adults *(Erwachsene)* and children *(Kinder),* as indicated by pictograms on the vending machines. Those using the S-Bahn should beware of boarding first-class cars with an ordinary ticket. If all this sounds confusing, you can purchase a 24-hour *(24-Stunden)* ticket, allowing unlimited rides in the inner zone for that period, at one of the ticket windows or from the machines.

WHEN TO GO:

Frankfurt may be explored in any season. The walk can be completed in about two hours, not including time spent visiting museums or sights. Most of the museums are closed on Mondays.

FOOD AND DRINK:

There is an enormous selection of eating places along the walking route, ranging from familiar fast-food outlets to some very elegant (and expensive) restaurants. A few good choices, in the sequence you will pass them, are:

> **InterCity Restaurant** (in the main train station) $$
> **Parkhotel Frankfurt** (Wiesenhüttenplatz 36, near the station), two restaurants, both $$$
> **Continental Hotel** (Baseler Str, 56, near the station) $$
> **Mövenpick** (Opernplatz, near the old opera), two restaurants, $$$ and $$
> **Jacques Offenbach** (Opernplatz, near the old opera) $$$

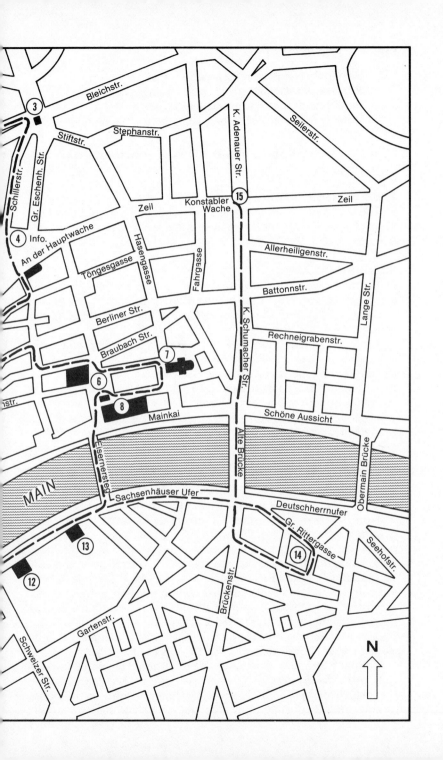

Heyland's Weinstube (Kaiserhofstr. 7) $$
Börsenkeller (Schillerstr. 11, near Hauptwache) $$
Café Hauptwache (Hauptwache) $$
Hotel Frankfurter Hof (Kaiserplatz), three restaurants, $$$ to $$

The Alt Sachsenhausen district (14) is lined with colorful restaurants and cafés.

TOURIST INFORMATION:

The tourist office, phone (069) 212-88-49, is in the north side of the main train station. There is a branch in the Hauptwache U-Bahn station, phone (069) 212-87-08.

SUGGESTED TOUR:

For the convenience of those staying out of town the walk beings at the 19th-century **main train station** (Hauptbahnhof) (1), the largest in Germany. You may want to spend a few minutes soaking up the atmosphere of this busy old terminal.

Cross the square in front of the station via an underground passage, which contains a wide variety of shops as well as U- and S-Bahn stations. From here follow Kaiserstrasse through a somewhat seedy eros zone until you come to a park. To your right is a modern theatre complex, used for operas and plays. Turn left and continue along Gallusanlage and Taunusanlage—the line of the old medieval town walls—to the **Old Opera House** (Alte Oper) (2). Built in 1880 in the Italian Renaissance style, it was destroyed by bombs in 1944 and has been restored as a very elegant concert hall.

Stroll down Hochstrasse to the 15th-century **Eschenheimer Gate** (3), a surprising sight amid all the office towers. This is the last surviving remnant of the city's medieval inner fortifications.

From here take Schillerstrasse to **An der Hauptwache** (4)—the very heart of modern Frankfurt. Beneath this huge open square lies a shopping center, complete with a tourist office and both U- and S-Bahn stations. Go down for a look, then come back to street level and visit **St. Catherine's Church** (Katherinenkirche) on the south side, where the poet Goethe was baptized. First built in the 14th century, it was reconstructed in 1681 and again in 1954. The very beautiful interior is noted for its contemporary stained-glass windows. In the center of the square, near the main subway entrance, stands the original *Hauptwache*, a guard house dating from 1729, now used as a café.

Continue on to the **Goethe House** (5), where Frankfurt's favorite son, Johann Wolfgang von Goethe, was born in 1749, and where he spent his childhood and adolescence. Whether you are a fan of Goethe or not, you will certainly enjoy a visit here if only to see how a well-

An der Hauptwache

to-do family lived in those times. The house was badly damaged during World War II, but has since been lovingly restored, using as much of the original materials as could be reclaimed from the rubble. An adjoining building houses a small museum devoted to the life of Germany's greatest literary genius. Both the house and the museum are open Mondays through Saturdays, from 9 a.m. to 6 p.m., closing at 4 p.m. from October through March. The complex is also open on Sundays, from 10 a.m. to 1 p.m. Don't miss seeing this—it is perhaps the most interesting sight in Frankfurt.

A short stroll from here leads to the **Römerberg** (6), a large and heavily restored old square lined with gabled buildings. The 15th-century Town Hall, known as the *Römer,* has an Imperial Hall *(Kaisersaal)* which you can see, although its sole attraction consists of some mediocre murals of all the Holy Roman emperors from Charlemagne on. While in the square, be sure to visit the tiny **Church of St. Nicholas** on the south side. Originally built in the 13th century, it is noted for its charming interior and a tower vaguely resembling a minaret.

Now follow Markt to the **Cathedral** *(Dom)* (7), built between the 13th and 15th centuries. Since 1356 all elections of German emperors

The Eiserner Steg and Skyline

were held here, and from 1562 until the dissolution of the Holy Roman Empire in 1806 it was also the site of all imperial coronations. There are several splendid works of art inside, including some fine 14th-century choir stalls and medieval altars.

From here on, it is one museum after another until you reach Alt Sachsenhausen—a destination which doesn't come to life until late afternoon. Naturally, you won't want to see them all, but the following descriptions should help you select.

Return to the Römerberg. At its very southern end stands the **Historical Museum** (8), located in a complex of buildings dating from the 12th century to the present. One of these, the Saalhofkapelle, was the chapel of the emperor Barbarossa, and is the oldest surviving structure in Frankfurt. The exhibitions, following a suggested itinerary, cover a vast variety of subjects including everyday life, wars, industry, transportation, politics,—just about everything that ever happened in the city. You could easily spend an entire afternoon here, although a fast visit can be made in an hour or so. The museum is open every day except Mondays, from 10 a.m. to 5 p.m.

Now walk around the corner to the Main River, where sightseeing boats depart at regular intervals. Cross the Eiserner Steg, an old iron footbridge dating from 1868, to the suburb of Sachsenhausen, which offers a broad choice of museums along its Schaumainkai. All of these are open from Tuesdays through Sundays, 10 a.m. to 5 p.m.; except the Bundespost Museum, which closes at 4 p.m.

The **Liebieghaus** (9) is Frankfurt's museum of sculpture. Housed in a former baronial mansion, the collection covers virtually the entire scope of the plastic arts, from ancient Egyptian through the Renaissance and baroque periods.

From here it is only a block to the **Städel Art Institute** (Städelsches Kunstinstitut) (10), which ranks as one of Europe's major art museums. Just about any painter you can think of is represented in this sweeping survey, from the Flemish Primitives to Picasso. The Städel is a must-see for any art lover.

The history of communications is thoroughly explored in the **Bundespost Museum** (11), a fascinating place to visit if you have an interest in postal matters, buses, radios, telephones, and the like.

Changing exhibitions concerning the customs of primitive people are featured in the **Museum of Ethnography** (Völkerkunde) (12).

Just beyond this is the **Decorative Arts Museum** (Museum für Kunsthandwerk) (13), housed in an 18th-century mansion. Its superb collection of beautiful furniture from the Middle Ages to the present day is absolutely delightful, as are the displays of porcelains, glassware, books, carpets, and so on.

By this time you are probably ready to sit down at a café for some liquid refreshment. Luck is on your side, since it is only a short stroll to **Alt Sachsenhausen** (14). The narrow pedestrians-only streets here are lined with colorful places to eat and drink, many of them featuring the apple wine (Ebbelwei) peculiar to Frankfurt. Be sure to poke into some of the hidden courtyards—this is where the more interesting establishments lurk. Prosit!

The easiest way back to central Frankfurt is via the Alte Brücke and Schumacher Strasse. This leads to the **Konstabler Wache** (15), where there are both U- and S-Bahn stations.

Mainz

The two-thousand-year-old city of Mainz is forever linked with one of the most significant achievements in western civilization. It was here, during the 15th century, that Johannes Gutenberg invented a method for producing movable type—a crucial event making possible the widespread dissemination of knowledge through printing. Naturally proud of its native son, the city has honored him with the marvelous World Museum of Printing, well worth the trip in itself.

Mainz has several other attractions, including a splendid 10th-century cathedral, which ranks among the largest and most ancient in Germany. Heavily bombed during World War II, some parts of the Old Town were beautifully restored, while in another section contemporary architects were given a free hand in creating bold new structures.

By getting off to an early start and cutting short the walking tour it is possible to combine this trip in the same day with one to Wiesbaden, Worms, or Darmstadt—all of which are easily reached by train. With its excellent transportation facilities, Mainz makes a good alternative base for exploring the Rhineland. It is very close to the Frankfurt airport.

GETTING THERE:

Trains to Mainz on the S-Bahn service *(route S-14, marked for Wiesbaden)* leave Frankfurt's Konstablerwache, Hauptwache, Taunusanlage, main station *(lower level)*, and airport station at frequent intervals. The journey takes about 45 minutes. Be sure to get off at the Mainz main station *(Hauptbahnhof)*, not at Süd or Nord. See ticketing instructions for the Frankfurt trip.

There are also a few regular express trains which depart from Frankfurt's main station *(street level)*, making the trip in less time. S-Bahn *(FVV)* tickets are not valid on these. Return service operates until late evening.

By car, leave Frankfurt on the A-66 Autobahn. Get off at the Wiesbaden-Erbenheim exit and head south on the B-455 across the Rhine to downtown Mainz. The total distance is 24 miles.

WHEN TO GO:

Mainz may be visited in any season, although it is more appealing in warm weather. All of the museums are closed on Mondays.

The Cathedral and Market Place

FOOD AND DRINK:

Mainz offers a nice variety of restaurants along the walking route. Some suggestions, in the order that you will pass or come close to them, are:

> **Haus des Deutschen Weines** (Gutenbergplatz 3) World-famous for its wine selections. $$
>
> **Zum Salvator** (Grosse Langgasse 4) $$
>
> **Rats und Zunftstuben Heilig Geist** (Rentengasse 2, near the printing museum) $$
>
> **Weinhaus Schreiner** (Rheinstr. 38) $
>
> **Hilton Hotel** (next to Rheingoldhalle), two restaurants, $$$ and $$
>
> **Walderdorff** (Karmeliterplatz 4, next to St. Christoph's) $$$
>
> **Hotel Mainzer Hof** (Kaiserstr, 98) Panorama restaurant, $$$

TOURIST INFORMATION:

The tourist office, phone (06131) 23-37-41, is located at Bahnhofstrasse 15, near the train station.

SUGGESTED TOUR:

Begin your walk at the **main train station** (1). The tourist office is nearby. Follow the map to the pedestrians-only **Market Place** *(Markt)*, an attractive large square which really comes to life when the farmers are in town. In its center stands a magnificent Renaissance fountain dating from 1526.

The huge six-towered **Cathedral** (Dom) (2), begun in 975, completely dominates the scene. Built over several centuries, it has a mixture of styles ranging from Romanesque to late baroque. Enter through the thousand-year-old bronze doors on the side portal and explore the interior. There is a choir at each end, an arrangement common in the Rhineland. Both of these have crypts, the eastern one being particularly interesting for its modern gold reliquary of the saints of Mainz. The cathedral is noted for its fine tombs of the archbishops, dating from the 13th to the 18th centuries.

A doorway along the south aisle leads through the cloister to the **Cathedral Museum**, where an extraordinary collection of medieval religious art is on display. You won't regret spending enough time for a careful examination of these treasures.

Leave the cathedral and circle around its eastern end, going by way of Grebenstrasse of the **Leichof**. From this lovely square you will have the best possible view of the church. Now stroll down Augustinerstrasse, a charming narrow street leading through the heart of the romantic old part of town. **St. Ignatius' Church** (3), a few steps beyond its lower end, has a remarkable outdoor Crucifixion statue from the 16th century.

Return to Holzstrasse and turn right to the majestic 14th-century **Wooden Tower** (Holzturm) (4), one of the few remaining relics of the former town fortifications. Continue straight ahead until you come to the Rhine, then make a left along its quay past the KD line pier (see chapter on Rhine Cruise).

A left here will lead you up steps to the strikingly modern **Town Hall** (Rathaus) (5), completed in 1973. Opposite this is the equally contemporary Rheingoldhalle, where concerts are frequently held. An elevated platform, complete with outdoor café, joins these together and spans busy Rheinstrasse next to the 13th-century Iron Tower (Eisenturm), another medieval town gate.

Follow the map through a sleek new shopping district to the **World Museum of Printing** (6), also known as the Gutenberg Museum. Exhibitions covering the entire scope of written communications throughout the ages are displayed on four floors of this modern structure. The museum's main treasure is its original Gutenberg Bible of 1452-55, kept in a vault which you may enter. More fascinating than that, though, is the reproduction of Gutenberg's printing shop where demonstrations of old techniques are given. Other areas are devoted to the development of alphabets, the history of paper, bookbinding, and even computerized phototypesetting. Opening times are daily from

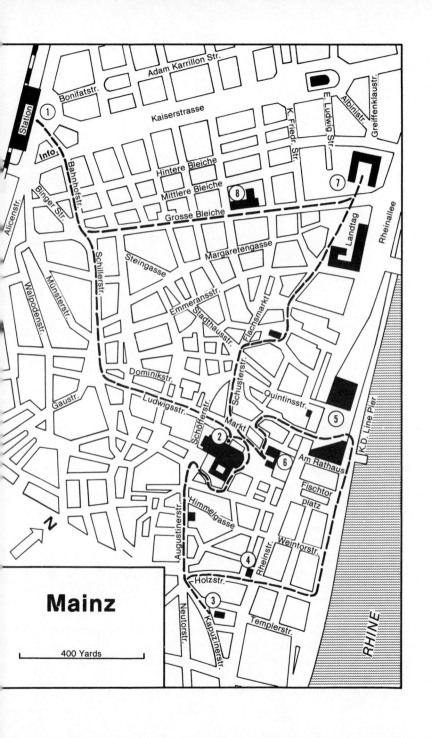

Bonifatstr.

Adam Karrillon Str.

Kaiserstrasse

Station

①

Info.

Binger Str.

Bahnhofstr.

Alicenstr.

Walpodenstr.

Münsterstr.

Gaustr.

Schillerstr.

Steingasse

Hintere Bleiche

Mittlere Bleiche

Grosse Bleiche

⑧

Margaretengasse

K. Friedr. Str.

E. Ludwig Str.

Albinistr.

Greiffenklaustr.

⑦

Landtag

Rheinallee

Rheinallee

Emmeransstr.

Stadthausstr.

Flachsmarkt

Dominikstr.

Ludwigsstr.

Schofferstr.

Schusterstr.

Quintinsstr.

⑤

K.D. Line Pier

Markt

②

Am Rathaus

⑥

Augustinerstr.

Himmelgasse

Fischtor platz

Weintorstr.

Rheinstr.

④

N

Holzstr.

Mainz

Neutorstr.

Kapuzinerstr.

③

Templerstr.

RHINE

400 Yards

The Town Hall

Tuesdays through Saturdays, 10 a.m. to 6 p.m., and on Sundays and holidays from 10 a.m. to 1 p.m.

Now return to the market place and walk down Schusterstrasse, circling around the ruins of St. Christoph's Church. From here a series of back streets leads to Deutschhaus Platz, fronted by the state parliament *(Landtag)* of Rhineland-Palatinate *(Rheinland-Pfalz)*, of which Mainz is the capital. In the square you will see an exact copy of the Jupiter Column, erected in A.D. 67 by the Romans. The original is in the Middle Rhineland Museum.

The **Roman-Germanic Museum** *(Römisch-Germanisches Zentralmuseum* (7), located in the former Electoral Palace of the 17th and 18th centuries, is just across the street. Archaeological finds from the stone age to the Carolingian period can be seen here every day except Mondays, from 10 a.m. to 6 p.m.

Stroll down the Grosse Bleiche to the **Middle Rhineland Provincial Museum** *(Mittelrheinische Landsmuseum)* (8), where the history of Mainz and the Rhineland from prehistoric times to the present is on display. The museum is open daily from 10 a.m. to 5 p.m., except on Mondays and holidays. From here it is a short walk back to the train station.

Wiesbaden

Kur und Kultur set the style in fashionable Wiesbaden, that elegant spa where the *belle époque* lingers on. Ever since the time of the Romans, who called it *Aquae Mattiacorum,* the wealthy and the powerful have been flocking here to partake of its healing waters and sophisticated aura. This is the kind of place where people still dress up at night—for the casino, the opera, the many splendid restaurants. But if all this seems a little rich for your blood, it needn't be. Wiesbaden is also a fairly large city, the state capital of Hesse, a center for conventions and business meetings, and, above all, a green town of manicured parks and gardens. A daytrip here won't cost very much, and offers a chance to enjoy yet another facet of German life.

It is possible to combine this trip in the same day with one to nearby Mainz. With its superb hotel and transportation facilities, Wiesbaden also makes an excellent alternative base for exploring the Rhineland, especially since it is so close to the Frankfurt airport.

GETTING THERE:

Trains to Wiesbaden on the S-Bahn service depart frequently from Frankfurt's Konstablerwache, Hauptwache, Taunusanlage, and main station *(lower level).* The S-1 line goes direct and takes about 45 minutes, while the S-14 line goes via the airport and Mainz, taking about one hour. Those without railpasses should note the ticketing instructions under the Frankfurt trip. Get off at Wiesbaden's main station, the very end of the line.

It is also possible to take a regular express train from Frankfurt's main station *(street level).* These take only about one-half hour for the trip, and are a nice option for railpass holders. S-Bahn *(FVV)* tickets are not valid on the expresses. Return trains run until late evening.

By Car, leave Frankfurt on the A-66 Autobahn. Get off at the Erbenheim exit and follow Berliner Strasse and Gustav Stresemann Ring into town. The total distance is 24 miles.

WHEN TO GO:

Wiesbaden may be visited at any time, although warm weather makes it considerably more attractive.

FOOD AND DRINK:

There are many good restaurants and cafés along the walking route. Some choices, in trip sequence, are:

Kurhaus Restaurants (in the Kurhaus) $$$

Hotel Nassauer Hof (Kaiser Friedrich Platz), two restaurants, both $$$

Mövenpick (Sonnenbergstr. 2) $$

Alt Prag (Taunusstr. 41) Czech cuisine. $$

Alte Münze (Kranzplatz 4, near Kochbrunnen) $$$

Dortmunder (Langgasse 34) A beer hall. $

TOURIST INFORMATION:

The tourist office has a branch in the train station, phone (06121) 31-28-45; and a main office at Rheinstrasse 15, at the corner of Wilhelmstrasse. You can phone them at (06121) 31-28-47.

SUGGESTED TOUR:

Begin your walk at the **main train station** (1). Cross the square via an underground passageway and walk through the park to Friedrich Ebert Allee. The **Wiesbaden Museum** (2) has a fine collection of art ranging from Old Masters through the 20th century, as well as some exceptionally lovely antique furniture. Just opposite this is the modern Rhein-Main Halle, used for exhibitions and conventions.

Continue along the elegant Wilhelmstrasse, passing the main tourist information office, and enter another park. Following the path around its pond will take you to the State Theatre, a 19th-century neoclassical opera house with a recent addition in the contemporary style. Now stroll into the **Kurpark** (3), a quiet oasis of dream-like beauty. Inviting paths lead beyond a small lake to secluded spots among the old shade trees. Outdoor concerts are given here during the summer, as well as other entertainments.

Leave the park and walk around to the **Kurhaus** (4), a rather ponderous neoclassical structure of 1907 which houses the gambling casino, a concert hall, restaurants and bars. Its superb tree-lined approach is bordered on the south by the Theatre Colonnade. On the north side is the elegant early-19th-century Brunnenkolonnade, where thermal waters are available.

Now follow the map to the **Kochbrunnen** (5). Set in an open square, this is the most famous of Wiesbaden's 26 hot saline springs. From here it is possible to make a side trip of about one mile to the base of the **Neroberg** (6), off the map but not too far to walk. You can also get there by bus (route #8). An amusing 19th-century rack railway *(Neroberg Bahn),* said to be the oldest in Germany, ascends the gentle hill during the summer season for a magnificent view of the town. Near

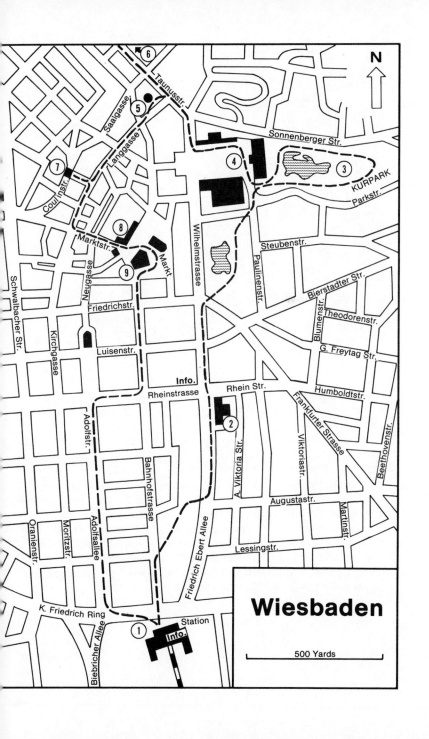

N

Taunusstr.

Sonnenberger Str.

Saalgasse

Langgasse

⑥

⑤

⑦

Cour..str.

④

③

KURPARK

Parkstr.

Steubenstr.

⑧

Marktstr.

Neugasse

Wilhelmstrasse

Markt

Paulinenstr.

Bierstadter Str.

Blumenstr.

Theodorenstr.

⑨

Friedrichstr.

G. Freytag Str.

Schwalbacher Str.

Kirchgasse

Luisenstr.

Info.

Rheinstrasse

Rhein Str.

Humboldtstr.

Adolfstr.

Bahnhofstrasse

②

A. Viktoria Str.

Frankfurter Strasse

Viktoriastr.

Beethovenstr.

Augustastr.

Martinstr.

Adolfsallee

Oranienstr.

Moritzstr.

Friedrich Ebert Allee

Lessingstr.

K. Friedrich Ring

Biebricher Allee

①

Station

Info.

Wiesbaden

500 Yards

The Kurhaus

the top there is a gorgeous "Greek Chapel," actually a Russian Orthodox church, erected in 1855 as a tomb for the Russian wife of Duke Adolf of Nassau.

Return to the Kochbrunnen and stroll down Langgasse to the **Römertor** (7), an old town gate. Parts of this are believed to date from the late Roman period. Continue along the pedestrians-only Langgasse and turn left into Marktstrasse. The Market Fountain, dating from 1537 and topped by a golden lion, stands in front of the former **Ducal Palace** *(Schloss)* (8), now the state parliament of *Land* Hesse.

Opposite this is the Renaissance-style Old Town Hall *(Altes Rathaus)* of 1609. Cross the square to the 19th-century **New City Hall** (9) and the splendid neo-Gothic Market Church, than walk through the market place. From here, follow the map through some pleasant neighborhoods back to the train station.

Rhine Cruise

For many visitors to Germany, the number-one attraction is a romantic cruise down the Rhine, steaming through its spectacular gorge past vineyards, castles, and the legendary Loreley. All of these sights are in the magnificent section between Rüdesheim and Koblenz, a part of the river which not only offers the best scenery but also the most frequent boat service.

Politically and economically, the Rhine is probably the greatest river on earth. For over two thousand years this watery main street of Europe has carried the trade of many nations along its 820-mile length from the Alps to the North Sea. It has been a border between opposing civilizations since the time of Julius Caesar. Legends inspired by its mysterious beauty have produced a treasure of art, literature, and music—especially in the stretch covered by this daytrip.

There are many possibilities for a cruise on the Rhine. The one described here is particularly good for travelers staying in Frankfurt. Those starting out from Mainz or Wiesbaden may prefer to board a boat there, while people making Koblenz or Cologne their base can do the trip in reverse, remembering that boats going in that direction are much slower due to the heavy current.

Most of the steamer service on this part of the Rhine is operated by the KD line, which accepts the Eurailpass on all boats except the much-too-speedy hydrofoil. Holders of the Eurail Youthpass must pay a small supplement to use express boats. Those with GermanRail Tourist Cards receive a substantial discount over the regular fares.

This trip can be combined in the same day with one to Koblenz by getting off to an early start. Alternatively, it is possible to start in Koblenz and go the other way by boat, winding up in Rüdesheim for an evening of wine drinking before taking a late train back to Frankfurt (or wherever).

GETTING THERE:

Trains to Rüdesheim leave Frankfurt's main station several times every morning, taking about one hour for the trip. A few of these require a change at Wiesbaden. Return service from Koblenz operates until late evening, and may require a change at Mainz.

By car, leave Frankfurt on the A-66 Autobahn and stay on it past Wiesbaden to Eltville. From there take the B-42 road into Rüdesheim. The total distance is about 45 miles. Those driving will, of course, have to return to Rüdesheim by train to pick up their car.

WHEN TO GO:

The KD line operates Rhine boat cruises from the beginning of April until the end of October, with more frequent sailings during the peak summer period. Good weather will greatly enhance your enjoyment of this trip. If possible, try to leave Frankfurt as early as 7 a.m. to make the best connections.

FOOD AND DRINK:

Meals and drinks are available abòard the boats at moderate prices. There is a wide selection of restaurants and cafés in both Rüdesheim and Koblenz, which are listed in the next two chapters.

TOURIST INFORMATION:

Information about boat cruises is available at all train stations, or you can call the KD line in Cologne at (0221) 2-08-80. Tourist information offices in Frankfurt, Mainz, Wiesbaden, Rüdesheim, Bingen, and Koblenz are listed in the sections dealing with those towns in this book.

SUGGESTED TOUR:

Travelers staying in **Mainz** (1) may prefer to board the boat there. The KD line pier is located near the town hall, as shown on the map for the Mainz trip. Alternatively, they could take a local train to Bingen (4) and pick up the cruise at that point—see the map on page 171.

Those making Wiesbaden their base have the option of getting on the boat at the KD line pier in **Wiesbaden-Biebrich** (2), easily reached by bus or taxi. It is also quite simple to get to Rüdesheim from Wiesbaden by train or bus.

For travelers staying in the Frankfurt area, the best starting point for a Rhine cruise is **Rüdesheim** (3). A map and description of that town will be found in the next chapter. The KD line pier is located a few blocks east of the train station, near the tourist information office. Several other companies also offer shorter Rhine cruises from here. Board the boat, which now crosses the river to the noted wine-ship-

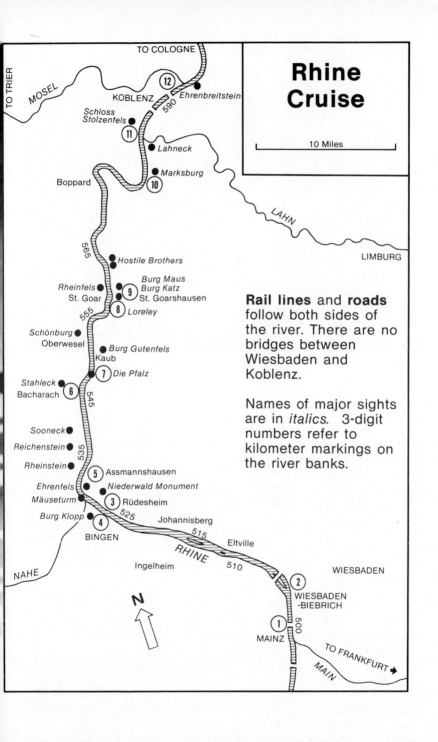

Rhine Cruise

10 Miles

TO TRIER

MOSEL

TO COLOGNE

KOBLENZ

⑫ Ehrenbreitstein

590

Schloss Stolzenfels

⑪

Lahneck

Marksburg

⑩

Boppard

LAHN

LIMBURG

565

Hostile Brothers

Burg Maus
Burg Katz
St. Goarshausen

Rheinfels
St. Goar

⑨

⑧ *Loreley*

555

Schönburg
Oberwesel

Burg Gutenfels
Kaub

⑦ *Die Pfalz*

Stahleck
Bacharach

⑥

545

Sooneck

Reichenstein

535

Rheinstein

⑤ Assmannshausen

Ehrenfels

Niederwald Monument

Mäuseturm

③ Rüdesheim

Burg Klopp

④

525

Johannisberg

515

Eltville

BINGEN

RHINE

510

NAHE

Ingelheim

WIESBADEN

②

WIESBADEN
-BIEBRICH

N

①

500

MAINZ

TO FRANKFURT →

MAIN

Rail lines and **roads** follow both sides of the river. There are no bridges between Wiesbaden and Koblenz.

Names of major sights are in *italics*. 3-digit numbers refer to kilometer markings on the river banks.

Die Pfalz

ping town of **Bingen** (4), also described in the next chapter.

As you sail down the Rhine you will make numerous stops and pass many famous sights. To identify these, refer to the *kilometer markings* on the banks of the river, which correspond to those on the map.

High atop a hill overlooking the river rises the colossal **Niederwald Monument,** described in the next chapter. The cruise now enters a long and fantastically beautiful stretch of the Rhine, beginning at the Binger Loch. You will soon pass the **Mäuseturm**, a small tower on a mid-stream island. Legend has it that a hated archbishop of Mainz was eaten alive here by mice during the Middle Ages. Directly opposite this, to the right, are the ruins of **Burg Ehrenfels**, a 13th-century fortress destroyed by the French in 1689.

The boat now stops at the romantic village of **Assmannshausen** (5), referred to in the next chapter. Across from this are three well-known castles; the first, to the left, being **Rheinstein**, built by robber barons in the 13th century. When Charlemagne's empire fell apart in the 9th century, the feudal lords who took over small bits of land set up castles to extort tolls from passing boats. In time these multiplied until just about every strategic location on the Rhine had a fortification. The next one, less than a half-mile to the right and overlooking the village of Trechtingshausen, is the 11th-century castle of **Reich-**

The Loreley

enstein. Beyond this is **Sooneck Castle**, dating from 1010. As is the case with many Rhine castles, these three were heavily restored during the wave of romanticism which swept 19th-century Germany.

The picturesque old wine town of **Bacharach** (6), whose name derives from that of the ancient god Bacchus, is an important stop for all boats. Its quaint streets are not visible from the river, however, as a medieval ring wall still blocks the view. A mile and a half downstream, **Die Pfalz** (7) rises as a strange apparition in midstream. If ever there was a good place to put a toll booth, this is it. Built in the 14th century and as forbidding today as ever, the castle is absolutely irresistible to photographers.

By this time, all of the German passengers will have gathered on the starboard side of the boat. They know what's coming next. When you hear them sing *"Ich weiss nicht was soll es bedeuten—,"* you are opposite the **Loreley** (8), a steep legend-haunted rock which occupies a peculiar place in the Teutonic psyche. It is said that in ancient times a lovely maiden sat at the top and lured boatmen to their deaths in the turbulent waters below. It is also reputed to be the hiding place of the Nibelung's golden treasure, immortalized in Wagner's opera *Das Rheingold*. One very real property of the narrow passage is its seven-fold echo, which some of the passengers may try to exploit.

St. Goarshausen (9) is the next stop on the right bank. It is possible to get off here and return on one of the fairly frequent trains back to Rüdesheim, Wiesbaden, or Frankfurt. Above the town rises the 14th-century Burg Katz, and to the left a rival castle of the same age, Burg Maus. Over on the left bank, the impressive 13th-century ruins of **Rheinfels Castle**—once the most powerful on the Rhine—stand guard over St. Goar. Overlooking Kamp are the twin castles of the **Hostile Brothers**, who in legend fought over the love of a fair maiden. Boppard, a stop for all boats, was founded by the Romans about A.D. 370. Parts of their fortifications still exist.

The best-preserved fortress along the Rhine gorge is **Marksburg** (10), just above the little town of Braubach, which dates from the 12th century. In all the battles which ravaged this area, Marksburg was never humbled. It withstood both the Thirty Years War and the French occupation, and it was not until 1945 that it sustained any damage from conflict. Restoration has since been completed.

Opposite the confluence of the Lahn River is the impossibly romantic palace of **Schloss Stolzenfels** (11), originally from the 13th century but heavily rebuilt in 1836 as a dreamy 19th-century vision of the Age of Chivalry. The kaiser lived there, and it suited his taste.

The end of your cruise is now in sight as the boat approaches **Koblenz** (12). Time permitting, this is a golden opportunity to explore a wonderful old town before heading for the train station. A map and walking tour will be found in the chapter beginning on page 173.

Rüdesheim

Wine lovers will rejoice in a trip to Rüdesheim, Germany's favorite wine village. The vintages here have been flowing for some two thousand years, ever since the Romans settled the area and began growing grapes. You can have a wonderful time sampling the result—some of Germany's (and the world's) best white wines—or in just exploring this delightful old town and its surroundings. Whatever you do, you won't be alone. Rüdesheim is *very* popular with tourists from all over the globe.

The suggested tour begins in the neighboring village of Assmannshausen and includes a ride across the Rhine to Bingen. If these don't interest you, it is entirely possible to spend the whole day in Rüdesheim and not get bored. Tipsy perhaps, but not bored. Parts of this trip can be combined in the same day with a Rüdesheim cruise, described in the preceding chapter.

GETTING THERE:

Trains depart Frankfurt's main station for Rüdesheim and Assmannshausen several times each morning. In addition, there are trains and buses from Wiesbaden, which can be reached by S-Bahn (see page 157). The direct trip takes about one hour. Return service operates until late evening. Be sure to check the schedules first, especially to determine whether the train you want also stops in Assmannshausen. If not, it is only a short distance by bus or taxi from Rüdesheim.

By car, leave Frankfurt on the A-66 Autobahn and stay on it past Wiesbaden to Eltville. From there take the B-42 road into Rüdesheim. The total distance is about 45 miles.

WHEN TO GO:

Rüdesheim may be visited anytime, although it is more attractive in the warmer seasons. The Brömserburg museum is open daily from March to mid-November. Many of the restaurants are closed in winter.

FOOD AND DRINK:

The Rüdesheim area offers a wide variety of restaurants and cafés in all price ranges. Some outstanding choices are:

Krone (Rheinuferstr. 10, Assmannshausen) $$$
Altes Haus (Lorcherstr. 5, Assmannshausen) $$
Lamm (Rheinuferstr. 6, Assmannshausen) $
Jagdschloss Niederwald (near top of chair lift) $$$
Felsenkeller (Oberstr, 39, Rüdesheim) $$
Traube-Aumüller (Rheinstr. 6, Rüdesheim) $$
Zum Bären (Schmidtstr. 24, Rüdesheim) $

In addition, there are many attractive wine taverns with food on and around the Drosselgasse.

TOURIST INFORMATION:

The tourist office in Rüdesheim is located at Rheinstrasse 16, near the KD Line pier. You can phone them at (06722) 29-62. In Bingen, they are at Rheinkai 21, phone (06721) 1-42-69.

SUGGESTED TOUR:

Those making the complete tour should begin at the **train station in Assmannshausen** (1). Follow the map through this romantic old village, whose existence was first documented in 1108. Oddly enough, it is the home of Germany's best *red* wines. The narrow streets lead past several half-timbered houses and an interesting late-Gothic church to the **chair lift** *(Seilbahn)* (2). Purchase a combination ticket to Rüdesheim and be seated for a comfortable ride to the Niederwald. Along the way you will have superb high-level views across the Rhine valley.

Getting off at the top, walk around past the **Jagdschloss** (3), a former hunting lodge of the dukes of Nassau. It is now a very attractive hotel and restaurant complete with another panoramic vista. From here take a leisurely stroll of about one-half mile or so along a forest road to the **Niederwald Monument** *(Denkmal)* (4), one of the most colossal statues on earth. A late 19th-century expression of overblown nationalism, it symbolizes the unification of Germany achieved in 1871 and is still deeply revered by the German people—although to foreign eyes it may seem somewhat amusing. The view across the Rhine is, of course, fabulous.

From here, take the nearby cable car *(Seilbahn)* down across the vineyards to its **lower station** (5) in Rüdesheim. Make a right on Oberstrasse to the **Brömserhof** (6), an aristocratic residence dating from 1542. The interior now features a curious exhibition known as Siegfried's Mechanical Music Cabinet, a collection of antique self-playing musical instruments.

Rüdesheim is world-famous for the **Drosselgasse**, a narrow lane that is usually jam-packed with hundreds of thirsty visitors. You will probably want to return here later to relax in one of its many colorful

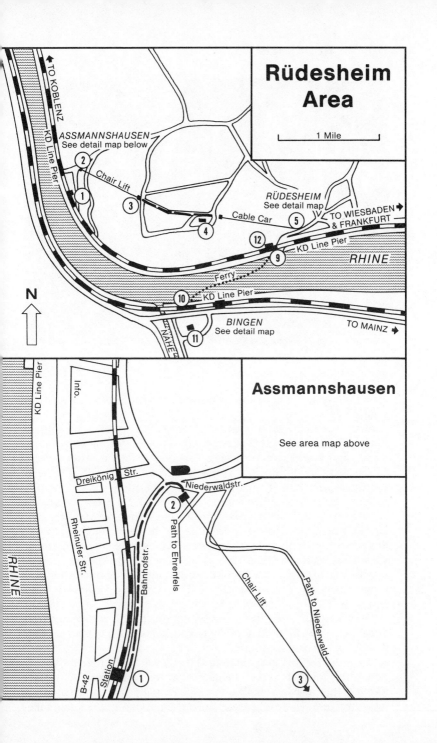

The Drosselgasse

wine taverns. Until then, however, there are several other sights worth seeing.

Continue to the bottom and turn left on Rheinstrasse, passing the tourist office. The Market Place *(Markt)* has an interesting 14th-century parish church which merits a visit. Beyond this, at the eastern end of Rheinstrasse, is the **Eagle's Tower** *(Adlerturm)* (7), built in the 15th century as part of the medieval defense fortifications.

Now return along the bank of the Rhine to the **Brömserburg** (8), an ancient castle built on late Roman foundations between the 11th and 14th centuries. Formerly a refuge for the archbishops of Mainz, this powerful structure now houses a fabulous wine museum, a must-see for any visitor to Rüdesheim. Displays here cover the entire scope of wine-making—and drinking—down through the ages. The museum is open daily from the beginning of March until mid-November, from 10 a.m. to 12:30 p.m. and 1:30-6 p.m.

A short stroll along the river brings you to the **passenger ferry dock** *(Personenfähre)* (9). From here you can take a quick boat ride to Bingen, just across the Rhine.

Near the **Bingen ferry landing** (10) you will find a tourist information office, located on the Rheinkai. Now follow the map up to **Burg Klopp** (11), a heavily rebuilt castle whose origins probably date from the Roman era. There is an exceptionally good view of the Rhine valley

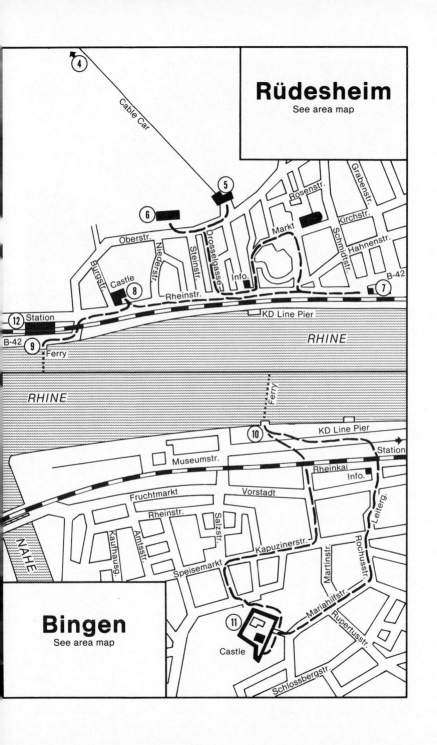

The Brömserburg

from here, but the main attraction is the Bingen Folk Museum *(Binger Heimatmuseum)*. Step inside to see some remarkable exhibits dating from prehistoric times until the Frankish period. Probably the most interesting of these is the collection of second-century Roman doctors' instruments. Opening times are from the beginning of April through mid-October; 9 a.m. to noon and 2-5 p.m. It is closed all day on Mondays.

Return to the ferry dock and Rüdesheim. The train station (12) is just across from the dock, but you will most likely want to enjoy a bit of wine sampling along the Drosselgasse before heading back to Frankfurt.

Koblenz

Relatively unknown to foreign tourists, Koblenz has long been a favorite destination for Germans. It was founded in 9 B.C. by the Romans as a stronghold guarding the confluence of the Rhine and Mosel rivers. For many centuries after that the town was a residence of the archbishops of Trier, and during the early 19th century actually became a part of France for a while. Although heavily bombed in World War II, Koblenz has been completely restored and today is a very charming and graceful medium-size city offering several delightful attractions.

A trip to Koblenz may be combined in the same day with a Rhine cruise—for which it makes a superb ending—or with Limburg, easily reached by train. With excellent rail and highway connections, it is also a fine base for travelers exploring the Rhine, Mosel, or Lahn regions.

GETTING THERE:

Trains leave Frankfurt's main station at least hourly for Koblenz. Most of them take about an hour and a half for the journey, and are of the IC class. There are also a few slower trains which require a change at Mainz. Return service operates until late evening.

By car, leave Frankfurt on the A-66 Autobahn to Wiesbaden, then cross the Rhine on the A-643 to Mainz. From there take the A-60 to Bingen and the A-61 into Koblenz. The total distance is 76 miles. A more scenic—but much slower—route is to follow either side of the Rhine from Wiesbaden or Mainz.

WHEN TO GO:

Koblenz is best visited in the warm seasons since most of its attractions are outdoors. The Middle Rhine Museum is closed on Mondays.

FOOD AND DRINK:

There are several good restaurants and cafés along the walking route. A few choices, in trip sequence, are:

Ratsstuben (Am Plan 9) $$
Weinhaus Hubertus (Florinsmarkt 54) $$
Café and Restaurant at Ehrenbreitstein Castle $$
Weindorf (in the wine village) $$

TOURIST INFORMATION:
The tourist office, phone (0261) 3-13-04, is directly across the street from the train station.

SUGGESTED TOUR:
Those arriving by boat should start at the Deutsches Eck (7) and work backwards to the Town Hall (2), then stroll down Rheinstrasse to the ferry landing and continue on to Ehrenbreitstein (8), the Schloss (9), and the Weindorf (10).

Assuming that you came by train, leave the **station** (1) and follow the map to the **Town Hall** *(Rathaus)* (2) in Jesuitenplatz. Formerly a Jesuit college, the magnificent 17th-century structure is built around a courtyard adorned with the amusing Schängelbrunnen, a modern fountain with a figure of a naughty boy who spits water at unwary bystanders. Beware.

A few steps away, reached via Braugasse, is the **Church of Our Lady** *(Liebfrauenkirche)* (3). Of Romanesque origin, it was rebuilt in the 13th century, and has a remarkably lovely interior with fine Renaissance tombs. Now stroll through Am Plan, a large open square lined with outdoor cafés, and go via Marktstrasse and Münzplatz to the 14th-century **Balduin Bridge** spanning the Mosel River. Three of its 14 original arches were destroyed by a bomb in 1945, and were replaced with a short modern section.

At the foot of this stands the handsome **Old Castle** *(Alte Burg)* (4), first erected during the 13th century but later extended in the Renaissance and baroque styles. It now houses the municipal library. From here, turn right and enter Florinsmarkt, a delightful square fronted by the 12th-century **Church of St. Florin**, built on Roman foundations.

The **Middle Rhine Museum** (5), a few yards to the left, occupies the early-15th-century Altes Kaufhaus. Step inside for a look at some superb art by regional painters, as well as antique furniture and artifacts. Opening times are from Tuesdays through Saturdays, 10 a.m. to 1 p.m. and 2:30-5:30 p.m.; and on Sundays and holidays from 10 a.m. to 1 p.m.

A short walk along the Mosel River leads to **St. Castor's Church** *(St. Kastor Kirche)* (6), first consecrated in 836 and renovated about 1200. It was here that Charlemagne's vast empire was divided up among his three grandsons in 843. The interesting interior features several art treasures including a particularly venerated Madonna painting. Surrounding the church are some very lovely gardens, offering nice views across the two rivers from its upper terrace. Next to this stands the Deutschherrenhaus, the only remaining structure of a complex belonging to the Teutonic Order of Knights, who first established themselves on German soil here in 1216.

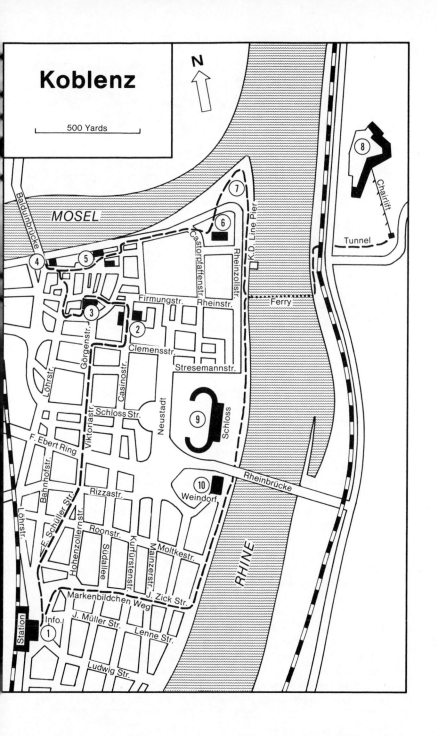

Koblenz

500 Yards

N

MOSEL

Baldulnbrücke

Castorpfaffenstr.

K.D. Line Pier

Rheinzollstr.

8

Chairlift

Tunnel

4

5

6

7

Firmungstr.

Rheinstr.

Rheinstr.

Ferry

3

2

Görgenstr.

Clemensstr.

Stresemannstr.

Löhrstr.

Casinostr.

Schloss Str.

Viktoriastr.

Neustadt

9

Schloss

F. Ebert Ring

Bahnhofstr.

Rizzastr.

10

Weindorf

Rheinbrücke

Löhrstr.

E. Schüller Str.

Hohenzollernstr.

Roonstr.

Südallee

Kurfürstenstr.

Mainzerstr.

Moltkestr.

J. Zick Str.

RHINE

Markenbildchen Weg

Station

Info.

1

J. Müller Str.

Lenne Str.

Ludwig Str.

Café at the Fortress of Ehrenbreitstein

The most famous sight in Koblenz is the **German Corner** *(Deutsches Eck)* (7), a spit of land at the confluence of the two great rivers. Until 1945, a huge equestrian statue of Kaiser Wilhelm I stood here; today only the 72-foot-high pedestal remains. A climb to its top will be rewarded with a stunning panoramic sweep across the neighboring landscape.

Now walk down to the ferry landing *(Fähre)* for a short ride across the Rhine to Ehrenbreitstein. On the other side turn left along the water, then right under the railway tracks and follow the signs for the chairlift *(Sesselbahn)*. You will first go through a short tunnel, then ride in an open chair to the citadel 400 feet above the Rhine.

The **Fortress of Ehrenbreitstein** (8) ranks second only to Gibraltar as the largest stronghold in Europe. First built in the 10th century, it was destroyed by the French in 1801 and later rebuilt by the Prussians during the early 19th century. Take the time to explore thoroughly its many passageways and hidden corners before succumbing to temptation and sitting down at the outdoor café in its main courtyard. Needless to say, the view down the Rhine valley is spectacular. Those with enough time may want to visit one or both of the two museums in the complex.

Return via the ferry to Koblenz and turn left along the Rheinanlagen, a very attractive river promenade. You will soon pass the **Elec-**

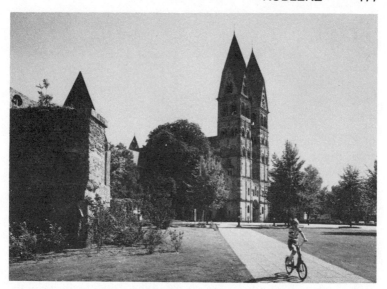

St. Castor's Church

tor's Palace *(Schloss)* (9) of 1786, which is now used for offices. Continue on to the **Wine Village** *(Weindorf)* (10). Built in 1925 as part of a wine fair, this compound of half-timbered houses is a joyful spot for imbibing—and a perfect place to end the day. From here it is only a short walk to the train station.

Trier

The greatest collection of Roman remains to be found anywhere north of the Alps is in Trier, which bills itself as Germany's oldest town. According to an ancient legend, this was founded around 2000 B.C. by Trebeta, son of Semiramis, the queen of Assyria. Historians say otherwise, although archaeological digs do reveal some trace of human habitation dating from that era. What is actually documented is that the town, then called *Augusta Treverorum,* was established in 16 B.C. by the Roman emperor Augustus near the site of an earlier Celtic settlement.

Whatever its true age, Trier is certainly a fascinating place. Several of its Roman structures remain in use today, along with well-preserved buildings from just about every era since. For centuries this city was among the most important in Europe; at one time second only to Rome. Those days have long since ended, and Trier is now a relatively minor provincial place. Although it is quite some distance from Frankfurt, the attractions are so compelling that a journey is more than worthwhile.

GETTING THERE:

Trains depart Frankfurt's main station or airport station fairly frequently in the morning for Koblenz, where you change to a train for Trier. Check the current schedule for the best connections. The total journey takes under three hours, and follows an exceptionally beautiful route along the Rhine and Mosel rivers. Return service operates as late as mid-evening.

By car, leave Frankfurt on the A-66 Autobahn, then take the A-3 (E-5) north past Limburg and head west on the A-48 to the Trier exit. The total distance is about 150 miles. A more scenic, if slower, route can be taken along the Mosel from Koblenz to Trier.

WHEN TO GO:

Trier can be visited in any season, but note that most of the major attractions are closed on Mondays from November 1st until March 31st, and every day during the entire month of December. Some of its museums close early on Sundays, and all day on major holidays. Train service is somewhat reduced on weekends.

The Porta Nigra

FOOD AND DRINK:

There is a good selection of restaurants along the walking route, particularly near the Porta Nigra, Hauptmarkt, and Kaiserthermen. Some choices are:

Hotel Porta Nigra (Porta Nigra Platz) $$$
Brunnenhof (in Simeonstift) $$
Zum Domstein (Hauptmarkt 5) $$
Brasserie (Fleischstr. 12) $$$
Europa Parkhotel (Kaiserstr. 29) $$
Hotel Deutscher Hof (Südallee 25) $

TOURIST INFORMATION:

The tourist office, phone (0651) 4-80-71, is next to the Porta Nigra.

SUGGESTED TOUR:

Leave the **main train station** (1) and walk down Bahnhofstrasse and Theodor Heuss Allee to the ancient **Porta Nigra** (2), the very symbol of Trier and one of the finest Roman relics anywhere. Built towards the end of the second century A.D. as a massive fortified gate, it was converted into a church about 1040 and restored to its original appearance by Napoleon in 1804, when Trier was a part of France. No mortar was used in its construction; instead, the stone blocks are joined by iron clamps. The name, meaning black gate, derives from its present color—the result of centuries of pollution. Stroll through the inner courtyard, where unsuspecting enemies were trapped from all sides. An exploration of its bulky interior can be made any day from 9 a.m. to 1 p.m. and 2-5 or 6 p.m., but not on Mondays between November 1st and March 31st, or at all during the month of December.

The tourist information office is located directly adjacent to this in the Simeonstift, an 11th-century cloister which also houses a restaurant and the interesting Städtisches Museum, devoted primarily to the history of Trier.

From here walk down Simeonstrasse past the very unusual **Dreikönigenhaus**, a nobleman's town residence dating from 1230. Note the strange location of its original entrance—at the second-story level where it could be reached only by a retractable ladder, a safety feature in those days of unrest.

Continue on to the **Hauptmarkt** (3). The stone cross in its center was erected in 958 as a symbol of the town's right to hold a market. Near this stands a lovely 16th-century fountain, while the entire busy scene is dominated by the Gothic Church of St. Gangolf. One particularly outstanding building is the Steipe, a colorful 15th-century banqueting house which is now home to the Ratskeller.

Now turn down Sternstrasse to the **Cathedral** *(Dom)* (4), a powerful fortress-like structure dating in part from Roman times. Over the centuries this was enlarged and rebuilt several times, the most visible changes having occurred during the 12th century. The interior is basically baroque and features a splendid treasury, which should not be missed. Its most precious possession is the Holy Tunic, alleged to have been worn by Christ.

Stroll through the cloisters, then visit the adjacent **Church of Our Lady** *(Liebfrauenkirche)* (5). One of the earliest Gothic churches in Germany, it was built in the form of a Greek cross during the 13th century, and is noted for its elegant, light-filled interior. Close to this is the **Bishop's Museum** (6) on Banthusstrasse. On display here are some fascinating fourth-century frescoes from the palace of the Roman emperor Constantine, discovered under the cathedral in 1945. There are also several medieval statues and other pieces of ancient religious art.

The enormous **Palastaula** (7), a few steps away, is the only surviving part of Constantine's great imperial palace. Once the throne room of the emperor, this colossal structure from about A.D. 306 now sees service as a Protestant church. Take a look inside, then walk around to the adjoining **Palace of the Electors**, an 18th-century rococo building presently used for government offices.

Paths through the palace gardens lead to the **Rhineland Museum**

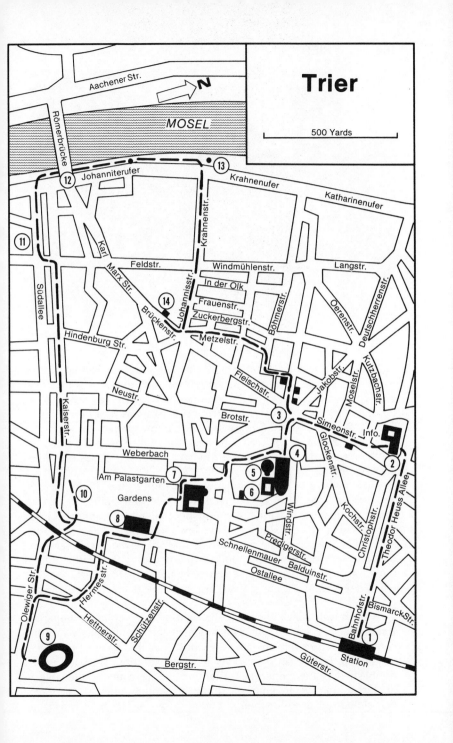

The Hauptmarkt

(Rheinisches Landesmuseum) (8), probably the best collection of Roman antiquities in Germany. Allow plenty of time to take it all in, from gold coins to mosaics to huge monuments. The displays also feature local archaeological finds dating from prehistory as well as a rich selection of medieval art. The museum is open Mondays through Fridays, 9:30 a.m. to 4 p.m.; on Saturdays from 9:30 a.m. to 2 p.m.; and on Sundays and holidays from 9 a.m. to 1 p.m., but closes on some major holidays.

Now follow the map to the **Amphitheatre** (9), the oldest Roman structure in Trier. Over 20,000 spectators once jammed its terraces to watch the gladiators fight, a form of spectacle which continued into the Christian era. Be sure to climb down into the cellars under the arena, and to examine the side chambers which served as cages. Much of the stone work was exploited as a quarry during the Middle Ages, but enough remains to imagine yourself back in the first century A.D., when it was built. Opening times are the same as for the Porta Nigra (2).

A short walk down Olewiger Strasse will bring you to the **Imperial Baths** *(Kaiserthermen)* (10). Not much of this extraordinary fourth-century structure remains above ground, but the maze of passage-ways below is truly fantastic and well worth exploring. The baths were established by the emperor Constantine and were among the largest in the entire Roman empire. Strangely enough, they were never completed nor used for their intended purpose. The ruins are open during the same times as the Porta Nigra (2).

Continue on to the second-century **Barbarathermen** (11) on Süd-allee. These baths were used for several centuries and were once larger than the Imperial Baths. Unfortunately, what little remains of their past glory is in derelict condition and requires a vivid imagination to visualize. Take a look from the street before deciding to enter. The opening times are the same as for the Porta Nigra (2).

The **Roman Bridge** *(Römerbrücke)* (12) is just a few steps away. Its stone piers were built in the second century A.D. and still carry the weight of heavy traffic. The upper parts, originally of wood, were replaced with masonry arches during the 14th century, and again in the 18th. Walk down to the path along the Mosel River and follow it past the Customs Crane *(Zollkran)*, dating from 1774, to the **Old Crane** *(Al-ter Kran)* (13), which goes back all the way to 1413. Both are in excellent condition, and their treadwheels can be seen by peeking in the windows.

Tourists of the World—Unite! And follow the map to the birth-place of Trier's most famous son. The **Karl Marx Haus** (14) is an international shrine for True Believers, a place where the political rhetoric is laid on heavily. A visit here is nevertheless quite interesting, and may be made from Tuesdays through Sundays, 10 a.m. to 6 p.m.; and on Mondays from 1-6 p.m. Between November and March the opening hours are reduced. Return to the train station via the 11th-century Frankenturm—one of the oldest surviving dwellings in Germany—and the Hauptmarkt (3).

Cologne
(Köln)

The skyline of Cologne is completely dominated by its magnificent cathedral, Germany's largest and one of the greatest on earth. This ancient city on the Rhine has long been in the center of things. Having begun life as a Roman camp in 38 B.C., it was raised to city status around A.D. 50 and given the name *Colonia Claudia Ara Agrippinensium*—a mouthful soon shortened to *Colonia*. After the fall of the Roman Empire this was Germanized to *Köln*, its official designation to this day. With nearly a million inhabitants, Cologne is now the fourth-largest metropolis in the nation (after Berlin, Hamburg, and Munich) and a world leader in commerce. Excellent transportation facilities make the city a good alternative base for exploring the Rhineland area north of Frankfurt.

GETTING THERE:

Trains, mostly of the IC class, leave Frankfurt's main station at least hourly for Cologne *(Köln)*, a journey of less than two and a half hours. Return service operates until mid-evening.

By car, leave Frankfurt on the A-66 Autobahn, then turn northwest on the A-3 (E-5), which goes directly to Cologne. The distance is 116 miles each way.

WHEN TO GO:

Cologne may be explored in any season, but avoid coming on a Monday, when most of the museums are closed. Except for the cathedral, these are the city's major tourist attractions.

FOOD AND DRINK:

Cologne has its own gastronomical delights such as Reibekuchen (potato pancakes and applesauce, often sold by street vendors—try some!) and Halber Hahn which, despite its name, is not half a chicken but a fancy cheese sandwich.

There is a very wide selection of restaurants in all price categories. Among the best, in trip sequence, are:

Hanse-Stube (in the Excelsior Hotel Ernst, between the cathedral and the train station) $$$

Alt Köln (Trankgasse 7, between the cathedral and the train station) A favorite old tavern. $$

Brauhaus Sion (Unter Taschenmacher 5, near the Diocesan Museum) Traditional fare. $

Früh (Am Hof 12, near the Diocesan Museum) Hearty food in a congenial atmosphere. $

Weinhaus im Walfisch (Salzgasse 13, south of Gross St. Martin Church) An old favorite. $$$

Ratskeller (Alter Markt, behind the Old City Hall) $$

Restaurant Bado-La Poêle d'Or (Komödienstr. 52, near the Municipal Museum) French cuisine, dining room $$$, bistro, $$

TOURIST INFORMATION:

The tourist office, phone (0221) 221-33-40, faces the front of the cathedral.

SUGGESTED TOUR:

The **main train station** (1) is located in the very heart of Cologne, just a few steps from the tourist office. Directly facing this is the **Cathedral** *(Dom)* (2), one of the world's most stupendous Gothic structures. Begun in 1248 on the site of an earlier cathedral—and a Roman temple—it was far from complete when construction came to a standstill in the early 16th century. After that, not much happened until a wave of romantic nationalism swept the country in the mid-19th century. In the end it was political rather than religious considerations which led to the final completion in 1880. The Protestant rulers of Prussia felt a need to placate the Catholic Rhineland, and the newly united nation would clearly benefit from a symbol embodying the spirit of medieval Germany in its Gothic design.

Enter the cathedral via its magnificent west portal. The sheer verticality of the nave is awesome, as are the medieval stained-glass windows, but the real treasures lie beyond the crossing. In a glass case behind the high altar you will find the most precious object of all. This is the **Reliquary of the Three Kings** *(Dreikönigenschrein)*, a 12th-century masterpiece of the goldsmiths' art alleged to contain the bones of the Magi, which were brought from Milan in 1164 by Emperor Frederick Barbarossa. It was the veneration of these relics during the Middle Ages which attracted countless pilgrims to Cologne and thus provided the impetus for building the present cathedral.

The medieval choir leading up to this has some outstanding stalls and statuary, while in the ambulatory there are two fabulous works of art. The first of these is the **Gero Cross,** dating from 976, which is regarded as the oldest existing monumental cross from the Middle Ages and is located in the Cross Chapel to the left of the choir. On the other side, in the Lady Chapel directly across the chancel, is the 15th-century **Dombild,** a triptych celebrating the Adoration of the Magi and the two patron saints of Cologne—Ursula and Gereon. More riches can be found in the **Treasury,** located just off the north transept. Before leaving the cathedral you may want to test your athletic ability by climbing over 500 steps to the top of the south tower for a fantastic view. Good luck.

Every time a hole is dug in Cologne there is a very real possibility of striking Roman ruins. An outstanding example of this happened in 1941, when workers were digging a bomb shelter next to the cathedral. What came to light was the wonderfully pagan **Dionysos Mosaic,** a 22-by-34-foot celebration of wine and revelry. In recent years the very modern **Roman-Germanic Museum** (3) was built around this to display a vast collection of local archaeological finds. Step inside and enjoy the marvelously inspired presentation of life in ancient Colonia, complete with room settings that look as though the Romans had just gone out for a stroll. No visitor to Cologne should miss seeing this museum, which is open daily except on Mondays and some holidays; from 10 a.m. to 5 p.m., and on Wednesdays and Thursdays until 8 p.m.

The small **Diocesan Museum,** just a few steps away on the same open square, may interest you with its exquisite collection of ancient and medieval religious art. Now follow the map to the nearby **Wallraf-Richartz Museum/Museum Ludwig** (4), which surely ranks among the greatest art galleries of Europe. This has recently moved into the stunning new cultural center between the cathedral and the Rhine, which also houses a magnificent concert hall. Allow plenty of time to peruse its many splendors—ranging all the way from the medieval to an exceptionally rich collection of American Pop art. On display are paintings by the Cologne masters of the 14th to 16th centuries, Rembrandt, Dürer, Cranach, Rubens, Van Dyck, and many others. The section devoted to modern art, called the Museum Ludwig, includes works by Picasso, Kandinsky, Dali, Max Ernst, Oldenburg, Rauschenberg, Warhol—to name a few. Opening times, not yet finalized, will probably be from 10 a.m. to 5 p.m., daily except Mondays; and until 8 p.m. on some evenings.

Return to the front of the cathedral and turn left onto the pedestrians-only Hohe Strasse. Follow this to Gürzenichstrasse, where you make a left. The Gürzenich building, dating from 1441, is still used for its original purpose—as a banqueting hall where festive occasions are held. Turn left on Martinstrasse and follow it to the **Old City Hall** (*Altes*

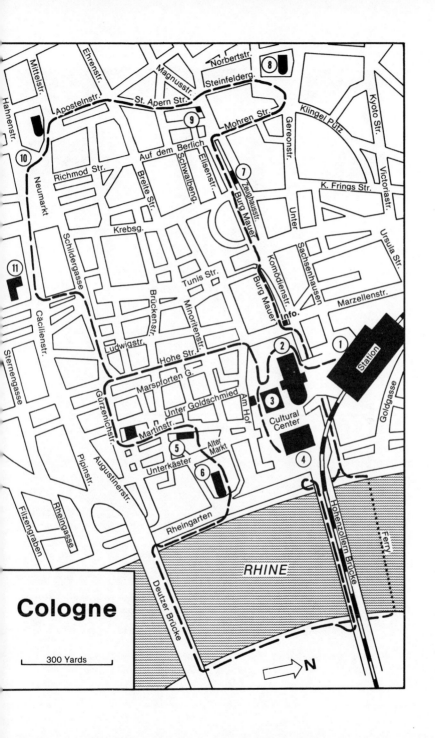

Cologne

300 Yards

N

Cologne Cathedral and the Cultural Center from the Rhine
(Photo by Klaus Barisch, Courtesy of Cologne Tourist Office)

Rathaus) (5), originally built in the 14th century but considerably altered since. Its Renaissance loggia is particularly attractive.

From here an alleyway leads to the Alter Markt with its amusing statue and on to the imposing **Gross St. Martin Church** (6). Along with the cathedral, this fortress-like structure—which was begun in 960 and completed in the mid-13th century—is a landmark of Cologne.

Now stroll through the Fisch Markt and along the river's edge, where a flight of steps will take you up to the Deutzer Bridge. Cross the Rhine on this and turn left on the path along its opposite bank. From here you will have a marvelous view of the renowned Cologne skyline. Return to the city either on the ferry shown on the map, or by walking across the footpath on the south side of the Hohenzollern railway bridge.

You have now seen most of the tourist attractions in Cologne. If time allows, a further exploration can be made by following the map to the **Municipal Museum** *(Kölnisches Stadtmuseum)* (7), located in a former arsenal. Displays here, including arms and armor, are concerned with the history of the city. Continue on to the **Church of St. Gereon** (8), which dates in part from Roman times. Many changes were made since then, making this a particularly fascinating structure to visit.

A short stroll down Steinfeldergasse will bring you to the **Roman Tower** *(Römerturm)* (9), a part of the original town walls built around A.D. 50. Although small, its mosaic brick patterns are highly intriguing. Now follow St. Apern Strasse, lined with elegant antique shops, and Apostelnstrasse to **Neumarkt** (10). This lively market square is dominated by the massive Church of the Holy Apostles, an 11th-century structure in the Rhineland Romanesque style.

One other attraction which you should definitely try to see is the **Schnütgen Museum** (11), housed in the desanctified 12th-century Church of St. Cecilia on Cäcilienstrasse. The superb collection of ancient religious artifacts, many of ivory, gold, or wood, are strikingly displayed in a setting of serene purity. From here you can return via Hohe Strasse to the train station.

Düsseldorf

Style is an elusive quality—you either have it or you don't. Düsseldorf does. Perhaps it's the French influence—during their occupation of the city Napoleon called it "my little Paris." Or maybe it's just money, the vast wealth generated in the nearby Ruhr valley. Whatever the reason, Düsseldorf is Germany's number one trend-setter in matters of fashion and life style. To stroll along the Königsallee, its elegant main street, is to witness another aspect of this kaleidoscopic nation—one which belongs as much to the world as to the *Vaterland*.

Düsseldorf was just a small fishing village until the 13th century, when it acquired city status and eventually became the residence of local nobility. It was their sophisticated affluence which attracted leading artists, musicians, and architects to this then-small town on the Rhine, especially during the early-18th-century reign of Elector Johann Wilhelm II. Within a century, Düsseldorf became a part of Napoleon's France, only to be taken over by Prussia in 1815. After another period of French occupation following World War I and the terrible destruction of World War II, the city re-emerged as the state capital of North Rhine-Westphalia as well as a leading center of commerce and culture.

GETTING THERE:

Trains depart Frankfurt's main station at least hourly for the under-three-hour trip to Düsseldorf. Most of these are of the IC class and may require a change at Cologne *(Köln)*. Return service operates until mid-evening.

By car, leave Frankfurt on the A-66 Autobahn, then head northwest on the A-3 (E-5) past Cologne to Düsseldorf. The total distance is 141 miles.

WHEN TO GO:

Düsseldorf may be visited at any time, but Mondays should be avoided if you plan to visit its splendid museums. The fashionable street life, especially on the Königsallee, is most enjoyable on warm, fine days.

FOOD AND DRINK:

The *Altstadt,* near the Rhine, is famous for its traditional taverns serving the city's noted dark-brown *Alt Bier* along with local special-

Along the Königsallee

ties. Many of the center-city restaurants cater to an international crowd and feature cuisine—and prices—to match. A few choices, in trip sequence, are:

Müllers und Fest (Königsallee 12) $$$

Benrather Hof (Steinstr. 1) $$

Schneider-Wibbel-Stuben (S.-Wibbelgasse 7, in the Altstadt) Seafood. $$$

Zur Auster (Bergerstr. 9) Seafood. $$

Zum Schiffchen (Hafenstr. 5, near Hetjens Museum) A traditional favorite. $$

Orangerie (Bilkerstr. 30, near history museum) $$$

TOURIST INFORMATION:

The tourist office is conveniently located opposite the train station. You can phone them at (0211) 35-05-05.

SUGGESTED TOUR:

Leave the **train station** (1) and follow Graf Adolf Strasse past the tourist office to the foot of the world-renowed **Königsallee**. This enormously wide tree-lined boulevard, locally known as the *Kö*, is split down the middle by a waterway which was once part of the town moat. The western side is lined with banks and offices, while the sunny east is a continuous row of posh shops, luxury restaurants, and sidewalk cafés. Besides the wealthy patrons, it is also the province of the *Radschläger,* a species of little boys unique to Düsseldorf. They cartwheel up and down the sidewalk, demonstrating a skill learned in school in the hopes of earning a small tip.

At its northern end, the Kö runs into a lovely park called the **Hofgarten** (2), reached via a passageway. Stroll this and note, to your right, the slab-sided Thyssen building—a modern high-rise which blends in well with its surroundings.

Cross a footbridge and continue along paths through another passageway to the **Goethe Museum** (3). Fans of Germany's greatest poet and playwright, who lived in Düsseldorf for a while, will enjoy seeing the many manuscripts, first editions, and memorabilia associated with his life. It is open every day except Mondays, from 10 a.m. to 5 p.m.; with Saturday hours being 1-5 p.m.

From here the map leads to the 14th-century **Church of St. Lambertus** (4), whose tower is curiously askew. Those attracted by museums may want to turn north along the Rhine to visit a fine pair. The first of these is the **State Museum of People and Economy** *(Landesmuseum Volk und Wirtschaft)* (5), a graphic presentation of social and economic conditions around the world. Opening times are Mondays to Fridays, 9 a.m. to 5 p.m.; and Sundays from 10 a.m. to 6 p.m. On Wednesdays it remains open until 8 p.m. Just beyond this is the **Fine Arts Museum** *(Kunstmuseum)* (6). Specializing in the 19th-century romantic painting of the Düsseldorf School and 20th-century German Expressionists, the collections also include a balanced selection of other styles ranging from Old Masters to contemporary works. In addition, there is an excellent display of glass from Roman times all the way up to Art Nouveau. The museum is open from Tuesdays through Sundays; 10 a.m. to 5 p.m.

Return along the river's edge to the **Castle Tower** *(Schlossturm)* (7), a 13th-century fortification now used as a Navigation Museum. You can see the models of inland shipping any day except Mondays, from 10 a.m. to 5 p.m.

A few steps beyond is the Town Hall *(Rathaus),* dating in part from 1573, and the **Market Place** *(Marktplatz)* (8) with its equestrian statue of the beloved elector Johann Wilhelm II, known in the local dialect as Jan Wellem. It was his leadership which put Düsseldorf on the map, so to speak, by attracting talent from all over the country. You are now in the oldest part of town, the *Altstadt.* Leading off from here is a maze of lively narrow streets lined with colorful old taverns—the perfect spot for lunch.

Now follow Bergerstrasse and Hafenstrasse to the **Hetjens Museum** *(Deutsches Keramikmuseum)* (9). Located in the former Nessel-

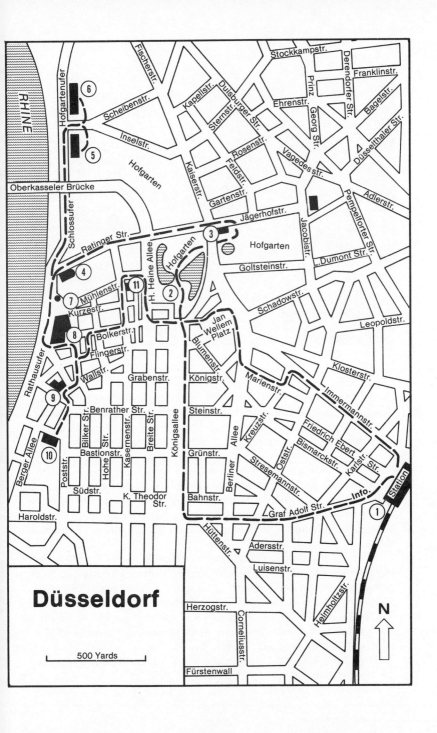

Düsseldorf

500 Yards

N

The Market Place

rode Palace, this incredible collection of ceramic objects from all over the globe spans 8,000 years of history. It is open every day except Mondays, from 10 a.m. to 5 p.m. Just beyond this is the **Museum of Municipal History** *(Stadtgeschichtliches Museum)* (10), housed in another 18th-century palace. Several centuries of local bygones are on display here, including furniture, art, and household objects.

Now stroll back towards the market place (8) and follow the map through some particularly interesting lanes in the Altstadt. The route passes an amusing musical clock on Schneider Wibbel Gasse, and the birthplace, at Number 53 Bolkerstrasse, of the famous poet Heinrich Heine.

A recent addition to Düsseldorf's cultural scene is the **State Gallery** *(Landesgalerie)* (11), a stunning curved structure in polished black granite located on Grabbeplatz. Enter it to enjoy the marvelous North Rhine-Westphalia Collection of 20th-Century Art, one of the finest displays of contemporary art anywhere in the world. The museum is open every day except Mondays, from 10 a.m. to 5 p.m.; and stays open until 8 p.m. on Wednesdays.

From here follow the map through Jan Wellem Platz and return to the train station.

Limburg

No, this is not the home of the malodorous cheese. *That* Limburg is in Belgium. What is served here is a feast for the eyes rather than the palate. Limburg an der Lahn, to use its proper name, is an extraordinarily well-preserved medieval town where twisting, dreamy lanes wind their way through half-timbered houses to one of the most unusual cathedrals you'll ever see. The view from the river is a scene right out of the Middle Ages—an old engraving come to life.

Yet Limburg is no backwater place. Set astride the Frankfurt-Cologne Autobahn and easily reached by train, it is essentially a thriving modern community which has successfully managed to keep its ancient heritage intact. Excellent rail and road facilities make it possible to combine a daytrip here with one to Koblenz.

GETTING THERE:

Trains on the S-Bahn service *(route S-2)* depart frequently from Frankfurt's Konstablerwache, Hauptwache, Taunusanlage, and main station *(lower level)* for Niederhausen, where you change to a local for Limburg. In addition, there are also a few through-trains leaving from Frankfurt's main station *(street level)*. The total trip takes a bit over one hour.

By car, leave Frankfurt on the A-66 Autobahn, then head north on the A-3 (E-5), getting off at the Limburg-Süd exit. The total distance is 46 miles.

WHEN TO GO:

Good weather is necessary to enjoy this trip, which can be taken any day. Rail service is reduced on weekends and holidays.

FOOD AND DRINK:

Limburg has several good restaurants, including:

Martin (Holzheimerstr. 2, behind station) $
St. Georg's Stube (Hospitalstr. 4) $$
Dom Hotel (Grabenstr. 57) $$

TOURIST INFORMATION:

The tourist office, phone (06431) 20-32-22, is behind the town hall at Hospitalstrasse 2.

In the Altstadt

SUGGESTED TOUR:

Leave the **train station** (1) and follow the map to the **Town Hall** *(Rathaus)* (2). The open square to the rear of this is enlivened by a contemporary fountain, a new municipal hall, and the beautiful 14th-century St. Anne's Church *(St. Annakirche)*—noted for its medieval stained-glass windows. The tourist office is located behind the church on Hospitalstrasse.

Now cross Grabenstrasse and enter the old part of town *(Altstadt)*. As you wander up Plötze through the Fischmarkt you will be engulfed in a world of half-timbered houses *(Fachwerkhäuser)*, many dating from the Middle Ages. Continue up Domstrasse to the **Cathedral** *(Dom)* (3), a startling sight of almost Oriental appearance. The seven-towered exterior is brightly painted in its original colors—mostly coral and white. Construction began around 1215 on the site of an earlier church, and was ready for consecration as early as 1235.

Step inside for a look at the famous superimposed galleries and the colorful 13th-century frescoes, which have been undergoing a painstaking restoration. While the outside of the building is Romanesque, its interior had already made the transition to Gothic during the relatively short period of construction.

Walk out into the **graveyard** (4) for a splendid panoramic view up and down the Lahn valley. Now stroll down a back alleyway to the

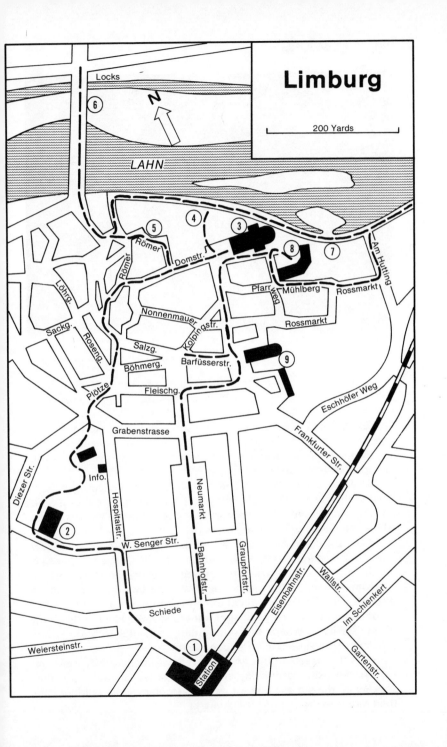

Limburg

200 Yards

Locks

⑥

N

LAHN

⑤ Römer
④
③
⑧
⑦
Römer
Domstr.
Am Hütting
Pfarr Weg
Mühlberg
Rossmarkt
Löhrg.
Nonnenmauer
Rossmarkt
Sackg.
Roseng.
Salzg.
Kolpingstr.
Böhmerg.
Barfüsserstr.
⑨
Plötze
Fleischg.
Grabenstrasse
Eschhöfer Weg
Diezer Str.
Info.
Frankfurter Str.
②
Hospitalstr.
Neumarkt
W. Senger Str.
Bahnhofstr.
Graupfortstr.
Eisenbahnstr.
Wallstr.
Im Schlenkert
Schiede
①
Weiersteinstr.
Station
Gartenstr.

View of the Cathedral from the Lahn

Römer (5). The house at Number 1 is said to be the oldest inhabited half-timbered house in Germany, and dates from 1296. Continue on past St. John's Chapel and cross the **Old Lahn Bridge** *(Alte Lahnbrücke)* (6), built of stone in 1315 and still carrying traffic. There is an excellent view of the cathedral from its far end. Tolls collected on this span were a considerable source of revenue to the town until finally being abolished in 1905.

Return across the bridge and follow the river's edge to the left. Beyond the base of the cathedral you will come to a picturesque **old mill** (7), whose waterwheel still turns. A little farther on there is a dock where cruises on the Lahn are offered.

Now turn down Am Huttig and make a right onto Rossmarkt. In one block bear right and climb Mühlberg to the **Castle** *(Schloss)* (8), a 13th- to 16th-century structure housing the Diocesan Museum.

From here follow the map to the **Town Church** *(Stadtkirche)* (9) on Bischofsplatz. Originally built in the 14th century, it has an interesting baroque interior which you might want to see. Adjacent to this is the Bishop's Palace, where the outstanding cathedral treasure *(Domschatz)* may be viewed at infrequent times.

All of the streets in this area are well worth exploring, especially Barfüsserstrasse, Kornmarkt, and Fleischgasse. Spend some time soaking up the atmosphere, or perhaps stopping at an outdoor café, then return to the station via Neumarkt.

Bad Homburg

Once the haunt of Europe's crowned heads, Bad Homburg is an elegant old spa located just eleven miles from downtown Frankfurt. Today, this genteel turn-of-the-century resort caters more to bankers than to kings, but its casino, hot springs, and lovely Kurpark maintain the ambiance of a world long vanished from most of contemporary Europe. Although this is reason enough for a visit, Bad Homburg also offers an intriguing castle—until 1918 the summer home of Kaiser Wilhelm II—and the utterly fascinating reconstructed Roman fortress dating from the second century A.D. at Saalburg.

GETTING THERE:

Trains on the S-Bahn service depart Frankfurt's Konstablerwache, Hauptwache, Taunusanlage, and main station *(lower level)* frequently for the twenty-minute ride to Bad Homburg. The route number is S-5, going in the direction of Friedrichsdorf. Return trains run until late evening.

By car, Bad Homburg is 11 miles from Frankfurt via the A-5 (E-4) Autobahn and the B-456 road.

WHEN TO GO:

This trip can be made at any time in good weather, but remember that the castle is closed on Mondays and a few major holidays.

FOOD AND DRINK:

Bad Homburg offers a broad range of restaurants and cafés, with several places right in the Kurpark. Some good choices are:

Maritim Hotel (in the Kurhaus on Ludwigstr.) $$$

Yuen's China-Restaurant (Kisseleffstr., by the Kurpark entrance) $$

Table (K. Friedrich Promenade, near Kurpark) $$$

Saalburg Restaurant (at Saalburg, near B-456 road) $$

TOURIST INFORMATION:

The tourist office, phone (06172) 121-30, is in the Kurhaus on Louisenstrasse.

SUGGESTED TOUR:

Before leaving the **train station** (1), check the schedule of buses going to Saalburg, which should be visited after seeing the town. Now follow the map on foot to the **Castle** *(Schloss)* (2). Built on the site of an earlier medieval fortification, of which only the 14th-century White Tower remains, the castle as it stands today was begun in 1680 by Landgrave Frederick II of Hesse-Homburg. Famed in literature as "*The Prince of Homburg,*" he created a baroque masterpiece which remained the home of his successors until 1866, when the principality was absorbed by Prussia. After that it became the favorite summer residence of Prussian kings and German emperors until the end of World War I.

Be sure to take the guided tour through the castle's interior, which is given in English on request. Unlike many palaces, this one has a rather homey, lived-in quality that is quite endearing.. The room settings have been left pretty much as they were when Kaiser Wilhelm II abdicated and fled into a Dutch exile in 1918. Visits may be made any day except Mondays or a few major holidays, from 10 a.m. to 5 p.m. The castle closes one hour earlier between November and February. Before leaving the grounds you should stroll out into the courtyard to see the ancient White Tower, which may be climbed.

Continue on past the market place and the modern Kurhaus—which houses the tourist office—to the large **Kurpark.** Laid out in the mid-19th century, this gorgeous park contains the hot springs which brought fame to Bad Homburg. Among its other attractions is the exotic **Siamese Temple** (3), presented by King Chulalongkorn of Siam after taking the cure.

Shady paths lead to the Kaiser Wilhelm Bad of 1890 and the **Casino** *(Spielbank)* (4), opened by the famous Blanc brothers of France in 1841. It was so successful that 25 years later they repeated themselves with a similar venture in Monte Carlo. The Russian author Feodor Dostoyevsky came here, lost a fortune, and wrote a novel about the whole experience called *The Gambler.* You can test *your* luck at the tables every day after 3 p.m., when roulette and baccarat are the games offered.

The spa gained immortality of a sort when Edward VII of England, then Prince of Wales, showed up wearing a new hat style which was quickly dubbed the homburg. A stroll down Brunnen Allee will bring you to the most popular (because of its high salinity) spring of them all, the **Elisabethenbrunnen** (5). Now walk over to the onion-domed **Russian Chapel** (6), built by another patron and member of the royal family, Czar Nicholas II.

Return to the train station via Friedrichstrasse and Bahnhofstrasse. From here a bus, leaving from platform 2 in front of the station, will

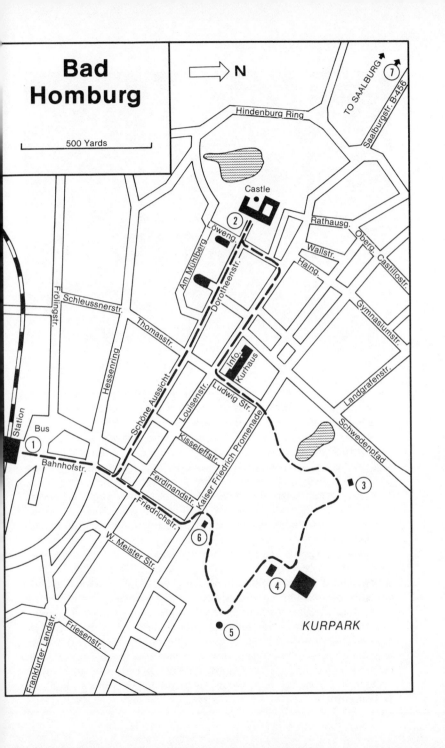

The Siamese Temple

take you on a ten-minute ride to Saalburg, certainly the most unusual sight in the area. Those with cars will, of course, want to drive the four-mile distance north on the B-456 road.

When the Romans invaded Germany in the first century A.D., they ran into a slight problem. The local tribes didn't like them. A defensive wall was clearly needed, and slowly one got built. Stretching some 340 miles between a point on the Rhine north of Koblenz to the Danube near Regensburg, this great engineering miracle was called the *Limes*. By A.D. 260, however, the fortifications were abandoned and the frontier moved back to the Rhine, where it remained until the fall of the empire.

Saalburg (7) was one of the many military camps along the Limes. Built in the early second century A.D., it later fell to ruin and became a convenient quarry during the Middle Ages. Archaeological excavations in the mid-19th century led to a total reconstruction under the leadership of Kaiser Wilhelm II between 1898 and 1907. What resulted is a fantastic, accurate re-creation of Roman life in the provinces. You will want to spend at least an hour exploring the camp and its museum, and take a short stroll to what remains of the great wall itself. An explanatory booklet in English is available, and the site is open daily from 8 a.m. to 5 p.m. Return by bus to Bad Homburg for a train to Frankfurt.

Marburg

Marburg is one of the few examples of a true medieval hill town in Germany. Its narrow, twisting lanes and steep stairways wind their way through a maze of half-timbered houses before finally reaching the ancient castle at its top. The climb can be exhausting, but there are several delightful rewards—and spots to rest—along the way.

A place of holy pilgrimage before the Reformation, Marburg became a center of liberal thinking afterwards. Martin Luther, Ulrich Zwingli, and others held their famous "Colloquy of Marburg" here in 1529, just two years after the world's first Protestant university was founded by the local margrave. That school is still going strong, and still attracts students by the thousands from all over the world. It is their presence which lends a youthful, vital, and international flavor to this otherwise peaceful old market town.

GETTING THERE:

Trains depart Frankfurt's main station almost hourly for Marburg, a run of about one hour. Return service operates until mid-evening.

By car, leave Frankfurt on the A-5 (E-4) Autobahn and get off at the Giessen-Nord exit. From there go to Lollar and take the B-3 north to Marburg. The distance is 58 miles each way. Park near the train station or St. Elizabeth's Church as driving in the old part of town is very difficult.

WHEN TO GO:

Marburg may be visited in any season, but avoid coming on a Monday or Tuesday, when some of the sights are closed.

FOOD AND DRINK:

A wide choice of restaurants in all price ranges will be found along the walking route, many of which feature foreign cuisines. Among the best known are:

Restaurant Atelier (Elisabethstr. 12) Italian cuisine. $$
Zur Sonne (Markt 11) $$
Stadthallen Restaurant (Biegenstr. 15, by the University Museum) $
Santa Lucia (Deutschhausstr. 35, near the University Museum) Italian cuisine. $$

TOURIST INFORMATION:
The tourist office, phone (06421) 20-12-49, is next to the train station.

SUGGESTED TOUR:
Leave the **train station** (1) and stroll down Bahnhofstrasse, turning left on Elisabethstrasse to **St. Elizabeth's Church** (2)—said to be the first purely Gothic church in Germany. Built in the 13th century, it once held the remains of St. Elizabeth, a former Hungarian princess married to the landgrave of Thuringia. When her husband died of the plague in 1227 she moved to Marburg and spent the rest of her short life caring for the sick and needy. After her death in 1231 and canonization in 1235, the church was erected by the Teutonic Order of Knights as a place of pilgrimage. It continued to serve that function until the Reformation, when one of her descendants, Landgrave Philip the Magnanimous—who had converted to Protestantism and founded the local university—abolished the cult of relics and had her bones removed for reburial elsewhere.

Step into the magnificent interior, which has several outstanding works of art devoted to St. Elizabeth. Don't miss her statue against the left wall near the crossing, her original tomb in the north transept, or especially her exquisite **golden shrine** in the sacristy to the left of the high altar. The south transept contains the tombs of the landgraves of Hesse, who were her descendants. One of these is particularly gruesome in its depiction of a worm-ridden corpse. On the way out, stop at the chapel under the north tower for a look at the tomb of President Paul von Hindenburg, the last leader of a democratic Germany prior to Hitler's rise to power.

A short side trip can be made from here to the tiny 13th-century **Chapel of St. Michael** (3) in the lovely pilgrims' cemetery. This involves a rather steep climb but offers a nice view of the castle.

Now follow Steinweg, an unusual street built on three parallel levels, and continue uphill on the pedestrians-only Neustadt and Wettergasse to the **Market Place** *(Markt)* (4). At the southern end of this stands the early-16th-century **Town Hall** *(Rathaus)*, famous for its clock which for centuries has signaled each passing hour with the simulated crow of a cock. Farmers' markets are held in front of this each Wednesday and Saturday. Beyond the fountain of St. George and the Dragon is the upper market, lined with colorful old houses. Walk through this and climb the steps at its north end.

A left at the top puts you on Landgraf Philipp Strasse, which continues ever upwards to the **Castle** *(Schloss)* (5). The strategic value of this lofty location was realized as far back as the 11th century, when it held a Franconian watchtower. The present structure, however, is a

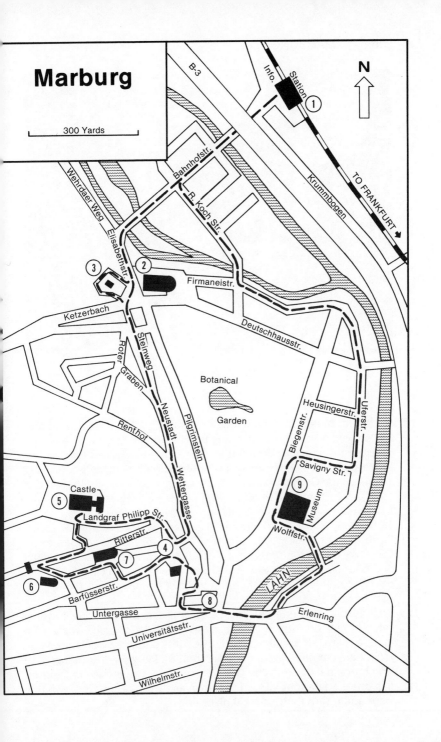

Marburg

300 Yards

N

B-3

Info.

Station ①

Krummbogen

TO FRANKFURT

Bahnhofstr.

Wehrdaer Weg

R. Koch Str.

Elisabethstr.

③

②

Firmaneistr.

Ketzerbach

Deutschhausstr.

Steinweg

Roter Graben

Botanical Garden

Neustadt

Heusingerstr.

Uferstr.

Pilgrimstein

Biegenstr.

Renthof

Wettergasse

Savigny Str.

Castle

⑨

Museum

⑤

Landgraf Philipp Str.

Ritterstr.

④

Wolffstr.

⑦

⑥

Barfüsserstr.

⑧

LAHN

Untergasse

Erlenring

Universitätsstr.

Wilhelmstr.

The Market Place

mixture of buildings dating from the 13th through the 16th centuries, during which time it underwent many changes.

Enter through a door in the courtyard and pick up an explanatory brochure in English. Three of the rooms are particularly interesting. These are the **Gothic Chapel,** now restored to its original 13th-century colors; the **Knights' Hall** *(Rittersaal);* and the **Landgrave's Study** with its memories of the famous dialogue between Luther and Zwingli in 1529. It was their failure to reach an agreement which helped split the Protestant movement into different sects. The castle is open from Tuesdays through Sundays, 10 a.m. to 1 p.m. and 2-5 p.m., closing one hour earlier in the winter season—when it is also closed on Sundays and holidays. Another part of the castle houses a small museum of cultural history.

Return to Landgraf Philipp Strasse and descend steps next to the café. A right on Ritterstrasse leads to the Kalbstor gate, where you make a sharp left past the picturesque 15th-century **Kugel Church** (6). From here continue on to the **Church of St. Mary** (7), a Lutheran parish church dating from the late 13th century. The terrace in front of this offers a fabulous view of the town and river valley. Go down the steps and return to the market place (4).

The Kugel Church

Now follow the map past the old buildings of the **Philipp University** (8) and cross the bridge over the Lahn. On the opposite bank there is a path which leads across a footbridge to the **University Museum** (9). Concerned with the history of art and civilization, this unusually fine museum is a must-see for any visitor to Marburg. It is open daily from 10 a.m. to 1 p.m. and 3-5 p.m., but closes on Tuesdays and some major holidays. The route shown on the map is an especially pleasant way to return to the train station.

Aschaffenburg

Perhaps Aschaffenburg is just too close to Frankfurt. Whatever the reason, it is almost always overlooked by tourists as they speed by on their way to Würzburg or beyond. This exceptionally pleasant small city on the Main has several attractions that make it worth at least a detour, including a huge and quite marvelous Renaissance palace. Much of the town is covered by enchanting parks, and there is a splendid abbey church and museum to see as well.

The curious thing about Aschaffenburg is that it is actually in Bavaria—although well beyond daytrip range of Munich. From the 10th century until the beginning of the 19th, it was under the control of the archbishops of Mainz. Napoleon made it a principality, but after his fall the town was incorporated into the kingdom of Bavaria. Badly devastated in World War II, Aschaffenburg today is a modern, albeit somewhat provincial, place which has managed to hang on to the best of a distinguished past. A trip here could be combined in the same day with one to Miltenberg.

GETTING THERE:

Trains leave Frankfurt's main station at about one-hour intervals for the 40-minute ride to Aschaffenburg. Return service operates until late evening.

By car, leave Frankfurt on the A-3 (E-5) Autobahn in the direction of Würzburg and get off at the Aschaffenburg-West exit. The distance is 25 miles.

WHEN TO GO:

Avoid coming on a Monday, when the palace is closed. Any other day is fine, although good weather will make this largely outdoor trip much more pleasant.

The Pompeianum and Johannisburg Palace

FOOD AND DRINK:

Aschaffenburg has a number of fine restaurants. Some good choices along the walking route are:

Hotel Zum Ochsen (Karlstr. 16)$
Schlossweinstuben (in the palace) $$
Ratskeller (Dalbergstr. 15) $$
Hotel Post (Goldbacher Str. 19) $$$
Aschaffenburger Hof (Frohsinnstr. 11) $$

TOURIST INFORMATION:

The tourist office, phone (06021) 304-26, is located at Dalbergstrasse 6, opposite the Town Hall.

SUGGESTED TOUR:

Leave the **train station** (1) and follow the map to the **Palace** *(Schloss Johannisburg)* (2). Built between 1605 and 1614 on the site of an earlier castle, it was the summer residence of the electors of Mainz until the Napoleonic period. Many kings and emperors stayed here during the course of their journeys. The palace later became an official residence of King Ludwig I of Bavaria after the town was incorporated into that kingdom. Allow at least an hour to wander through its many rooms, which are filled with superb art, antique furniture, and various artifacts. The main floor has a fascinating collection of finely detailed architectural models of classic Roman structures, all rendered in cork during the early 19th century. Go upstairs to see the rest of the treasures. Opening times are from 9 a.m. to noon and 1-5 p.m., Tuesdays through Sundays, with somewhat reduced hours between October and March.

The palace **gardens,** overlooking the banks of the Main, convey a Mediterranean atmosphere that is at once more Italian than German. Stroll through them to the **Pompeianum** (3), a reproduction of the villa of Castor and Pollux in ancient Pompeii. It was built in the mid-19th century for King Ludwig I, who fancied the classical era.

Now walk through what little remains of the old part of town, taking the route via Pfaffengasse, Dalbergstrasse, and Stiftsgasse. This will bring you to the Town Hall *(Rathaus),* across the square from the tourist office.

Aschaffenburg's other major sight is the **Church of SS. Peter and Alexander** *(Stiftskirche)* (4). Dating from the 12th century and much altered over the years, it contains an unexpectedly rich treasure of art including a *Lamentation* by Matthias Grünewald and a *Resurrection* by Lucas Cranach the Elder. The Romanesque cloister, which can be entered from the adjacent museum, is especially lovely. Leave the church proper and visit the **Municipal Museum,** housed in the former chapter house. More works of outstanding religious art are displayed here, along with a collection of china.

Continue down Sandgasse to **Schöntal Park** (5), a shady and romantic spot laid out in 1780 in the English style. On one side of the pond you will pass the ruins of an ancient monastery. The park ends at the medieval Herstallturm tower. To the right of this is a very modern shopping center, called the City Galerie. The nicest way back to the station is via the tree-lined Weissenburger Strasse, making a right onto Erthalstrasse.

NEARBY SIGHT:

A very charming short excursion can be made on foot or by car to **Schönbusch Park** (6), a tranquil place of idyllic beauty. To reach it, cross the Main River on the Willigisbrücke and walk out Kleine Schönbuschallee, a distance of not quite two miles. Cars can get there via Darmstädter Strasse. The main attraction, besides the small temples, gazebos, and follies surrounded by ponds and meandering lanes, is the **Little Palace** *(Schlösschen),* an 18th-century pleasure retreat of the archbishops.

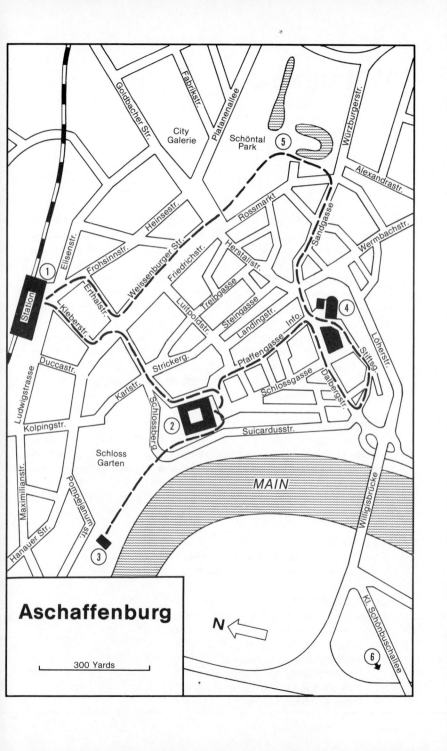

Miltenberg

If a contest were held to choose the most beautiful small town in Germany, Miltenberg would certainly be among the top contenders. Its market place is so astonishingly picturesque that it seems to belong to another world—or a long-forgotten dream.

The Romans had a camp here in the second century A.D. as part of their great defensive wall called the Limes. Around 1200 a castle was begun by the archbishops of Mainz to protect the growing trading post which connected the Rhine-Main area with an overland route to the Danube. The town prospered during the Middle Ages, changed hands several times and ultimately, in 1816, was annexed to Bavaria. Much of old Miltenberg, including its castle, has survived intact to delight us today. A visit here could be combined in the same day with one to Aschaffenburg.

GETTING THERE:
Trains depart Frankfurt's main station about 7 a.m. and around noon for Miltenberg. One of these requires a change at Aschaffenburg. The trip takes an hour and a half, and return service operates until early evening.

By car, leave Frankfurt on the A-3 (E-5) Autobahn, then turn south on the B-469 at Stockstadt. The distance is about 50 miles.

WHEN TO GO:
Visits to Miltenberg should be made between April and October, on any day except Mondays—when the sights are closed.

FOOD AND DRINK:
Miltenberg is very popular with German tourists, and so offers a good choice of restaurants. Among the best are:
Jagd-Hotel Rose (Hauptstr. 280) $$
Schönenbrunnen (Mainstr. 75) $$
Brauerei Keller (Hauptstr. 66) $$
Fränkische Weinstube (Hauptstr. 111) $
Altes Bannhaus (Hauptstr. 211) $$$

The Market Place

TOURIST INFORMATION:
The tourist office, phone (09371) 672-72, is in the town hall on Engelplatz.

SUGGESTED TOUR:
Leaving the **train station** (1), follow Brückenstrasse and cross the bridge spanning the Main. Boat trips are offered nearby. Turn right and stroll along the water's edge, then make a left to the **Market Place** *(Marktplatz)*. One of the most beautiful sights in Germany, this open square is lined with an amazing array of half-timbered houses *(Fachwerkhäuser)*. The Renaissance fountain in its center dates from 1583, while on the left is the **Town Museum** (2), located in the former 16th-century seat of administration. Step inside for a look at the town's history and traditional folk arts. The museum is open from April through October, daily except Mondays, from 10 a.m. to noon and 2-4 p.m.

Now walk uphill through the old town walls to the **Mildenburg Castle** (3), a medieval stronghold built between the 13th and 16th centuries. The view from its tower is spectacular and well worth the climb. In the courtyard you will find the fascinating *Toutonenstein,* a carved

View from Mildenburg Castle

stone monument from early Germanic times. The castle may be visited from April through October, but not on Mondays.

Descend the hill via the other path and return to the market place. On its north side stands the 14th-century **St. James' Parish Church** *(Pfarrkirche St. Jakobus)* (4), which contains several splendid works of art. The twin towers were added in 1820.

The Hauptstrasse is lined with an impressive variety of old buildings, many of which are half-timbered. Walk past the **Old Town Hall** *(Altes Rathaus)*, a 14th-century stone structure, and continue on to the **Gasthaus zum Riesen** (5). Claiming to be Germany's oldest inn, its guest register reads like a *Who's Who* of European history. The present structure dates from 1590, but some questionable documents seem to show that the inn was doing business since the 12th century and has sheltered Frederick Barbarossa and other greats. In any case, it's a nice place to stay.

Just beyond this is the Engelplatz, where the tourist office is located in the town hall. The baroque 17th-century **Franciscan Church** (6), on its north side, is a worthwhile stop before spending the rest of your time poking around the narrow alleyways which add so much interest to this ancient town.

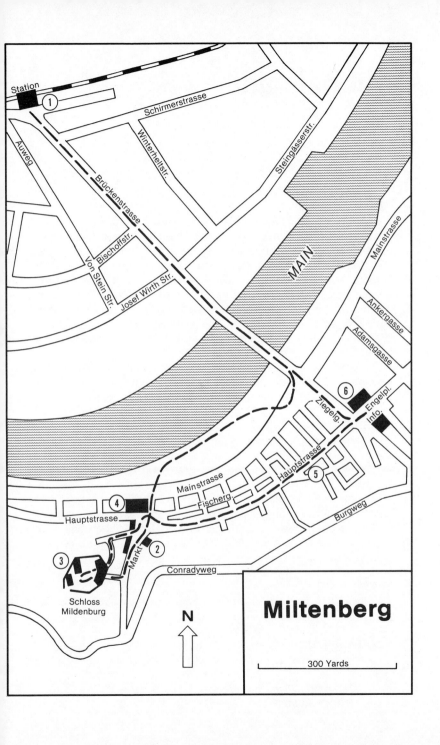

Station

Schirmerstrasse

Auweg

Winterhellstr.

Brückenstrasse

Steingasserstr.

Bischofstr.

Von Stein Str.

Josef Wirth Str.

MAIN

Mainstrasse

Ankergasse

Adamsgasse

Ziegelg.

Engelpl.
Info.

Mainstrasse

Fischerg.

Hauptstrasse

Hauptstrasse

Markt

Burgweg

Conradyweg

Schloss
Mildenburg

N

Miltenberg

300 Yards

① ② ③ ④ ⑤ ⑥

Michelstadt

The heart of the Odenwald is Michelstadt, a town of extraordinary beauty set in the enchanted forest of the Nordic god Odin; where once the Nibelungs hunted and Siegfried was killed by Hagen's spear. Or at least in legend. Today's Odenwald is a vacation paradise for the citizens of nearby Frankfurt. The history of its settlement began in Roman times, when the area had to be defended against Teutonic hordes. Michelstadt was first mentioned in A.D. 741 and soon became a place of some importance. The splendid medieval structures which still grace its narrow lanes are a reflection of the great prosperity which blessed the town during the Middle Ages.

By getting off to an early start, it is possible to combine this trip with one to Darmstadt. Those with cars could choose to visit Miltenberg instead.

GETTING THERE:

Trains depart Frankfurt's main station about 8 a.m. and noon for the 75-minute ride direct to Michelstadt. There is direct return service in the early evening. You can also get there by changing trains at Darmstadt.

By car, leave Frankfurt on the A-5 (E-4) Autobahn and head south past Darmstadt, getting off at the Bensheim exit. Continue east on the B-47 road—the famous Nibelungenstrasse—into Michelstadt, a total distance of about 50 miles. Shorter routes are possible but not as attractive.

WHEN TO GO:

Michelstadt may be visited at any time in good weather. Some sights are closed on Mondays.

FOOD AND DRINK:

Michelstadt has quite a few good restaurants, among the leading being:

Drei Hasen (Braunstr. 5) $$
Grüner Baum (Gross Gasse 17) $

The Market Place and Town Hall

TOURIST INFORMATION:
The tourist office, phone (06061) 741-46, is on the Markt Platz.

SUGGESTED TOUR:
Leave the **train station** (1) and follow the map to the **Market Place** *(Markt Platz)*. In its center there is an ornamental fountain dedicated to St. Michael which has been bubbling away since 1575. The **Town Hall** *(Rathaus)* (2), directly opposite, is one of the most photographed sights in Germany. Built in 1484, its steeply pointed roof and spired oriel windows resting on massive oak supports combine to form a vision that seems to have been lifted right out of the pages of a fairy tale. The scene is further enhanced by colorful half-timbered houses lining the square, and by the tower of its 15th-century church. During the warm months, outdoor café tables allow you to take it all in while enjoying a drink. The tourist office is adjacent.

Turn right and visit the medieval **Thieves' Tower** *(Diebsturm)* (3) before crossing the old dry-moat to the public gardens. Stroll through these and into the **Burghof** (4), a courtyard whose origins date from Carolingian times. The present buildings mostly date from the 16th

Fürstenau Castle

century and now house an interesting Toy Museum *(Spielzeug Museum)* and the Odenwald Museum, whose exhibits range from Celtic finds to the sword of the last town executioner.

Now walk over to the **Town Church** *(Stadtkirche)* (5), a late-Gothic structure begun in 1461. Step inside to see the beautiful old tombs, then follow the map down Mauerstrasse. Along the way you will pass an intriguing 18th-century synagogue before going through the restored town walls. Turn left in the gardens, re-enter the walls, and return to the market place.

Two fascinating sights lie just outside the town proper. To reach them, return to the train station (1) and continue on until you come to a creek. A trail to the right leads past a lovely old watermill to **Fürstenau Castle** (6). Begun in the 13th century, it grew over the years into a place of immense charm. The magnificent ornamental arch between two of the structures was added in 1588. Although the castle is still a private residence, you can wander around the courtyards and visit the tiny museum.

A path from the central courtyard takes you over the moat to **Einhard's Basilica** (7), an ancient stone church of impressive proportions built in the 9th century by Charlemagne's friend and biographer, Einhard. Once in a state of ruin, it has now been partially restored and may be visited. From here you can retrace your steps back to the train station.

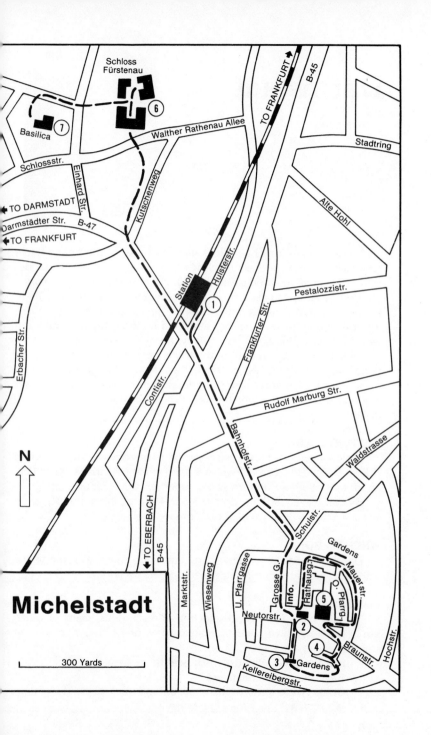

Schloss Fürstenau

6

Basilica

7

Walther Rathenau Allee

Stadtring

Schlossstr.

Einhard Str.

Kutschenweg

TO FRANKFURT

B-45

Alte Hohl

← TO DARMSTADT

Darmstädter Str. B-47

← TO FRANKFURT

Pestalozzistr.

Erbacher Str.

Station

1

Hülsterstr.

Frankfurter Str.

Rudolf Marburg Str.

Contistr.

Bahnhofstr.

Waldstrasse

N

↑ TO EBERBACH

B-45

Schulstr.

Gardens

Mauer str.

Michelstadt

Marktstr.

Wiesenweg

U. Pfarrgasse

Grosse G.

Info.

Rathausg.

O. Pfarrg.

5

Hochstr.

2

Neutorstr.

4

Braunstr.

300 Yards

3

Gardens

Kellereibergstr.

Darmstadt

Creativity has long been the hallmark of Darmstadt, one of those rare places where intellectual curiosity is given a full chance to develop. This medium-sized city in the foothills of the Odenwald is among the leading European centers of science, literature, and the arts. There are no tourist attractions in the ordinary sense, but travelers with an interest in architecture will be captivated by its highly unusual—and world-famous—buildings, particularly those in the *Art Nouveau* style.

An extraordinary amount of the city is devoted to parks, while the pedestrians-only business district has a light and airy quality about it. A baroque palace and three splendid museums round out this easy daytrip from Frankfurt, which could be combined with a visit to Michelstadt.

GETTING THERE:

Trains leave Frankfurt's main station frequently for the 15-minute ride to Darmstadt. There are also S-Bahn commuter trains which take about one-half hour. Return service operates until late evening.

By car, leave Frankfurt on the A-5 (E-4) Autobahn and head south to Darmstadt, a distance of about 22 miles.

WHEN TO GO:

Darmstadt may be visited at any time, but note that some of the museums are closed on Mondays and others on Fridays.

FOOD AND DRINK:

The city has a fairly good selection of restaurants, many of which are in the downtown pedestrian area. Some of the better choices, in trip sequence, are:

Maritim Hotel (Rheinstr. 105, near the train station) $$$
Ratskeller (Marktplatz 8) $$
China Restaurant (Mühlstr. 60, behind Marktplatz) $$
Weinmichel (near the State Museum) $$

The Wedding Tower and Russian Chapel

TOURIST INFORMATION:
The tourist office, phone (06151) 13-27-82, is just outside the train station. There is another office, phone (06151) 13-27-80, at Luisenplatz.

SUGGESTED TOUR:
Begin your tour at the **main train station** (1). From here it is a rather uninteresting one-mile walk to downtown, which can be avoided by taking a streetcar or bus to the spacious **Luisenplatz** (2), site of the stunning new City Hall and the towering Ludwig monument.

Walk straight ahead to the **Market Place** *(Marktplatz)*, where outdoor farmers' markets are held. On its south side you will see the **Old City Hall**, erected in 1598 in the Renaissance style. Dominating the square is the massive **Palace** *(Schloss)* (3), home of the rulers of the Grand Duchy of Hesse-Darmstadt until 1918. Parts of the palace were once a medieval castle, but many changes and additions made between the 16th and 19th centuries have greatly altered its appearance. Stroll through the main portal to its inner courtyard, where you will find the entrance to the **Palace Museum** *(Schlossmuseum)*. Guided tours lasting about an hour are conducted through the beautifully restored rooms, whose treasures include a noted Madonna by Hans Holbein the Younger, works by local artists, furniture, costumes, and carriages. The museum is open from Mondays through Thursdays, 10 a.m. to 1p.m. and 2–5 p.m.; and on Saturdays and Sundays from 10 a.m. to 1 p.m.

Now follow the map along a garden path to the **Mathildenhöhe** (4). Developed around the turn of the century as an artists' colony by the visionary Grand Duke Ernst-Ludwig, this low hill overlooking the city is famous for its unusual structures. Rising above all is the very symbol of Darmstadt, the **Wedding Tower** *(Hochzeitsturm)*, an acknowledged masterpiece of Art Nouveau *(Jugendstil)* architecture built in 1906 but appearing to be much younger than that. Next to this, the gold-domed **Russian Chapel** of 1899 seems wildly out of place—a strong addition to an already surrealist landscape. Built by Czar Nicholas II for his Hessian bride, it is still used as an Orthodox church and may be visited. A stroll around the precincts will reveal many other visual surprises.

From here you can take a pleasant walk by heading east past the railway line to the tranquil **Rosenhöhe Park** (5). Go through the lion-topped gateway of 1914 and wander past the secluded artists' homes, then return to the center of town via the Mathildenhöhe.

Back at the palace (3), turn north and visit the **Hessian State Museum** *(Hessiches Landesmuseum)* (6). The exhibitions in this huge institution—one of Europe's oldest—encompass a wide scope of subjects ranging from art to natural history. Of particular interest are the outstanding collections of medieval, Renaissance, and modern paintings. Allow at least an hour to sample the highlights, and be sure to see the marvelous display of Art Nouveau *(Jugendstil)* objects. The museum is open from Tuesdays through Sundays, 10 a.m. to 5 p.m.

Continue on through the **Herrngarten** (7), a lovely city park in the English style. At its far end is **Prince George's Palace** (8), an early-18th-century summer residence of the dukes. It now houses an exquisite collection of porcelain, which may be seen from Mondays through Thursdays, 10 a.m. to 1 p.m. and 2–5 p.m.; and on Saturdays and Sundays from 10 a.m. to 1 p.m. The side of the palace facing the park has an immensely charming garden which should not be missed.

Return to Luisenplatz (2) and visit the bold new Luisen Center on its south side. This large structure is home to the new city hall and an indoor shopping center. Amble through it and continue south on Wilhelminenstrasse to **St. Ludwig's Church** (9), an imposing 19th-century building with an enormous dome modelled on the Pantheon in Rome. Take a look at its unusual interior, then return to Luisenplatz where you can board a streetcar or bus back to the train station.

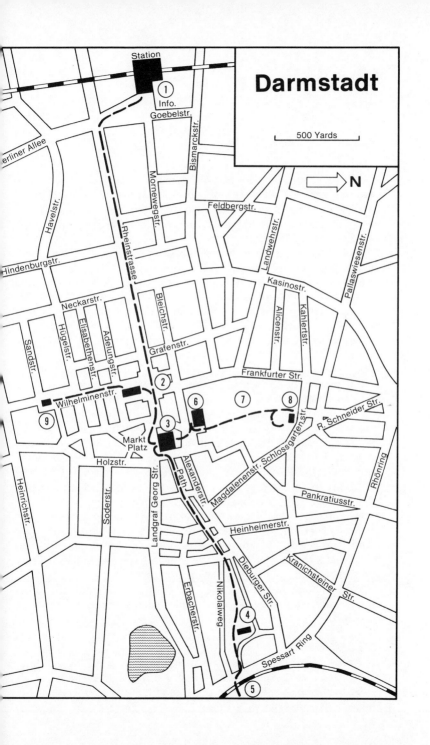

Heidelberg

More a romantic state of mind than an actual place, old Heidelberg has captured the hearts of countless tourists. First-time visitors are often filled with a sense of *deja-vu*, the feeling that somehow they've been here before. In their thoughts they probably have—for who hasn't heard of *The Student Prince?*

Half a million years ago these hills were home to the Heidelberg Man, a pre-human whose jawbone was found nearby. Celtic tribes settled the area around 400 B.C., were succeeded by Teutons, and eventually by the Romans. A series of rival kingdoms followed, monasteries were built, and in 1196 the first documented reference to *Heidelberch*—then the political center of the Palatinate—was made.

Heidelberg University, the oldest in Germany, dates from 1386. During the Reformation it became a stronghold of Protestantism. In 1622, at the height of the Thirty Years War, General Tilly's Catholic army captured the town after a destructive two-month siege.

In an effort to bring peace to the Rhineland, the new ruler, Karl-Ludwig, married his daughter to the Duke of Orléans—the brother of France's Louis XIV. When Karl-Ludwig's son died heirless in 1685, the "Sun King" claimed the Rhineland-Palatinate as his own, precipitating a war which left Heidelberg almost totally leveled. Later rebuilt in stone, the town lost status when the court moved to Mannheim in 1720. The final blow to its castle came in 1764 in the form of a lightning bolt which reduced it to the ruin it is today.

Heidelberg's glory faded in those last smoldering ashes; but its university lived on, eventually escaping into a never-never land of romanticism—a world of writers, artists, poets, and musicians. This was the *milieu* of the Student Prince; the ambiance of beer drinking, songs, and duels which still fires the imagination of today.

With its many hotels and good transportation, Heidelberg makes an excellent alternative base for exploring the Rhineland south of Frankfurt.

GETTING THERE

Trains depart Frankfurt's main station frequently for the one-hour ride to Heidelberg. Return service operates until late evening.

By car, take the A-5 (E-4) Autobahn all the way from Frankfurt to Heidelberg, a distance of 56 miles.

WHEN TO GO:
Heidelberg may be visited any time. The Palatinate Museum is closed on Mondays and the Student Jail on Sundays and holidays.

FOOD AND DRINK:
This much-visited town offers a huge variety of restaurants in all price ranges. Among the best choices are:
Kurfürstenstube (in Europäische Hotel, Nadler Str.) $$$
Museum Restaurant (in the Palatinate Museum) $$
Perkeo (Hauptstr. 75) $$
Hotel zum Ritter (Hauptstr. 178) $$
Scheffeleck (F.-Ebert Anlage 51, near St. Peter's) $$
Weinstube im Schloss (by the castle) $$
You may want to join the rest of the tourists in one of the historic student inns. The most famous are:
Roter Ochsen (Hauptstr. near Karlsplatz) $$
Sepp'l (Hauptstr. near Karlsplatz) $$

TOURIST INFORMATION:
The tourist office, phone (06221) 213-41, is in front of the train station.

SUGGESTED TOUR:
Start your tour at the **main train station** (1). The tourist office is located just outside this. From here it is a rather boring one-mile walk to **Bismarck Platz** (2), where the Old Town begins. You may prefer to take a streetcar or taxi instead.

Continue down the pedestrians-only Hauptstrasse to the **Old University** (3) on Universitäts Platz. This is the oldest surviving building of the school, having been erected in the early 18th century. Walk around to its rear façade and visit the **Student Jail** *(Studentenkarzer)* at Number 2 Augustinergasse. The lockup was used until 1914 for the incarceration of campus rowdies, who got to spend anywhere from one to five weeks on bread and water for their misdeeds. Actually, serving time here was considered a mark of honor and, given the cleverness of students, the water usually turned out to be beer. Many of the "convicts" immortalized their enforced leisure by covering the cell walls with amusing graffiti, which can be seen today.

Escaping from the pokey, stroll across to the New University, built in 1931 with American funds. In its courtyard you will find the 14th-century **Witches' Tower** *(Hexenturm)* (4), all that remains of the medieval town walls. Now climb a few steps and turn right on Seminarstrasse to the **University Library** *(Universitäts-Bibliothek)* (5). If you get here during the opening hours *(10 a.m. to noon, closed Sundays*

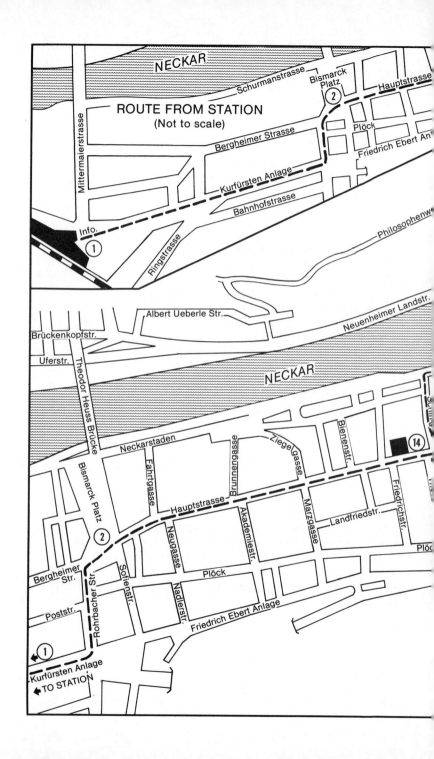

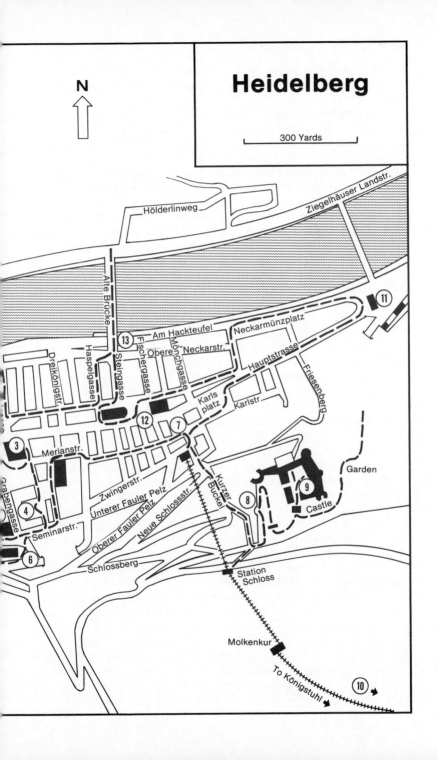

and holidays) you will be able to visit its exhibition gallery, containing a priceless collection of medieval manuscripts and illuminations along with other treasures.

St. Peter's Church (6), dating from the 15th century, serves the academic community. Wander through its tranquil yard and follow the map past the Jesuit Church of 1712 to **Kornmarkt** (7), from which you get a lovely view of the castle. The 18th-century Prinz Karl Inn on the west side of the square is now a town hall annex but in its heyday housed such luminaries as Mark Twain, Kaiser Wilhelm I, and Bismarck.

At the corner of Burgweg stands the house of Count Graimberg, a French artist who was responsible for the preservation of the castle ruins during the 19th century. Just a few steps beyond is the lower station of the mountain railway *(Bergbahn)*. Board this and ride up to the castle *(Schloss)*. Alternatively, you could walk up the rather steep Kurzer Buckel.

You are now at Heidelberg's stellar attraction, its **Castle.** Follow the path to the **Rondell** (8), once a gun battery and now an excellent spot for closeup views of the town below. Beyond it lies the remains of the **Fat Tower** *(Dicker Turm)*, which was blown up by the French in 1689. Return along the other path through the **Elizabeth Gate,** built in 1615—allegedly in one night—by Friedrich V as a present for his wife, Elizabeth Stuart, the daughter of England's James I.

Stroll over to the castle's main entrance and cross the moat into the **courtyard** (9). From here you can take a one-hour guided tour through the complex, partly in a state of ruin and partly restored. If you don't feel up to this, at least see the **Great Vat** *(Grosses Fass)*, which may be visited separately. This is the world's largest wine cask, once guarded by the court jester Perkeo, a dwarf with a monumental capacity for the juice. A statue of him—glass in hand—may be seen opposite the vat. Another attraction which can be visited without taking the tour is the **German Pharmaceutical Museum** *(Deutsches Apotheken Museum)*, a fascinating collection of ancient apothecary equipment complete with an alchemist's laboratory. Outside again, a walk through the beautiful **gardens,** originally laid out around 1620, will complete your visit to the castle.

An interesting side trip can be made by returning to the mountain railway and riding it all the way up to the **Königstuhl** (10), changing cars at Molkenkur along the way. The panoramic view from here is spectacular.

Return to town via the mountain railway or the Kurzer Buckel, a narrow stepped lane leading back to Kornmarkt (7). Now turn right and follow Karlstrasse to Karlsplatz. Opposite this, on Hauptstrasse, are two famous old student inns—the Roter Ochsen and Sepp'l. Con-

The Courtyard of Heidelberg Castle

tinue on to **Karlstor** (11), a neoclassic archway from 1775. Turn left and walk along the river, noting the locks which enable Rhine traffic to reach as far as Stuttgart, then make a left on Leyergasse and right onto Heiliggeiststrasse.

Marktplatz (12), the main square, is the scene of the farmers' market held on Wednesday and Saturday mornings. It bustles with activity on other days as well, with several outdoor cafés in good weather. On its east end is the baroque **Town Hall** *(Rathaus)*, which features a daily *glockenspiel* recital at 7 p.m. Walking along the south side of the church, you will come to the **Haus zum Ritter.** Now a hotel, it was built in 1592 by a wealthy merchant and was the only mansion to survive the French invasion of 1693. Its fantastically elaborate façade is well worth studying.

The **Church of the Holy Ghost** *(Heiliggeist Kirche)*, dominating the square, also made it through the devastation. Erected during the early 15th century, it was both Protestant and Catholic from 1705 until 1936; the two faiths being separated by a wall between the nave and choir. The unusual merchants' stalls along the outside walls have been there since medieval days.

Stroll through Fischmarkt and follow Steingasse to the **Old Bridge** *(Alte Brücke)* (13). Four earlier bridges had occupied this same site since the Middle Ages, all succumbing to flood, ice, or fire. The pres-

The Church of the Holy Ghost

ent span was completed in 1788, blown up in 1945, and rebuilt in 1947. Walk across it for the classic view of Heidelberg.

Now follow the map through colorful old streets to the **Palatinate Museum** *(Kurpfälzisches Museum)* (14), housed in an early-18th-century mansion, the Palais Morass. Among the best of the smaller German museums, its collections range from a jawbone cast of the original Heidelberg Man of a half-million years ago—the earliest evidence of man in Europe—through Roman finds and goes all the way up to Romantic and contemporary art. The real treasure, however, is the Altarpiece of the Twelve Apostles, carved by the renowned Tilman Riemenschneider in 1509. The museum is open from 10 a.m. to 5 p.m., every day except Mondays. From here it is an easy walk back to Bismarck Platz (2), where you can board a streetcar, take a taxi, or hike back to the train station.

Worms

For over a thousand years, Worms played a pivotal role in German history—and has the monuments to prove it. Although the town had been settled since the Stone Age and was a major Roman garrison, its time of glory really began in the 5th century A.D. when the Burgundians made it their capital. Out of this cloudy past came the greatest of German epics, the *Nibelungenlied,* replete with such heroes and villains as Siegfried, Brünnhilde, Gunther, Hagen, and even Attila the Hun. Twisted almost beyond recognition in Richard Wagner's *Ring Cycle,* the original legend takes place mostly in and around Worms, and is partly based on historic events.

The town flourished when Charlemagne made it a major center of the Holy Roman Empire. Slowly losing prestige as succeeding emperors became weaker, it had its final moment on the world stage in 1521 when Martin Luther's incipient Reformation was solidified at the Diet of Worms. Events after that, especially the Thirty Years War and the French Revolution, reduced Worms to the status of a small market town. World War II brought vast destruction, but in the decades since then the town has prospered and grown. Happily, most of its ancient treasures survived intact and today make Worms a fascinating place to explore. This trip can be combined in the same day with one to Mainz.

GETTING THERE:

Trains depart Frankfurt at frequent intervals for Mainz, where you change for Worms. Refer to page 152 for more details. The total journey takes up to an hour and a half. Return service operates until mid-evening. Be sure to check the schedule as there are other possible routes.

By car, leave Frankfurt on the A-5 (E-4) Autobahn, then a switch to the A-67 and head south to the Lorsch exit. From here take the B-47 road into Worms. The total distance is about 50 miles.

WHEN TO GO:

A visit to Worms may be made at any time, but note that the museums are closed on Mondays and holidays.

FOOD AND DRINK:
Worms has a fair selection of restaurants, of which the best-known are:

Dom Hotel (Obermarkt 10) $$
Domschänke (Stephengasse 16) $$
Kriemhilde (Hofgasse 2) $

TOURIST INFORMATION:
The tourist office, phone (06241) 250-45, is at Neumarkt 14, behind the cathedral.

SUGGESTED TOUR:
Leave the **main train station** (1) and follow Wilhelm Leuschner Strasse to Lutherplatz. The massive **Luther Monument** (2), erected in 1868, is inscribed with the famous words *"Here I stand, I cannot do otherwise. God help me. Amen."* It commemorates Martin Luther's appearance before the Diet of Worms in 1521, which is regarded as the turning point of the Reformation. At his feet are other leaders who set out to reform the Church—Hus, Savonarola, Waldo, and Wycliffe.

Continue on to **St. Peter's Cathedral** *(Dom)* (3), one of the glories of the High Romanesque style. Begun in the 11th century, it has an outstanding interior with fine sculptures and an 18th-century baroque high altar by Balthazar Neumann.

While in the area, you may want to visit the small **Heylshof Museum** (4), located in a mansion on the site of the former Bishop's Palace. The collection includes 15th- to 19th-century paintings and sculptures, porcelains, ceramics, and medieval stained glass. Opening hours are 10 a.m. to noon and 2–5 p.m., every day except Mondays; with reduced hours in the winter season.

Now stroll down the shady Lutherring to the **Jewish Cemetery** *(Judenfriedhof)* (5), in use since the 11th century and the oldest in Europe. A walk through this highly evocative spot with ancient tombstones recalls the time when Worms was a major center of Jewish culture.

The Andreasring leads around a corner to the former 12th- to 13th-century St. Andrew's Monastery, which now houses the **Municipal Museum** *(Museum der Stadt Worms)* (6). Step inside to see magnificent displays encompassing the entire long history of Worms, from prehistoric days to the present. Visits may be made any day except Mondays, from 10 a.m. to noon and 2–5 p.m.

Walk straight ahead past the Romanesque Church of St. Magnus, begun in the 9th century and now the oldest Lutheran church in southwest Germany. The route reveals a splendid view of the cathedral, then continues on to the tourist office, the Siegfried Fountain,

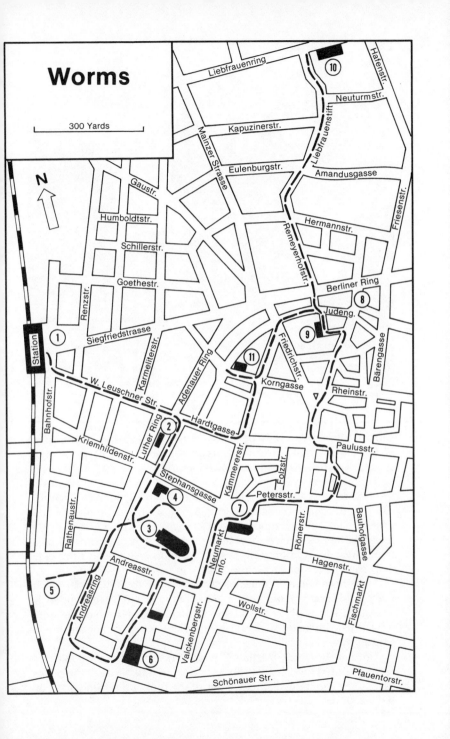

St. Peter's Cathedral

and the colorful **Market Place** *(Marktplatz)* (7). Next to this is the **Church of the Holy Trinity** *(Dreifaltigkeitskirche)*, an 18th-century baroque structure with an exceptionally nice interior.

Follow the map along a complicated route through Old Worms to the 11th-century **Raschi Tor** (8), a medieval gate in the old town walls. Close to this is the oldest **synagogue** (9) in Germany, originally built in 1034, with a 13th-century women's synagogue added next to it. The Jewish community once accounted for 30 percent of Worms' population. There is an interesting Jewish museum just behind this; open daily except on Mondays, from 10 a.m. to noon and 2–5 p.m.

From here you could make a short side trip to the **Church of Our Lady** *(Liebfrauenkirche)* (10), a 15th-century church surrounded by vineyards. This is where the original *Liebfrauenmilch* wine comes from, not the pale imitation sold as Liebfraumilch—which can be any Rheinhessen wine at all.

Continue on to **St. Martin's Church** (11), dating from the 12th century and noted for its beautiful west portal. A walk through the pedestrians-only shopping district will finish the tour and return you to the train station.

Baden-Baden

There are very few places in the world like Baden-Baden. By far the most elegant spa in Germany, it was known as the "summer capital of Europe" during the 19th century. Today it caters less to aristocracy than to wealthy businessmen and celebrities, but its gold-plated ambiance remains as glittering as ever. To go there is to experience an aspect of Germany that is quite at odds with the usual image of bustling cities, quaint old villages, and natural splendor.

The Romans, who loved to take baths, were here first. From the moment they set eyes on its hot springs the place became known as *Aquae Aureliae*. Their emperor Caracalla came for the cure, and was followed by countless other crowned heads down through the centuries. What really put Baden-Baden on the map, though, was not the healing waters but the casino, opened in 1838. This attracted the international set, particularly those from nearby France. Since World War II Baden-Baden has regained its prestige, and is now on an equal footing with Monte Carlo.

GETTING THERE:

Trains depart Frankfurt's main station several times in the morning for the two-hour ride to Baden-Baden. Some of these require a change at Mannheim. There is also an alternative route via Mainz. Return service operates until mid-evening.

By car, leave Frankfurt on the A-5 (E-4) Autobahn and stay on it all the way to the Baden-Baden exit, 112 miles away.

WHEN TO GO:

You can visit Baden-Baden at any time, although it is much more pleasant in warm weather when the gardens are in bloom. A few minor sights may be closed on Mondays.

FOOD AND DRINK:

The town has a great many restaurants, some of which are quite elegant. Less expensive places can be found around Leopoldsplatz and into the Old Town. In trip sequence, the most noted are:

Stahlbad (Augustaplatz) $$$
Boulevard Terrassen (in the Kurhaus) $$

Münchner Löwenbräu (Gernsbacher Str. 9) $$
Zum Nest (Rettigstr. 1) $$
Schwarzwald Grill (in the world-renowned Brenner's Hotel $$$

TOURIST INFORMATION:
The tourist office, phone (07221) 27-52-00, is on Augusta Platz.

SUGGESTED TOUR:
The **train station** (1) is quite a distance from the town. Take a bus—or a taxi—from the front of the station to **Augusta Platz** (2), where the tourist office is located. Here you can purchase an inexpensive one-day card *(Tageseintrittskarte)* entitling you to free entry to the spa concerts and the Pump Room—including all the hot mineral water you can drink—as well as a few minor attractions.

Follow the map across the Oos stream to the **Kurhaus** (3), a white colonnaded building of 1821. Its splendid interior houses the **Casino,** ballroom, a theatre, a restaurant-café, and other facilities. Guided tours through the luxurious casino are held daily between 10 a.m. and noon. Gambling, which includes roulette, baccarat, and blackjack, begins at 2 p.m. and lasts until early morning. Proper dress—meaning jacket and tie for men—is required at that time. There is a small entrance fee but no obligation to gamble.

In front of the Kurhaus you will notice a bandstand where spa concerts are given daily in good weather—otherwise they are held indoors. You may want to check the posted schedules and perhaps come back for one of these. Now continue on to the **Pump Room** *(Trinkhalle)* (4), a marvelously elegant 19th-century building whose colonnade features frescoes of Black Forest legends. Step inside and sample the healing waters.

From here you can take a pleasant side trip up the Michaelsberg to the **Romanian Chapel** *(Stourdza-Kapelle)* (5), a lovely spot with nice views.

Now follow the map into the colorful old part of town. Stroll down the pedestrians-only Lange Strasse and turn left on Gernsbacher Strasse to the **Town Hall** *(Rathaus)* (6), then around to the market place. The **Collegiate Church** *(Stiftskirche)* (7), partly dating from the early 13th century, contains some exceptional works of art including a remarkable sandstone crucifix of 1467 and the highly ornate tomb of Margrave Ludwig Wilhelm, both of which are in the chancel.

Leave the church and climb the steps opposite to the 15th-century **New Palace** *(Neues Schloss)* (8), home of the excellent Zähringer Museum. Paintings, porcelains, china, and exquisite objects of art are well displayed in several magnificent room settings. Walk around to

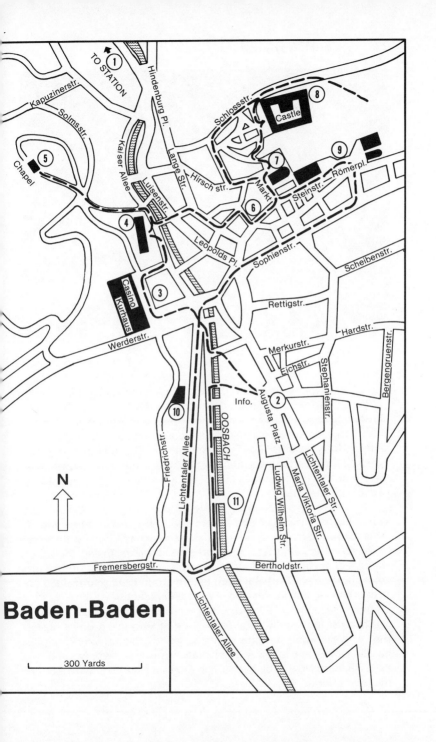

Baden-Baden

300 Yards

Along the Oos Stream

the palace gardens for a good panoramic view of Baden-Baden.

Return to town via Schloss Strasse and Marktplatz to the Fried-richsbad, where many of the spa's hydrotherapy facilities are located. Next to this, covered by a modern structure, are the ruins of the 2nd-century **Roman Baths** *(Römische Badruinen)* (9). Go in for a fascinating stroll through the excavations, then walk around Römerplatz past the strikingly contemporary Augustabad, another of the spa's water-cure establishments.

From here, the tree-lined Sophienstrasse brings you back to the Kurhaus area. Cross the Oos stream and turn left onto the world-famous **Lichtentaler Allee,** a fashionable promenade lined with exotic trees. You will soon pass a small **art museum** *(Kunsthalle)* (10) which features changing exhibitions. The path continues on for quite a distance, but you will probably want to turn around and return along the stream before reaching its end at the Lichtental Abbey.

In any case, be sure to go by the renowned **Brenner's Park Hotel** (11), almost universally regarded as one of Europe's poshest hostel-ries. An anachronism in this changing world, it still retains the quiet elegance of an age long vanished, and in its way is the very symbol of Baden-Baden. Now stroll back to the Augusta Platz and board a bus to the train station.

Triberg

The legendary Black Forest lies tucked away in a remote corner of Germany often overlooked by foreign tourists. Simple geography keeps them away. One glance at the map shows you how difficult it is to include this enchanted region—known in German as the *Schwarzwald*—into any practical itinerary. But that doesn't rule out sampling at least a bit of its magic on a lengthy but delightful daytrip from the Frankfurt area.

Triberg is probably the best spot for a first-time visit to the Black Forest. It has just about everything—waterfalls, mountain trails, a *gemütlich* atmosphere, good restaurants, and a fabulous museum filled with cuckoo clocks. It is also fairly easy to reach by rail, and not too difficult by car. You could, of course, make the journey more worthwhile by staying in the region for a few days and including trips to Baden-Baden and Freiburg.

GETTING THERE

Trains leave Frankfurt's main station in the morning—*but not later than about 8:30 a.m.*—for Offenburg, where you change to another train for Triberg. The entire journey takes about three hours. A change at Mannheim en route to Offenburg may be necessary. Return connections operate until early evening.

By car, leave Frankfurt on the A-5 (E-4) Autobahn and head south to the Offenburg exit, then continue on the B-33 road into Triberg. The total distance is 185 miles.

WHEN TO GO:

Triberg should be visited in the warm season, when trails to the waterfalls are open. Rail service is somewhat reduced on weekends. Good weather is important for this outdoor trip.

FOOD AND DRINK:

There are many good places to eat and drink in this popular resort, some quite inexpensive. Among the best choices are:

    Parkhotel Wehrle (Marktplatz) $$$
    Hotel Pfaff (Hauptstr. 85) $$
    Zur Lilie (near the waterfalls) $
    Hotel Tanne (Wallfahrtsstr. 35) $$
    Café Ketterer (Friedrichstr. 7, by the Kurhaus) $$

TOURIST INFORMATION:
The tourist office, phone (07722) 812-30, is in the Kurhaus (8).

SUGGESTED TOUR:
Leave the **train station** (1) and follow the map uphill to the **Market Place** *(Marktplatz)* (2). A few yards to the right of the main street the Gutach stream pokes its rushing waters between a clutter of inns, restaurants, and shops—none very elegant but all quite appealing. The **Town Hall** *(Rathaus)* (3) is worth a short visit for its richly carved wooden interiors.

Continue uphill on Hauptstrasse and enter the woods. In a few yards you will see an attractive café with a small watermill. Just beyond this is a **tollhouse** (4) where you pay a small fee to visit the waterfalls. From this point upwards, the Gutach stream tumbles down over seven cascades into a romantic glen for a drop of over 500 feet, making it the highest *Wasserfälle* in Germany.

Slowly climb the path alongside the rushing torrent until you reach the very top. There are many places to rest along the way. Once there, descend a short distance to a bridge with a sign pointing the way to the Wallfahrtskirche. Cross it and pass another tollhouse, but do not give up your ticket as you may want to re-enter the park. You are now on the Panorama Weg, a woodland trail with stunning views of the surrounding mountains and forests. Going past an onion-domed church, you will soon come to a **boating pond** (5), where an outdoor café invites you to stop for lunch or a drink by the water's edge.

Now follow the map to the **Church of Our Lady of the Fir-Trees** *(Wallfahrtskirche)* (6), which you saw from the path. Built in 1705, this small pilgrimage church has a marvelously baroque interior. Its beautifully carved high altar is particularly outstanding.

Continue down the street to the **Local Museum** *(Heimatmuseum)* (7). Here you can get a good impression of Black Forest life in the hard times before the region became a tourist center. Woodcarving, clockmaking, and mining were the predominant industries, and all are well represented in the museum. Individual rooms re-create the workshops and homes of long ago, while a hundred-foot-long tunnel offers a small taste of what the mines must have been like. The most fascinating exhibits, however, are the mechanical music machines, ranging from huge orchestrions to tiny bird-call boxes. Many of these can be operated by inserting a coin, and are an absolute delight to watch and hear. The most famous products of the Black Forest—cuckoo clocks—are also displayed in great variety. Triberg is a good place to purchase one of these noisy contraptions, should you feel so inclined.

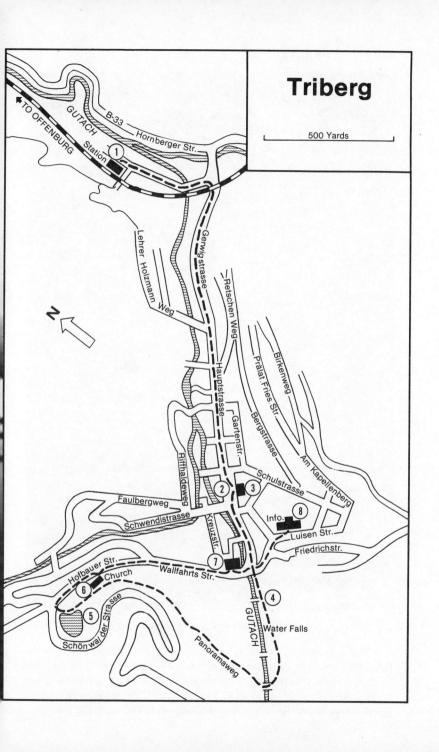

The Waterfalls (Photo Courtesy of Triberg Tourist Office)

Crossing the Hauptstrasse, walk down Luisenstrasse to the **Kurhaus** (8) a modern structure which houses a concert hall, a restaurant, and the tourist office. Here you can rest in a pleasant garden and get more information for a possible longer stay in the region. Be sure to allow enough time for the return walk down to the train station.

Freiburg

One of Germany's most appealing cities remains virtually unknown to foreign tourists. Located in the extreme southwest corner of the country, Freiburg is so far off the beaten path that few travelers even consider going there. Those who do are in for a real discovery. This delightful place on the edge of the Black Forest is not only exceptionally attractive, but also has plenty of character—and eccentricities. Where else do mountain streams run down the gutters of the streets? How many other towns, for that matter, have a mountain right in their very center? But its main attraction lies in the sunny disposition of its people, who manage to be easy-going and yet cosmopolitan at the same time; a heritage, no doubt, from over four centuries of Austrian rule as well as strong ties to nearby France and Switzerland.

GETTING THERE:

Trains, mostly of the IC class, depart Frankfurt's main station several times each morning for the two-and-a-half-hour ride to Freiburg. Be sure to leave by about 8:30 a.m. A change at Mannheim might be necessary. Return service operates until early evening.

By car, Freiburg is 168 miles south of Frankfurt via the A-5 (E-4) Autobahn. Use the Freiburg-Nord exit.

WHEN TO GO:

Freiburg claims to get more sunshine than any other city in Germany. Visits may be made at any time, but some sights are closed on Mondays.

FOOD AND DRINK:

This is a place which abounds in good restaurants. A few of the best choices are:

Ratskeller im Kornhaus (Münsterplatz 11) $$
Weinstube zur Traube (Schusterstr. 17) $$$
Schlossberg Dattler (top of the cable car) $$
Greiffenegg-Schlössle (Schlossbergring 3) $$
Zum Roten Bären (Oberlinden 12, claims to be Germany's oldest inn) $$$

A very inexpensive lunch can be had from one of the many vendors at the farmers' market in Münsterplatz, held daily except on Sundays.

TOURIST INFORMATION:
The tourist office, phone (0761) 216-32-89, is at Rotteckring 14.

SUGGESTED TOUR:
Leave the **main train station** (1) and follow Eisenbahnstrasse to the tourist office at the corner of Rotteckring. Continue down the pedestrianized Rathausgasse to **Rathausplatz** (2), a very charming old square bordered on the west by both the new and old town halls. The statue in its center is of a Franciscan friar, Berthold Schwarz, who is supposed to have invented gunpowder here in 1353. Enter the picturesque courtyard of the **New Town Hall** *(Neues Rathaus)*, which was created by linking together two 16th-century houses. A carillon plays folk tunes here each day at 12:03 p.m.

Turn right on Franziskanerstrasse and pass the 13th-century St. Martin's Church, noted for its beautiful Gothic cloisters. Opposite this is the famous **Haus zum Walfisch.** Originally built in 1516 as a home for Emperor Maximilian I, it later served as a refuge for the humanist, Erasmus of Rotterdam, and is now a bank. Note the magnificent oriel window above its doorway.

Continue on to the **Cathedral** *(Münster)* (3), widely regarded as one of the great masterpieces of Gothic architecture. Its superb 380-foot-high **tower,** which may be climbed on any day except Mondays, is among the very few in Germany to have been completed during the Middle Ages. Construction began around 1200 and took over 300 years to complete, resulting in a rather engaging mixture of styles. The interior has several excellent works of art, including an outstanding early-16th-century painting on the high altar, another altarpiece—by Hans Holbein the Younger—in the University Chapel to the right, and a vast expanse of luminous stained glass dating from the 14th century.

A lively farmers' market is held in the adjacent area every day except Sundays and some holidays, from 7 a.m. to 1 p.m. Outdoor cafés line the square in good weather, making this a wonderful place to sit down and enjoy all the activity. Some of the buildings here have survived the ages to delight us today, especially the blood-red, turreted 16th-century **Merchants' Guild House** *(Kaufhaus)* on the south side.

Now follow the map to the lower station of the **Schlossberg cable car** *(Seilbahn)* (4), which carries you to the top of Freiburg's downtown mountain. Purchase an "up" ticket *(Bergfahrt)* only, since you will be walking down. Stroll along the trail overlooking the city and descend to the medieval **Swabian Gate** *(Schwabentor)* (5), a part of

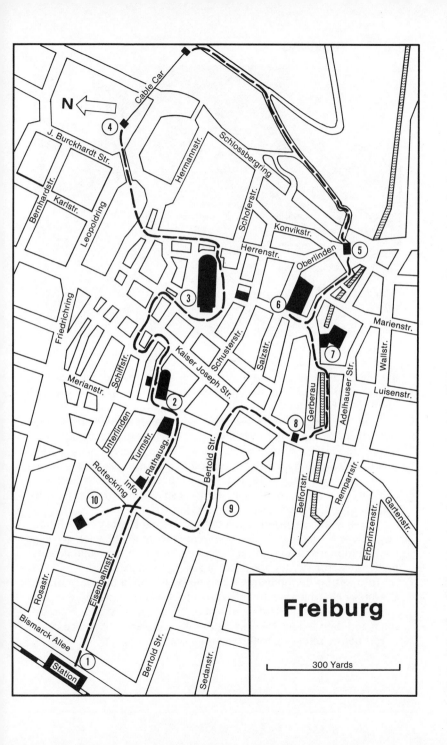

N

J. Burckhardt Str.

Cable Car

Hermannstr.

Schlossbergring

Bernhardstr.

Karlstr.

Leopoldring

Schoferstr.

Konvikstr.

Herrenstr.

Oberlinden

Friedrichring

Schiffstr.

Kaiser Joseph Str.

Schusterstr.

Salzstr.

Marienstr.

Wallstr.

Merianstr.

Unterlinden

Turmstr.

Rathausg.

Bertold Str.

Gerberau

Adelhauser Str.

Luisenstr.

Info.

Rotteckring

Belfortstr.

Rempartstr.

Erbprinzenstr.

Gartenstr.

Rosastr.

Eisenbahnstr.

Bismarck Allee

Bertold Str.

Sedanstr.

Station

Freiburg

300 Yards

Münsterplatz and the Cathedral

the old fortifications. Take a look at the street leading into town—Oberlinden—which has the characteristic *Bächle,* or little streams running in the gutters.

From the gate, the route goes through a colorful old district alongside a canal to the **Augustiner Museum** (6). Housed in a former 13th-century monastery, its magnificent collections span over ten centuries of art. At least an hour will be needed to even sample the treasures on display, including works by some of the most illustrious names in painting. The museum is open from Tuesdays through Sundays, 10 a.m. to 5 p.m.; and until 8 p.m. on Wednesdays.

You may be interested in the nearby **Natural History and Ethnology Museum** *(Natur and Völkerkundemus Museum)* (7), also occupying an old monastery. Continue along the canal to the magnificently medieval **Martinstor** (8), the other surviving town gate.

Turn left on Bertholdstrasse and go by the main buildings of the **University** (9), which was founded as far back as 1457 and is now among the leading centers of higher education in Germany. Wander around them and then follow Rotteckring to **Colombi Park** (10), a nice place to rest before returning to the train station.

Section IV

The North

Northern Germany is a world apart—and all too often overlooked. You won't find many castles here, or towering mountains. The landscape is mostly flat and sometimes even bleak. More akin to Scandinavia—or Holland—than to Bavaria, its true beauty lies in its people, and the intriguing civilization they have created over the centuries.

This is the land of the great merchant cities, a prosperous place which developed around trade rather than kings or the Church. Its inhabitants have always been fiercely independent; attuned more to the outside world than to the *Vaterland*.

Hamburg is the natural center of the north. Superb accommodations, a cosmopolitan atmosphere, and excellent transportation make it the ideal base for probing this fascinating region. Before setting out on any adventures, however, you should really take a look at the great metropolis itself—the subject of the next chapter.

Most of the daytrips in this section can also be made from Hannover, which is centrally located and enjoys equally good transportation. Ambitious travelers may want to combine the trips to Lüneburg and Celle in the same day.

Hamburg Tour

Proudly proclaiming itself as the Free and Hanseatic City of Hamburg, Germany's greatest port and second-largest metropolis—after Berlin—is a state in its own right. It possesses its own parliament and has never had much use for kings, emperors, or even archbishops. Merchants run the show here, as they have since the founding of the Hanseatic League in the 13th century. The goal of its citizens is to make money—a trait they were always quite adept at.

Hamburg is perhaps best known for its notorious St. Pauli district and the famous Reeperbahn, an area filled with fleshpots and raunchy bars. Yet this is only a very small part of a very large picture. It is also one of the continent's most elegant cities, as well as a leader in culture and the arts. A visit to its bustling port facilities is always exciting. Virtually nothing of the city's ancient history has survived the great fire of 1842 and the wholesale devastation of the last war, but in its place a handsome new metropolis has risen—one whose many facets are at least partially explored in the suggested tour which follows:

GETTING AROUND:

The route shown involves about five miles of walking, which can be reduced by using the excellent public transportation system *(HVV)* part of the way. This consists of U-Bahn subways, S-Bahn subways (which continue on as commuter trains), buses, and ferries. A map and instructions are available at the tourist information office next to the main train station. The system operates very much the same as Frankfurt's (see page 145), and the same rules generally apply. One-day passes can be purchased at the tourist offices or from vending machines in the stations.

WHEN TO GO:

Hamburg is at its best between April and September, although even the winter season is much milder than you might expect. The museums are closed on Mondays.

FOOD AND DRINK:

Great restaurants abound in this internationally minded city; some of them very expensive. Among the best choices along the walking route, in the sequence you will pass them, are:

Hotel Vier Jahreszeiten-Restaurant Haerlin (Neuer Jungfernstieg 9) $$$
Alsterpavilion (Jungfernstieg 54, on the water) $$
Schümann's Austernkeller (Jungfernstieg 34) $$$
Ratsweinkeller (in the Rathaus) $$
Zum Alten Rathaus (Börsenbrücke 10, near the Rathaus) $$$
Deichgraf (Deichstr. 23) $$$
Nikolaikeller (Cremon 36) $$
Überseebrücke (Vorsetzen, overlooking the harbor) $$$

In addition, there are many popular-priced restaurants in the Jungfernstieg, Rathaus, and St. Pauli dock areas.

TOURIST INFORMATION

The tourist office, phone (040) 24-87-00, is just outside the main train station, with a branch in the station.

SUGGESTED TOUR:

Begin your walk at the **Jungfernstieg** (1), easily reached on foot or by U- or S-Bahn subway. This elegant boulevard is bordered on the north by the Binnenalster, a large boat basin created centuries ago by damming up the Alster river. Delightful cruises through a complex network of waterways are available here, but this treat is better saved for the end of the day.

Stroll through the lovely Alsterarkaden to the **City Hall** *(Rathaus)* (2). Built in the Renaissance style during the 1890s atop some 4,000 oak piles, its 367-foot-high tower dominates the adjacent market place. Guided tours through the richly, if heavily, decorated interior are conducted frequently. While these don't visit all 647 rooms, they do take a full hour.

Now follow the map past the stock exchange *(Börse)* and along several ancient canals, including Hamburg's first harbor, the 700-year-old Nikolai Fleet. The ruined **Church of St. Nicholas** (3), originally dating from 1195 and rebuilt several times, was destroyed during World War II and is now preserved as a monument. Its steeple, at 482 feet, is the third-highest in Germany.

Cross the pedestrian bridge spanning busy Ost-West Strasse and wander down **Deichstrasse,** an intriguing street lined with old merchants' homes—many of which are now occupied by restaurants specializing in traditional Hamburg dishes. A stroll over Hohe Brücke and around **Cremon** (4) will take you past old warehouses and a former crane on the edge of the harbor.

Continue along the route to Number 10 Krayenkamp and enter its courtyard. The 17th-century **Mercers' Guild Houses** (5) were built to house widows of guild members, and have been restored as restau-

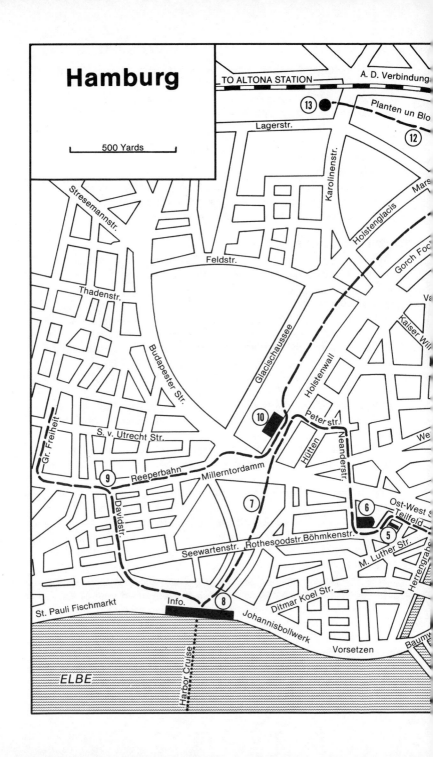

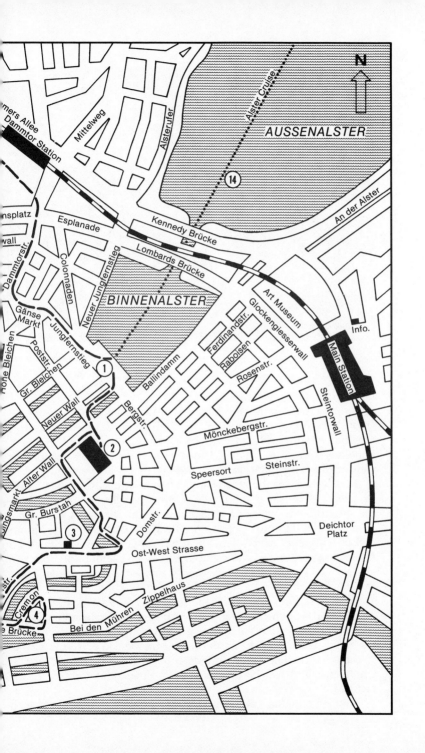

Along the Canals

rants, art galleries, and boutiques.

From here it is only a few steps to **St. Michael's Church** (6), a marvelously baroque structure from the 18th century. Take a look at its spacious interior and then ride the elevator to the top of its tower. Popularly known as "Michel," this spire offers the best panoramic view of Hamburg and its vast harbor.

Now follow Neanderstrasse and Peterstrasse past some beautifully restored old houses. A left on Holstenwall brings you into a park on the site of the former town walls. Stroll by the **Bismarck Monument** (7) and continue down steps to the **St. Pauli Docks** (8). The harbor cruises *(Hafenrundfahrt)* offered by the HADAG company are the most fascinating part of a visit to Hamburg. They take about one hour and give you an excellent closeup view of the port's extensive facilities. Don't miss this!

From here the route enters the notorious St. Pauli district, where prostitution is open and legal. You will be perfectly safe as long as you stick to the main streets and don't go looking for trouble. Walk down Davidstrasse and note the barrier sealing off the end of Herbertstrasse to the left. A police notice forbids entry to women and children. If you're male and over 18 you can go in for a peek, but don't try to take pictures.

Turn left onto the world-famous **Reeperbahn** (9), a wide street lined

The Mercers' Guild Houses

with sleazy bars and porno shops. The tamer night spots, which are still pretty raw, are on the Grosse Freiheit—the street of "great freedom." Return on the Reeperbahn to Millerntor Platz. Along the way you will pass the Panoptikum, an interesting wax-works museum.

Continue on to the **History Museum** *(Hamburgische Geschichte)* (10). The fine exhibits here are concerned with shipping through the ages, development of the port, and reproductions of Old Hamburg. Those whose ancestors emigrated from northern Europe between 1850 and 1914 may be interested in stopping first at the **Historic Emigration Office** in the museum, where complete records on all persons who passed through Hamburg en route to America are kept. These can be traced within an hour for a reasonable fee if you already know your ancestor's name and year of emigration. The search can be made without the dates but will take longer and cost more. The museum is open from 10 a.m. to 5 p.m., every day except Mondays.

The route now leads through a lovely park to the **Old Botanical Gardens** (11), where you can wander through tropical plants in a large climate-controlled structure. A little farther on is the delightful **Planten un Blomen Park** (12), whose strange-sounding name is in the old Hamburg dialect. The **Television Tower** *(Fernsehturm)* (13) offers splendid views from its observation deck, reached by elevator. There is also a revolving restaurant.

On the Harbor Cruise

Now return to Jungfernstieg (1), either on foot or by subway from Stephansplatz. Several boat cruises are available from the landing alongside the Alster Pavilion. Of these, the least expensive and longest, but perhaps the most interesting, ride is to take one of the regular commuter ferries which make stops along the Binnenalster and **Aussenalster** (14) and then continue up the creeks to the north. The one-day transit pass is valid on this, with a small surcharge. Just ride all the way out to the end, and come back on the same boat. Try to get an outdoor seat for the best views. This is the perfect end to a busy day of exploring.

NEARBY SIGHTS:

Hamburg has several other attractions, which are best saved for another day. Among them are the **Art Gallery** *(Kunsthalle)* and the **Museum of Arts and Crafts** *(Kunst und Gewerbe)* at either end of the main train station. **Hagenbeck's Zoo** *(Tierpark)*, reached via the U-2 subway, is world-renowned. If you happen to be in town on a Sunday morning, you may want to visit the **Altona Fish Market** around 8 a.m. (or earlier) for some excitement. The show is over by 10, and it can be reached by U- or S-Bahn to Landungsbrücken.

Bremen

Standing defiantly in Bremen's market place is a tall statue of the valiant knight Roland. With sword drawn, he stares at the medieval cathedral opposite, as he has done since 1404. His bearing summarizes the attitude of most *Bremers*. These are a people who do not like to be told what to do—not by the Church, not by the government, not by anyone. Still calling itself the Free Hanseatic City of Bremen, this ancient seaport has its own parliament and is, in fact, Germany's smallest self-governing state.

Bremen's history goes back at least 1,200 years. In 787, during the reign of Charlemagne, it was made the seat of a bishop. Already a major shipping center, the growing town joined the Hanseatic League in 1358. Along with Hamburg and Lübeck, it virtually controlled northern trade and grew very rich as a result. Further independence came in 1646 when Bremen became a free imperial city, and later a sovereign city-state—a status it held well into this century.

Despite its size, Bremen is an eminently walkable city. Just about everything of interest lies in the compact area between the train station and the river, while the fascinating docks can be seen at closeup range on a boat tour.

GETTING THERE:

Trains depart Hamburg's main station frequently for the one-hour run to Bremen. Most of these may also be boarded a few minutes earlier at Hamburg's Altona or Dammtor stations. Return service operates until late evening.

By Car, leave Hamburg on the A-7 (E-3) Autobahn; then change to the A-1 (E-3), which goes to Bremen. The total distance is 74 miles. There are several parking lots near the train station.

WHEN TO GO:

The best time to visit Bremen is between the end of March and the end of October, when the harbor tour operates. The major museums are closed on Mondays.

FOOD AND DRINK:

Bremen is famous for its good food. In trip sequence, some choice restaurants are:

Ratskeller (in the Rathaus) Very famous, has over 600 German wines. $$
Deutsches Haus-Ratsstuben (Am Market 1) $$
Das Flett (Böttcherstr. 3) $$
Martini (Böttcherstr. 2) $$
Beck's in'n Snoor (Im Schnoor 36) Several dining rooms, different menus. $$
Comturei (Ostertorstr. 31) Historical building. $$$

There are also several good inexpensive restaurants, mostly around the pedestrian area.

TOURISTS INFORMATION:
The tourist office, phone (0421) 363-61, is just opposite the train station.

SUGGESTED TOUR:
Leave the **main train station** (1) and walk across the square to the tourist office, where you can confirm schedules for the town hall and harbor tours. Continue straight ahead and cross the old city moat. Until the early 19th century, Bremen was surrounded on three sides by defensive bastions—since replaced by lovely gardens and waterways.

Stroll down Sögestrasse, a pedestrians-only shopping street, past a charming group of bronze pigs which children love to climb. At the end bear left to the 13th-century **Church of Our Lady** *(Liebfrauenkirche)* (2). A delightful flower market is held each morning along its outer walls.

Just a few more steps and you are in one of Europe's most beautiful market squares, the *Marktplatz*. To the left stands the elegant **Town Hall** *(Rathaus)* (3), dramatically proclaiming the wealth of Old Bremen. Originally built in 1409, it was given a magnificent new façade in the Weser Renaissance style during the early 17th century. On its west side, near the church, you will find a statue of the Bremen Town Musicians—a donkey, dog, cat, and cock who figured in the famous fairytale by the Brothers Grimm.

Enter the Town Hall and take the free half-hour guided tour of its Upper Hall, the richest interior in this affluent city. The splendid spiral staircase of 1620, Renaissance decorations, and wonderful models of early sailing ships are its main attractions. Tours are held on Mondays through Fridays at 10 a.m., 11 a.m., and noon; and on Saturdays and Sundays at 11 a.m. and noon; except during civic functions. Between November and February there are no weekend tours.

A huge **statue** of the knight Roland, symbol of Bremen's independence, stands proudly in the market square. Since 1404 he has guarded

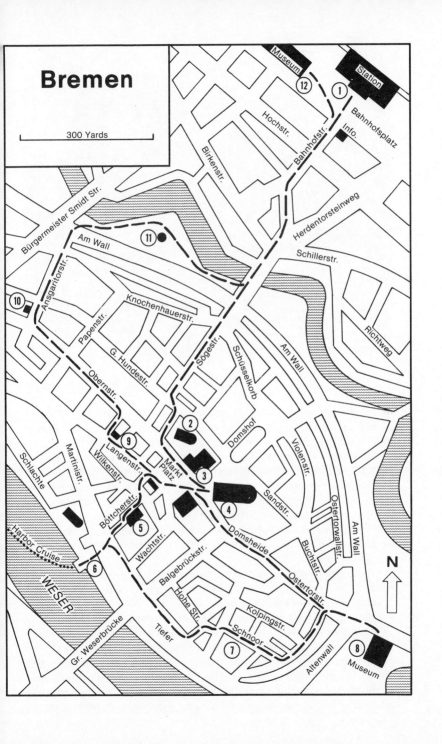

Bremen

300 Yards

Museum
Station
Bahnhofsplatz
Info.
Hochstr.
Bahnhofstr.
Herdentorsteinweg
Birkenstr.
Schillerstr.
Bürgermeister Smidt Str.
Am Wall
Ansgaritorstr.
Knochenhauerstr.
Richtweg
Papenstr.
Sögestr.
Schüsselkorb
Am Wall
G. Hundestr.
Obernstr.
Domhof
Violenstr.
Martinistr.
Langenstr.
Wilkenstr.
Markt platz
Sandstr.
Ostertorwallstr.
Am Wall
Schlachte
Böttcherstr.
Wachtstr.
Domsheide
Buchstr.
Ostertorstr.
Harbor Cruise
Balgebrückstr.
WESER
Gr. Weserbrücke
Tiefer
Hohe Str.
Schnoor
Kolpingstr.
Altenwall
Museum

N

The Town Hall and Cathedral

its citizens against encroachment by the Church or anyone else who would attempt to rule them. Roland was obviously successful at this task, for his face wears a smile of self-satisfaction.

St. Peter's Cathedral *(Dom)* (4) towers over the square. Begun in 1042, it occupies the site of an earlier church built in 787 at the request of Charlemagne. Be sure to see its oldest parts, the crypts, and especially the Lead Cellar *(Bleikeller)* which contains nine curiously preserved corpses dating from the 16th to the 18th centuries. This is open from May through October. The cathedral itself is closed between noon and 2 p.m., and cannot be visited on Saturday afternoons or Sunday mornings.

The modern structure next to the cathedral is Bremen's own parliament. To the right of it is the **Schütting,** a 16th-century merchants' guild house in the Flemish style.

Now stroll over to the famous **Böttcherstrasse,** a crowded narrow passage teeming with visual excitement. Once a tradesmen's alleyway, it was transformed during the 1920s into an idealistic art center by the wealthy coffee merchant Ludwig Roselius. On your left is the stunning **Paula Becker-Modersohn House** (5), a museum dedicated to the early Expressionist painter who worked in the Bremen area. In addition to her works, there are changing exhibitions of other modern

On the Harbor Cruise

artists. The museum connects internally with the **Roselius House,** a 16th-century mansion filled with masterpieces of North German art. Just outside this a porcelain carillon plays tunes at noon, 3 and 6 p.m.

Continuing along Böttcherstrasse, you will pass other buildings of the development, many of which house shops, restaurants, and cafés. The overall style is a strange blend of Gothic and *Jugendstil,* an overpowering combination rarely encountered. Stop in at the Atlantis House for a look at its unusual spiral staircase.

Stroll down to the **Martini Dock** (6), where you can take a fascinating 75-minute cruise *(Hafenrundfahrt)* of Germany's second-largest harbor. Boats operate between late March and the end of October; departing daily at 10 and 11:30 a.m., and 1:30, 3:10, and 4:30 p.m.

When you return, take a look at the unusual 13th-century Martini Church, just a few steps away. Then follow the map to the **Schnoor district** (7). In the late Middle Ages this was home to Bremen's fishermen. Little changed over the past three centuries, it has been restored and is now inhabited by craftsmen and artists. Wander down its main alleyway, Im Schnoor, and explore the labyrinth of narrow passageways and tiny squares which cut off to the sides. The area is filled, as you might expect, with cafés, restaurants, galleries, and boutiques.

In the Schnoor

While in the area, you may want to visit the **Art Gallery** *(Kunsthalle)* (8). Its collections are particularly rich in Old Masters, French Impressionists, and works of contemporary German painters. Opening times are from 10 a.m. to 4 p.m., daily except on Mondays; and on Tuesday and Friday evenings from 7-9 p.m.

Now return to the market square and head down Langenstrasse. Note the magnificent **Weights and Measures Office** *(Stadtwaage)* (9), erected in 1587. A right on Grosse Waagestrasse leads to Obernstrasse, a pedestrians-only shopping street. Turn left and then make a right on Ansgaritorstrasse, passing the 17th century **Gewerbehaus** (10). Beyond the busy thoroughfare, Am Wall, lie peaceful gardens which replace the former fortifications. Stroll along the pathway to the last **windmill** (11) in the Old Town.

From here it is only a short walk to the **Overseas Museum** *(Übersee Museum)* (12), featuring interesting displays of exotic cultures and world trade. Visits may be made between 10 a.m. and 6 p.m., daily except on Mondays. The train station is right next to this.

Schleswig

Schleswig is haunted by memories of the Vikings, who founded their great trading post here over a thousand years ago. Even today, the town seems more Danish than German. Relatively few foreign tourists find their way to this ancient settlement, but those who do are in for a delightful experience.

Located at the end of a long arm of the Baltic, Schleswig was the link which enabled trade to cross the Jutland peninsula from the North Sea, thus avoiding dangerous waters to the north. Then known as *Sliesthorp* or *Haithabu,* the town was first mentioned in 804. Two centuries later it moved to the opposite bank of the Schlei and prospered throughout the Middle Ages. A cathedral and a castle got built, both of which dominate Schleswig today. The town's greatest attraction, though, lies in its charming provincial character—and in the opportunity to sample a small taste of Scandinavia while remaining in Germany.

GETTING THERE:

Trains depart Hamburg's Altona station several times in the morning for the less-than-two-hour trip to Schleswig. There is an S-Bahn connection to Hamburg's main station. Check the schedules carefully. Return service operates until early evening.

By Car, Schleswig is 77 miles north of Hamburg on the A-7 (E-3) Autobahn. Get off at the Schleswig-Jagel exit and continue into town, parking near the cathedral. You will probably prefer to drive to Gottorf Castle.

WHEN TO GO:

The summer season is the best time to visit Schleswig. Avoid coming on a Monday or major holiday, when the castle is closed. Good weather will greatly enhance your enjoyment of this trip.

FOOD AND DRINK:

Schleswig offers a good selection of restaurants. Some choices, in trip sequence, are:

>   **Strandhalle** (Strandweg 2, near the cathedral) $$
>   **Skandia** (Lollfuss 89, en route to the castle) $$
>   **Schloss Keller** (in Gottorf Castle) $$
>   **Waldhotel** (Stampfmühle 1, behind castle) $$

TOURIST INFORMATION:

The tourist office, phone (04621) 81-42-26, is at Plessenstrasse 7, near the cathedral. Ask them about the new Viking Museum at Haithabu (8).

SUGGESTED TOUR:

Schleswig's **train station** (1) is located a little over a mile and a half from the old part of town *(Altstadt)*. You can get there by bus or taxi, although the walking route on the map is very pleasant. In either case, begin at the tourist office, just a block from the cathedral.

St. Peter's Cathedral *(Dom)* (2) is an unusually attractive brick Gothic structure. Begun about 1100, it was not completed until the 15th century and only acquired its present tower in the late 19th. Enter by the south portal, which is capped by a marvelous stone tympanum from 1170. In the chancel you will see the renowned **Bordesholm Altar,** carved from oak during the early 16th century by Hans Brüggeman. A masterpiece of the woodcarvers' art, it contains some 392 figures. Other treasures include the noted *Blue Madonna* painting on a pillar on the north side of the nave, fine medieval cloisters, and some outstanding 13th-century frescoes.

Now follow the map along the harbor to the picturesque fishermen's district of **Holm** (3). Its lanes, very reminiscent of Scandinavia, are lined with quaint cottages. Stroll down some of the narrow passageways leading to the water's edge, then take a look at **St. John's Convent** (4), which was founded in the 12th century.

Return to town via Norderholmstrasse and Fischbrückstrasse. The **Rathausmarkt** (5) is a lovely open square bordered by the 18th-century town hall. Continue up Lange Strasse and turn left into Kornmarkt. From here the pedestrians-only Stadtweg and Lollfuss lead to the castle.

Gottorf Castle *(Schloss)* (6) was first built around 1150, although virtually all of the present structure dates from the 16th and 17th centuries. For over 400 years it was home to the dukes of Schleswig-Holstein-Gottorf, a dynasty which gave Russia its czars in the 18th century. Today it houses the two major museums of Schleswig-Holstein, which are worth the trip in themselves. One admission covers both.

The **Prehistorical Museum** contains one of the most fantastic archaeological finds in Germany, the 4th-century **Nydam Boat,** on display in a separate building next to the castle. Discovered in 1863, this remarkably well-preserved craft required 36 rowers to man its oars, and is of the type used by the Angles and Saxons on their conquest of Britain. Other exhibits, some here and others in the castle, include prehistoric corpses, runic stones, and Viking artifacts.

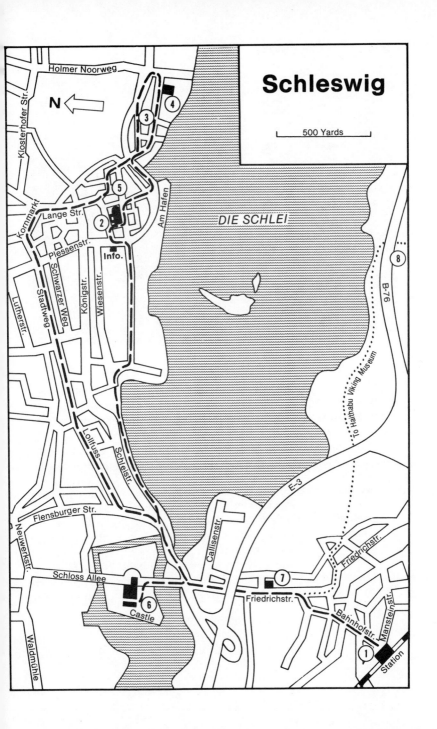

Schleswig

500 Yards

N ⟵

Holmer Noorweg

Klosterhofer Str.

DIE SCHLEI

Kornmarkt

Lange Str.

Plessenstr.

Info.

Schwarzer Weg

Königstr.

Wiesenstr.

Stadtweg

Lutherstr.

Am Hafen

Lollfuss

Schleistr.

B-76

To Haithabu Viking Museum

Flensburger Str.

Neuwerkstr.

Schloss Allee

Castle

Waldmühle

Callisenstr.

E-3

Friedrichstr.

Friedrichstr.

Bahnhofstr.

Mansteinstr.

Station

The Harbor at Holm

Also in the castle is the splendid **Schleswig-Holstein State Museum,** which has rich collections of local art and culture from the Middle Ages to the present. Among the most outstanding rooms are the Gothic "King's Hall" and the Renaissance chapel. Allow at least an hour to sample some of its treasures. Both museums are open daily except on Mondays, from 9 a.m. to 5 p.m.; closing an hour earlier between November and the end of March.

You can return to the train station by bus from the corner of Gottorfstrasse. Those walking the half-mile distance may want to stop at the **Municipal Museum** *(Stadt Museum)* (7), located in a 17th-century mansion on Friedrichstrasse. Its interesting displays are concerned with local history. From here it is only a short walk to the station, or you could continue on to the new **Haithabu Viking Museum** (8) at the nearby "Haddeby Noor" archaeological digs. It is open from 10 a.m. to 4 p.m., daily except on Tuesdays. Ask the tourist office for directions.

Lübeck

Free and Imperial Lübeck, Queen of the Hansa; in the Middle Ages the capital of the Hanseatic League and one of the most powerful mercantile cities on earth. What a place it must have been at the height of its glory! Fortunately for the traveler, its gradual decline and a location well off the mainstream of German life have combined to preserve much of the city's medieval flavor. Here you can still walk back in time to another age when its merchants brought untold prosperity to the mighty little republic which rose from the ruins of the Holy Roman Empire.

Lübeck was founded in 1143 as a trading post on an easily defended island in the Trave and grew in importance, becoming a Free Imperial City in 1226. Gradually, however, expanding trade with the New World favored ports on the North Sea. This, along with the collapse of the Hanseatic League in the 17th century, weakened Lübeck's position. It slowly became a backwater port, no longer rich enough to rebuild, and had to be content with remaining in the fabric of its medieval past. The final blow came in 1937, when the proud old city lost its last claim to independence. Since the end of World War II it has shared in Germany's rebirth, and is now a frontier town of sorts—being only a stone's throw from the East German border.

GETTING THERE:
   Trains depart Hamburg's main station at about one-hour intervals for the 45-minute run to Lübeck. Return service operates until late evening.
   By car, Lübeck is 41 miles form Hamburg via the A-1 (E-4) Autobahn.

WHEN TO GO:
   Lübeck is a city for all seasons. The museums are open from 10 a.m. to 4 p.m., daily except on Mondays.

FOOD AND DRINK:
   The city is well endowed with restaurants evoking an Old-World atmosphere. Among the best-known are:

The Holstentor

Stadtrestaurant (in the train station) $$
Ratskeller (in the town hall) $$
Lübecker Hanse (Am Kolk 3, by St. Peter's) $$$
Das Schabbelhaus (Mengstr. 48) World-famous. $$$
Schiffergesellschaft (Breite Str. 2) Historic. $$

TOURIST INFORMATION:
   The tourist office, phone (0451) 723-00, is on the market place by the town hall, with a branch in the train station.

SUGGESTED TOUR:
   Leave the **main train station** (1) and follow the map to the **Holstentor** (2), a gigantic fortified gate built in 1477. This symbol of Lübeck's former power now houses an intriguing museum of the city's history. Be sure to see the large model of the town as it appeared in 1650, as well as the grim torture chamber in the basement. To the right of the gate, along the water, stands a colorful row of warehouses from the 16th and 17th centuries. Salt from Lüneburg was once stored here before being exported to Scandinavia.
   Cross the bridge and continue on to **St. Peter's Church** (Petri-kirche) (3). Built between the 13th and 15th centuries, it was badly damaged during World War II and is being rebuilt. Its tower, however, has been restored and may be ascended by elevator for a marvelous view.

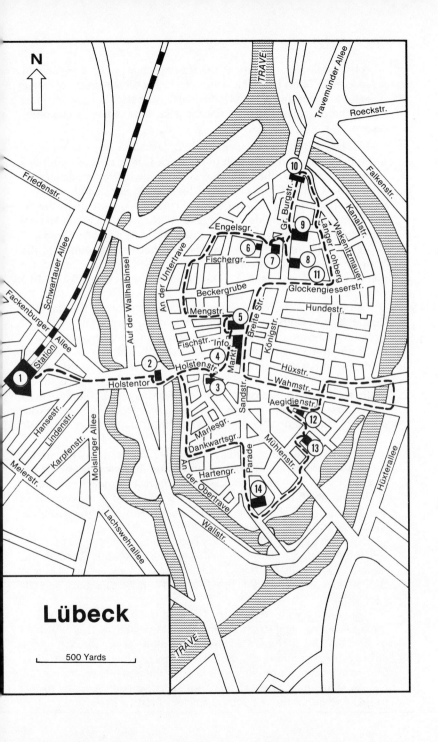

N

TRAVE
Travemünder Allee
Roeckstr.
Falkenstr.
Friedenstr.
Schwartauer Allee
Auf der Wallhalbinsel
An der Untertrave
Engelsgr.
Gr. Burgstr.
Kanalstr.
Wakenitzmauer
Langer Lohberg
6
10
9
Fischergr.
7
8
Beckergrube
11
Glockengiesserstr.
Mengstr.
Hundestr.
Fischstr.
5
Breite Str.
Königstr.
Info.
4
Markt
2
Holstenstr.
Sandstr.
Hüxstr.
Holstentor
3
Wahmstr.
Fackenburger Allee
Station
1
Aegidienstr.
12
Hansestr.
Lindenstr.
Moislinger Allee
Marlesgr.
Dankwartsgr.
Parade
Mühlenstr.
13
Meierstr.
Karpfenstr.
An der Obertrave
Hartengr.
14
Hüxterallee
Lachswehallee
Wallstr.

Lübeck

500 Yards

TRAVE

A left off Kohlmarkt leads to the **Market Place** (4), bordered by the splendid old **Town Hall** *(Rathaus)*. This highly ornate structure with its needle-like spires and arcaded promenade was begun in 1250 and modified in the centuries since. The tourist office is on the north side of the square.

St. Mary's Church *(Marienkirche)* (5), just a few steps away, is the finest in Lübeck and a triumph of the Brick Gothic style. Serving as a prototype for many other churches in the Baltic region, it was erected during the 13th and 14th centuries. Its Briefkapelle chapel, with star vaulting supported by only two slender columns, is particularly lovely. The composer Buxtehude was organist here; both Bach and Handel came to hear him play. During the war, St. Mary's was bombed and two great bells fell, smashed to bits, and became imbedded in the floor under the south tower. The pieces were left there as a silent memorial to the war dead. St. Mary's is open daily from 10 a.m. to 3 p.m.

Opposite the church, at Number 4 Mengstrasse, is the baroque **Buddenbrooks House** where Thomas Mann was born in 1875. It played a role in his novel of the same name, and is now occupied by a bank. Continue down the street past the Schabbelhause, a pair of elegant merchants' homes at numbers 48 and 50, which house a world-famous restaurant. Now follow the map through some interesting old streets to the **Mariners' Guild House** *(Haus der Schiffergesellschaft)* (6). Built in 1535, it is now home to an historic restaurant noted for its splendid interior, whose ambiance recalls the glorious days of the Hanseatic League.

St. James' Church *(Jakobikirche)* (7) is directly across the street. A visit to this dark, atmospheric 14th-century hall church—noted for its Gothic organs—will be in complete contrast to others in Lübeck. Under the north tower there is a chapel dedicated to sailors lost at sea. It contains a lifeboat, the sole survivor of the 1957 shipwreck when a local barque went down with all hands.

Walk through the little alleyway between the church and its vicarage and then turn right on Königstrasse. The **Behnhaus Museum** (8), located in a magnificent 18th-century mansion, specializes in 19th- and 20th-century art, particularly the works of Friedrich Overbeck and Edvard Munch.

Now retrace your steps to the **Heiligen Geist Hospital** (9), one of the most outstanding structures in town. It was built in 1286 as a charity hospital and later used as an old-age home. The entrance opens directly into a spacious chapel. Next to this is a huge hall containing four rows of tiny rooms which were once the patients' quarters. You can examine some of these medieval stalls, whose proximity to the chapel underlines the religious character of charity in those days. It is

The Tov Hall

open from 10 a.m. to 4 p.m., daily except on Mondays.

Grosse Burgstrasse leads to the 15th-century **Burgtor** (10), a fortified gate which defended the only land approach to Lübeck. Walk under it and follow the map through a quiet old part of town. Along Glockengiesserstrasse you will pass several examples of the residential alleys and courtyards (*Wohngänge* and *Höfe*) for which the city is noted. Beginning in the late Middle Ages, these were built to alleviate an increasing demand for space on a small island. The **Füchtingshof** (11) at Number 25 is a particularly nice one.

Turn left on Breite Strasse, a pedestrians-only shopping street, and note the elegant 16th-century Dutch Renaissance staircase on the side of the town hall. Another left on Wahmstrasse leads to Balauerfohr. From here a pleasant side trip can be made by following the route on the map through a park on the far side of the river.

The small 13th-century **Aegidien Church** (12), is famous for its magnificent Renaissance rood screen. Now stroll down St. Annen Strasse to **St. Anne's Museum** (13). Housed in a former convent, it has a fabulous collection of ecclesiastical art and period room settings which should not be missed.

Continue on the the recently restored **Cathedral** *(Dom)* (14). Built between the 12th and 15th centuries, its delightful interior is well worth a visit before heading back to the station via the route on the map.

Lüneburg

It was salt that made Lüneburg rich. This well-preserved medieval town dates from the discovery of its saline springs at least a thousand years ago. In those days salt was needed for food preservation, especially in Scandinavia—which has no deposits of its own and borders on a distinctly un-briny sea, the Baltic. From Lüneburg, the Old Salt Road led to Lübeck, where the white gold was put on ships headed for ports as distant as Russia.

Lüneburg joined the Hanseatic League in the 14th century and became immensely wealthy. Fine homes, churches, and public buildings were constructed, mostly of brick. Then, in the 16th century, trade began to decline. The Thirty Years War and the plague decimated its population. After that the town remained a poor, backwater place until fairly recent times, when new industry and the development of its spa brought a measure of prosperity. Today, the town remains much as it was in the 15th and 16th centuries, a living museum of life in the late Middle Ages. This trip can be combined in the same day with one to Celle.

GETTING THERE:

Trains depart Hamburg's main station frequently for the half-hour trip to Lüneburg. These same trains can also be boarded a few minutes earlier at Hamburg's Altona and Dammtor stations. Return service operates until late evening.

By car, leave Hamburg on the A-7 (E-4) Autobahn and head south to the B-4 road, which will take you to Lüneburg. The total distance is 34 miles.

WHEN TO GO:

Lüneburg may be visited at any time, but avoid coming on a Monday if you want to see the museum or the inside of the town hall.

FOOD AND DRINK:

Some choice restaurants, in trip sequence, are:

> **Bremer Hof** (Lünerstr. 13) $$
> **Scheffler** (Bardowickerstr. 7) $$
> **Ratskeller** (in the town hall) $$
> **Wellenkamp's Hotel** (Am Sande 9) $$$

Mills by the Old Port

TOURIST INFORMATION:
The tourist office, phone (04131) 322-00, is in the town hall.

SUGGESTED TOUR:
Leave the **train station** (1) and follow the map to the colorful **Old Port** (2) on the Ilmenau River. On your left, looking like a fantastic bird, is the **Old Crane** *(Alter Kran)*, a strange wooden contraption built in 1797. Similar cranes stood here since at least the 14th century. There are some ancient warehouses in the same area and, across the harbor, a group of 16th-century merchants' houses. Stroll along Am Fischmarkt and cross the tiny footbridge over the millstream. One of the old watermills here continues to grind flour as it has done for centuries.

Walk straight ahead and turn right on Rotehahnstrasse. Midway down the block, at Number 14, is the **Roter Hahn** (3), a medieval old-folks' home. Step into its very lovely courtyard, then continue on to **St. Nicholas' Church** (4), consecrated in 1409 and noted for its star-vaulted ceiling.

A left on Bardowicker Strasse leads to the **Market Place** (5), with its Luna Fountain of 1530. Outdoor farmers' markets are held here on Wednesdays and Saturdays. The splendid **Town Hall** *(Rathaus)*, facing the square, has an ornately decorated façade. Actually a complex of

The Market Place and Town Hall

buildings dating from the 13th through the 18th centuries, it is considered to be among the finest in Germany. Guided tours through its magnificent interior are held several times daily, except on Mondays. For specific times, ask at the tourist office located on the side facing the square.

Now follow the map to **St. Michael's Church** (6) on Johann Sebastian Bach Platz, where the great composer got his start at the age of fifteen as a boy soprano. From here you can make a pleasant side trip to the **Kalkberg** (7), a small mound which offers a good view of the town.

Continue down Auf der Altstadt, Schlägertwiete, and Heiligengeiststrasse. This ancient part of town has been slowly subsiding as the salt deposits below are extracted. Some of the houses lean at odd angles and cracks develop in their walls.

You are now at Am Sande, a large open area lined with some beautiful old buildings. The most outstanding of these is **St. John's Church** *(St. Johannis Kirche)* (8), a 14th-century brick structure with a slightly skewed tower. Go inside for a look at the fine altarpiece and choir stalls, and especially at the famous ''Bach'' organ.

At this point you may want to stroll around the picturesque streets between here and the market place, or follow the map to the **Museum of the Principality of Lüneburg** (9), whose superb displays are concerned with local history and culture. The train station is only a few blocks away.

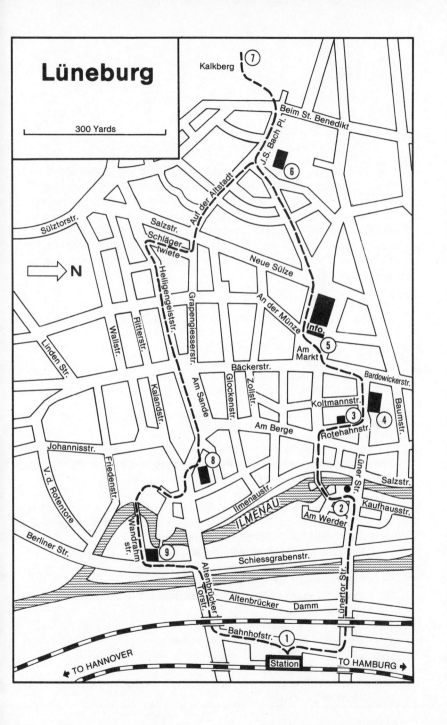

Celle

If Celle were in Bavaria, it would be mobbed with tourists. Fortunately, its location on the fringe of the Lüneburg Heath has spared it that fate. Pronounced *Tz-ella*, this delightful old town has a refreshing atmosphere, a lightheartedness often missing in other holdovers from the Middle Ages. This is a place to savor, not for any famous sights—there are precious few—but for its remarkable enjoyable ambiance. A trip here could easily be combined in the same day with one to Lüneburg.

GETTING THERE:

Trains depart Hamburg's main station several times in the morning for the one-and-a-half-hour ride to Celle. These same trains may be boarded a few minutes earlier at Hamburg's Altona or Dammtor stations. Return service operates until late evening.

By car, leave Hamburg on the A-7 (E-4) Autobahn and head south to the Soltau-Süd exit, then follow the B-3 road south to Celle. The total distance is 74 miles.

WHEN TO GO:

Celle may be visited at any time, but a fine day in the warm season will make it much more enjoyable. The castle is closed on Saturday afternoons and the museum on Sunday afternoons.

FOOD AND DRINK:

The town offers a fine selection of restaurants in all price ranges. Among the best choices, in trip sequence, are:

    Historischer Ratskeller (in the town hall) $$
    Schwarzwaldstube (Bergstr. 14) $$
    Städtische Union Celle (Thaerplatz) $$
    Hotel Fürstenhof-Endtenfang Restaurant (Hannoversche Str. 55) $$$

Along the way you will pass several nice cafés, some with outdoor tables, as well as less expensive restaurants.

TOURIST INFORMATION:

The tourist office, phone (05141) 230-31, is located on Schlossplatz, just in front of the castle.

The Duke's Castle

SUGGESTED TOUR:

The **train station** (1) is about one mile from the old part of town. Although you can get there by bus or taxi, the walk—going through a park most of the way—is actually very pleasant.

Turn left on Schlossplatz to the impressive **Duke's Castle** *(Schloss)* (2), formerly the residence of the dukes of Brunswick and Lüneburg. Begun in 1292 as a fortification, it was later rebuilt in the Renaissance and baroque styles. The castle has a strange relationship with British royalty. Sophie-Dorothea, the daughter of the last duke to live in Celle, was married to her cousin, the elector of Hannover, who in 1714 became the German-speaking King George I of England. He later divorced her for infidelity and had her imprisoned for life, but before that unhappy event they had two children. One of these became England's George II and the other, Sophie, the mother of Frederick the Great. George III fits into the story, too. His sister, Caroline Mathilda, married the mentally unstable king of Denmark, and later had an affair with one of his ministers. For this she was banished for life to Celle Castle, where she died in 1775.

Enter the castle and take one of the guided tours through its splendid interior, which are conducted about once an hour between 9 a.m. and 4 p.m., every day except Saturday afternoons. The most interesting rooms are the kitchen, the highly eccentric Renaissance **chapel,** and the magnificent baroque **court theatre**—still in use today.

The **Bomann Museum** (3), just across the street, has an utterly fascinating display of life in Lower Saxony. Reconstructed farm houses, utensils, costumes, and toys compete for your attention with a sizeable collection of art and antiques. Be sure to see all of the floors, including the basement, and don't miss the charming **Biedermeier house** in the courtyard, reached from an upper floor of the museum. Opening hours are from 10 a.m. to 5 p.m., every day except Sunday afternoons.

Now follow the Stechbahn, once a medieval tournament ground, to the **Town Church** *(Stadt Kirche)* (4). This was consecrated in 1308 and renovated in the baroque style during the 17th century. The dukes are buried here, along with the unfortunate Caroline Mathilda. A trumpet is played from its tower every day at 7:30 a.m. and 6:30 p.m.

From here the narrow Kalandgasse leads past the Old Latin School of 1602 to Kanzleistrasse. Make a right and stroll down to the Markt, where a carillon with revolving figures plays tunes at 10 a.m., 11 a.m., noon, and 3, 4, and 5 p.m. Continue along Schuhstrasse, a gorgeous pedestrians-only street lined with restored half-timbered houses. A colorful farmers' market is held on Wednesday and Saturday mornings at Brandplatz.

Return via Neue Strasse, again lined with a profusion of ancient houses, to the **Town Hall** *(Rathaus)* (5). This ornately elegant structure was begun in the 14th century and enlarged in the 16th. Note the fabulous north façade with its Weser Renaissance gable.

Continue up Zöllnerstrasse, a pedestrian shopping street with medieval houses, interesting shops, and outdoor cafés. At its end turn right and wander down Mauernstrasse to the **Hoppener House** (6) at the southwest corner of Poststrasse. Built in 1532, this is the most ornate dwelling in a town jam-packed with elaborately decorated houses. Its richness sums up what Celle is all about. Restoration here has been carried out to such an extent that it begins to take on an unreal character. The Middle Ages could never have been this colorful, but the fantasy created is very inviting.

Now follow the map to the **French Park** *(Französischer Garten)* (7), a thoroughly delightful spot to relax. At its far end you will come to the **Bee Institute** *(Bieneninstitut)* (8), a state facility devoted to research on apiculture. Visitors are welcome from Mondays through Fridays, except on holidays. Before returning to the station you will probably want to spend more time just wandering around the streets.

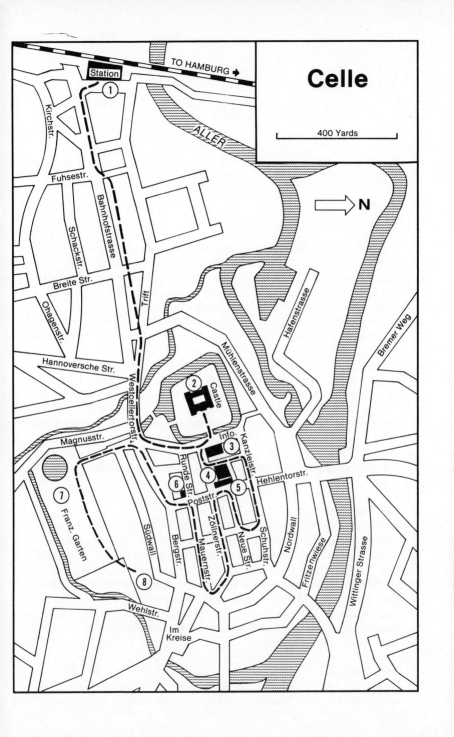

TO HAMBURG →

Celle

400 Yards

N

Station

ALLER

Kirchstr.
Fuhsestr.
Schackstr.
Breite Str.
Ohagenstr.
Bahnhofstrasse
Trift
Hannoversche Str.
Westcellertorstr.
Magnusstr.
Mühlenstrasse
Hafenstrasse
Bremer Weg
Castle
Info.
Kanzleistr.
Hehlentorstr.
Runde Str.
Poststr.
Nordwall
Franz. Garten
Südwall
Bergstr.
Zöllnerstr.
Mauernstr.
Neue Str.
Schuhstr.
Fritzenwiese
Wittinger Strasse
Wehlstr.
Im Kreise

① ② ③ ④ ⑤ ⑥ ⑦ ⑧

Goslar

Easily one of the most fantastic medieval towns in Germany, Goslar lies tucked away at the foot of the Harz Mountains—miles from the nearest Autobahn and near the end of a minor rail line. Relatively few foreign tourists venture this far off the beaten path, but those who do are in for a visual treat which rivals even Rothenburg.

Goslar is over a thousand years old—and looks it. Virtually untouched by time, it was the favorite residence of the Holy Roman emperors during the 11th and 12th centuries. Rich deposits of silver, lead, copper, and even some gold brought great wealth; and in the 13th century the prospering town joined the Hanseatic League. By 1340 it had become a Free Imperial City, remaining powerful well into the 16th century. After that, however, religious wars and the loss of its mining rights to the Duke of Braunschweig brought on the inevitable decline. Goslar went into a long sleep, from which it did not awaken until the 19th century. Today, the mines are once again active, but the real gold comes from vacationing Germans, who flock to the nearby mountains by the thousands.

GETTING THERE:

Trains depart Hamburg's main station in the morning for either Hildesheim or Hannover, where you can change to a local for Goslar. The trip takes about three hours. Be sure to check the current schedules carefully, preferably the day before, as an early start is necessary.

By car, leave Hamburg on the A-7 (E-4) Autobahn and head south past Hannover and Hildesheim to the Rhüden exit. From there take the B-82 road east into Goslar. The total distance is about 150 miles. Those driving may want to make Goslar a stop on a trip between central and northern Germany.

WHEN TO GO:

Goslar may be visited at any time. The major sights are open daily, except the Goslarer Museum, which closes on Sunday afternoons.

The Kaiserworth and Town Hall

FOOD AND DRINK:
Being the center of a popular resort area, Goslar offers a fine selection of restaurants. Some noted choices are:

Der Achtermann (Rosentorst. 20, near the station) $$
Schwarzer Adler (Rosentorstr. 25, near the station) $$
Kaiserworth (on the Markt Platz) $$
Das Brusttuch (Hoher Weg 2) $$
Weisser Schwan Balkan Grill (Münzstr. 11) $$

TOURIST INFORMATION:
The tourist office, phone (05321) 28-46, is at Markt Platz 7.

SUGGESTED TOUR:
Leave the **train station** (1) and follow the map to the **Markt Platz** (2), where the tourist office is located. An outdoor farmers' market is held here on Tuesdays and Fridays until 1 p.m. In the center of the square stands a 13th-century fountain adorned with the town's emblem, an imperial eagle. On the east side, a carillon with mechanical figures puts on a free show depicting the history of mining in the region at 9 a.m., noon, 3, and 6 p.m. Outdoor café tables are set up in the square during the summer. The 15th-century **Kaiserworth,** now a hotel, is a remarkably picturesque structure. Take a look at its famous Ducat Man, a somewhat obscene carved figure of a man excret-

ing golden coins, below the statue of Abundance on the side near the corner.

The **Town Hall** *(Rathaus)* (3), on the west side of the square, also dates from the 15th century. Enter it by way of the outdoor staircase and visit the **Chamber of Homage** *(Huldigungssaal)*, a small room covered with lavish medieval decorations. A noted 16th-century gospel book and several splendid examples of the silversmiths' art are displayed as well.

Now stroll over to the **Market Church** (4). Begun in the 12th century, it was expanded over the years and contains some wonderful Romanesque stained-glass windows, a 16th-century brass baptismal font, and other treasures. Next to this, at the corner of Hoher Weg, stands the 16th-century **Brusttuch** (5). One of Goslar's most outstanding dwellings, this curiously named structure is now an inn.

From here the route leads to the **Siemens House** (6), the ancestral home of the famous industrialist family. Built in the 17th century, this mansion may be visited between 9 a.m. and 12:30 p.m., Mondays through Saturdays, but not on Wednesdays. Just ring the doorbell for entry.

Continue via Bergstrasse, Forststrasse, and Frankenberger Strasse through a delightful square to the **Frankenberg Church** (7). Originally built in the 12th century, it was remodeled during the 1700s and is renowned for its 13th-century murals and elaborately decorated nuns' gallery.

The walk now goes through a very colorful old part of town along the Gose stream, across which is the **Imperial Palace** *(Kaiserpfalz)* (8). Once a residence of the Holy Roman emperors, it was the scene of many imperial diets until the 13th century. The immense structure was first built around 1050, altered many times, and almost completely reconstructed during the late 19th century as a memorial to the First Reich. Enter the enormous **Imperial Hall** *(Reichssaal)* with its romantic 19th century murals depicting great events in German history. A leaflet describing the pictures in English is available. While there, be sure to see the 12th-century **Chapel of St. Ulrich,** the final resting place for the heart of Heinrich III, an 11th-century emperor. The rest of him is buried in Speyer. Visits to the palace may be made any day; from 9:30 a.m. to 5 p.m. between May and September; 10 a.m. to 4 p.m. during March, April, and October; and 10 a.m. to 3 p.m. from November to February.

Goslar once had a cathedral, but this was demolished in 1820. All that remains today is its 12th-century **north porch** *(Domvorhalle)* (9), which can be visited. From here you may want to make a side trip along traces of the medieval walls to the **Zwinger** (10), an ancient bastion containing a small museum and a café.

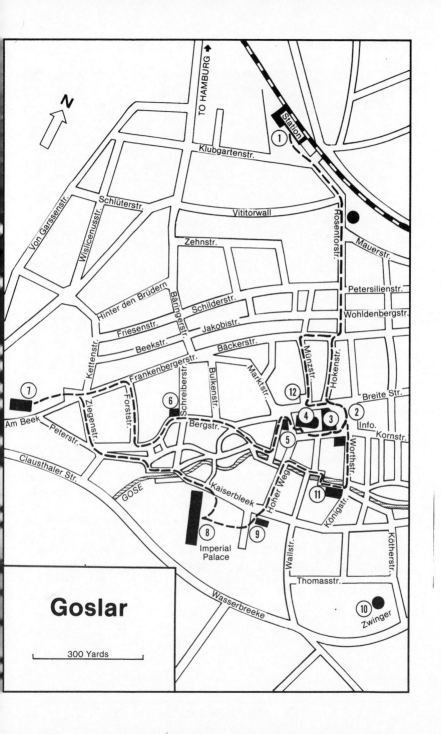

Goslar

300 Yards

N

TO HAMBURG

Station ①

Klubgartenstr.

Von Garssenstr.

Schlüterstr.

Wislicenusstr.

Vititorwall

Zehnstr.

Rosentorstr.

Mauerstr.

Petersilienstr.

Wohldenbergstr.

Hinter den Brüdern

Baringerstr.

Schilderstr.

Friesenstr.

Jakobistr.

Beekstr.

Bäckerstr.

Kettenstr.

Frankenbergerstr.

Schreiberstr.

Bulkenstr.

Marktstr.

Münzstr.

Hokenstr.

Breite Str.

⑦

Forststr.

⑥

⑫

④ ③

②

Info.

Am Beek

Ziegenstr.

Bergstr.

⑤

Kornstr.

Petersstr.

Worthstr.

Clausthaler Str.

GOSE

Kaiserbleek

Hoher Weg

⑪

Königstr.

Köthersstr.

⑧

⑨

Imperial
Palace

Wallstr.

Thomasstr.

Wasserbreeke

⑩

Zwinger

Corner by the Goslarer Museum

Walk down Hoher Weg and turn right just across the stream, passing a charming old mill. The **Goslarer Museum** (11), a few steps beyond, has fascinating displays of life in old Goslar as well as treasures from the former cathedral—particularly the 11th-century Crodo Altar. Don't miss seeing this. The museum is open from 10 a.m. to 5 p.m., Mondays through Saturdays, and until 1 p.m. on Sundays. Between October and May it closes for lunch from 1-3 p.m.

Return to the market place (2), where several outdoor cafés invite you to stop for a rest. On the way back to the station be sure to go through the **Schuhhof** (12), a marvelous square lined with half-timbered houses, and continue on via Münzstrasse, where there is an interesting new museum of pewter figures *(Zinnfiguren)* at Number 11.

Index

Boat Cruises, Casinos, Castles and Palaces, Cathedrals, Lakes, Mountains, Museums, and Roman Relics are listed individually under those category headings. *Names of persons are in italics.*